EDITED BY
JESSICA JACOBSON AND
PENNY COOPER

# PARTICIPATION IN COURTS AND TRIBUNALS

Concepts, Realities and Aspirations

Foreword by the Rt Hon Sir Ernest Ryder

BRISTOL
UNIVERSITY
PRESS

First published in Great Britain in 2020 by

Bristol University Press
University of Bristol
1-9 Old Park Hill
Bristol
BS2 8BB
UK
t: +44 (0)117 954 5940
e: bup-info@bristol.ac.uk

Details of international sales and distribution partners are available at bristoluniversitypress.co.uk

British Library Cataloguing in Publication Data
A catalogue record for this book is available from the British Library

ISBN 978-1-5292-1129-0 hardcover
ISBN 978-1-5292-1131-3 ePub
ISBN 978-1-5292-1130-6 OA ePdf

Cover design by blu inc, Bristol
Cover image credit: macu-ic-PbN_Gl_ZoMk-unsplash
Printed and bound in Great Britain by CPI Group (UK) Ltd,
Croydon, CR0 4YY
Bristol University Press uses environmentally
responsible print partners.

# Contents

List of Boxes, Figures and Tables     iv

Notes on Contributors     v

Acknowledgements     vii

Foreword by Rt Hon Sir Ernest Ryder     ix

one     Introduction     1
*Jessica Jacobson*

two     Policy and Practice Supporting Lay Participation     19
*Gillian Hunter*

three     Conceptualising Participation: Practitioner Accounts     65
*Amy Kirby*

four     Observed Realities of Participation     103
*Jessica Jacobson*

five     Looking Ahead: Towards a Principled Approach to Supporting Participation     141
*Penny Cooper*

Index     177

# List of Boxes, Figures and Tables

## Boxes

| | | |
|---|---|---|
| 1.1 | Definitions | 5 |
| 3.1 | Conceptualisations of participation | 70 |
| 3.2 | Providing and eliciting information | 71 |
| 4.1 | Observations and court users | 104 |
| 4.2 | Summaries of observed hearings | 108 |
| 4.3 | Efforts to humanise care proceedings in the Family Court | 126 |

## Figure

| | | |
|---|---|---|
| 1.1 | Major first-instance courts and tribunals in England and Wales | 6 |

## Tables

| | | |
|---|---|---|
| 3.1 | Breakdown of respondents by jurisdiction and role | 68 |
| 5.1 | Comparing approaches to ground rules hearings | 149 |
| 5.2 | Ten Points of Participation as a provisional framework for court user guidance | 163 |

# Notes on Contributors

**Penny Cooper** is Visiting Professor at the School of Law at Birkbeck, University of London, and Senior Research Fellow at Birkbeck's Institute for Crime & Justice Policy Research (ICPR). She has held professorial posts at three other universities in London and was an Associate Dean at the law school at City, University of London until 2012. She co-founded and chairs the leading website 'The Advocate's Gateway', created ground rules hearings and devised the English witness intermediary model. She is co-editor of the leading text *Vulnerable People and the Criminal Justice System*, published by Oxford University Press in 2017. Penny has been a barrister since 1990, is based at 39 Essex Chambers, London and specialises in witness preparation for commercial cases.

**Gillian Hunter** is Senior Research Fellow at ICPR. Prior to joining ICPR in 2003, she worked on health-based social research at the Centre for Drugs and Health Behaviour, then based at Imperial College, London. Her current research interests focus on access to justice and victims', witnesses' and defendants' experiences of the criminal justice system. Her publications include *Inside Crown Court: Personal Experiences and Questions of Legitimacy* (Policy Press, 2015, with Jessica Jacobson and Amy Kirby). She has also recently conducted research on problem-solving approaches in the Youth Court and evidence-based practice in policing and crime reduction.

**Jessica Jacobson** is Director of ICPR and Professor of Criminal Justice at Birkbeck. She was formerly a researcher in the Home Office and also worked for many years as an independent policy researcher and consultant. She undertakes research and publishes on many aspects of the justice system, including prisons, sentencing and the work of the courts more widely. Her recent publications include *Inside Crown Court: Personal Experiences and Questions of Legitimacy* (Policy Press, 2015, with Gillian Hunter and Amy Kirby) and *Imprisonment Worldwide: The Current Situation and an Alternative Future* (Policy Press, 2016, with Andrew Coyle, Helen Fair and Roy Walmsley).

**Amy Kirby** is Lecturer in the Department of Criminology at Birkbeck. She was awarded a PhD from the University of Surrey in 2019 for her study of lay participants' perceptions of the legitimacy of the criminal courts, funded by the Economic and Social Research Council. Over the last decade, her research and teaching has focused on a range of criminal justice oriented topics, including: the criminal courts and sentencing, 'court culture', legitimacy, victimology, youth justice and joint enterprise. She is co-author of *Inside Crown Court: Personal Experiences and Questions of Legitimacy* (Policy Press, 2015, with Jessica Jacobson and Gillian Hunter).

# Acknowledgements

This book is the culmination of an ambitious, wide-ranging research project, to which a great many people contributed. We would like to express our sincere gratitude to all the individuals across our research sites who took time out of busy work schedules to assist with the research by offering practical support and taking part in research interviews. We are grateful also to Dr Bina Bhardwa, Helen Fair and Dr Emily Setty who were part of the research team which conducted the interviews and court observations; and also to Emily Setty for her contribution to the policy review conducted as part of the study.

We received invaluable advice and guidance from a judicial reference group and project steering group. For their insightful comments on drafts of this volume, we would especially like to thank Dr Bina Bhardwa, Professor Mike Hough, Dr Camillia Kong, Professor Grainne McKeever, Alex Ruck Keen, Jenny Talbot, David Wurtzel, the anonymous Bristol University Press reviewer and several members of the judiciary.

For their approval of and assistance with research access, we wish to thank the Judicial Office, the Ministry of Justice National Research Committee, the HMCTS Data Access Panel, Cafcass, Cafcass Cymru, the Citizens Advice Witness Service and the Personal Support Unit (now Support Through Court). We are also grateful to the Commission on Justice in Wales, and particularly its Chair Lord Thomas of Cwmgiedd and Secretary Andrew Felton, for their support and help with access to relevant services and individuals in the research site in Wales.

Thanks are also due to the following individuals who facilitated Penny Cooper's visits and supported research about jurisdictions outside England and Wales, findings from which are reported in Chapter Five: Tim Barraclough, Angelica Blasi, Laura Cilesio, Kristy Crepaldi, Professor Coral Dando, Sheriff Alistair Duff, Elron Elahie, Adrienne Finney, Judge Jennie Girdham, Veronica Holland, Justice Iain Morley, Carolina Puyol, Dr Liz Spruin, Justice V. Georgis Taylor-Alexander, Heidi Yates and colleagues at ACT Human Rights Commission and DCI Peter Yeomans.

This project was generously funded by the Nuffield Foundation. The Nuffield Foundation is an independent charitable trust with a mission to advance social well-being. It funds research that informs social policy, primarily in education, welfare, and justice. It also funds student programmes that provide opportunities for young people to develop skills in quantitative and scientific methods. The Nuffield Foundation is the founder and co-funder of the Nuffield Council on Bioethics and the Ada Lovelace Institute. The Foundation has funded this project, but the views expressed are those of the authors and not necessarily the Foundation. Visit www.nuffieldfoundation.org.

# Foreword

I am delighted to introduce the findings of this major research project funded by the Nuffield Foundation. I am very grateful to Jessica Jacobson, Penny Cooper, Gillian Hunter and Amy Kirby for the quality of the work that has been undertaken and for the collaboration that this has involved between the academy, the judiciary and those representing courts and tribunals users.

The authors' central thesis is that people should be able to participate effectively in the court and tribunal proceedings that directly concern them. The project involved 159 interviews with judges, lawyers, court staff and other practitioners and over 300 hours' observational research conducted in criminal and family courts and employment and immigration and asylum tribunals. The study shows that practitioners do, by and large, make sincere efforts to help lay users participate in proceedings; yet many barriers to participation remain which can leave users marginalised in hearings. It is the responsibility of all those who work in courts and tribunals to understand these barriers and take steps to help users overcome them – this study provides insight and practical suggestions.

The researchers are correct to call on policy makers, judges and other practitioners to use and further elaborate on the *Ten Points of Participation* that have emerged from this study. The researchers also make the case for international collaboration and much-needed research with users themselves. As discussed in the final chapter, the findings of this study not only have relevance to the way we conduct face-to-face hearings, but also to COVID-19 remote hearings and future plans for the use of technology in courts and tribunals.

The researchers have studied national and international court and tribunal practice in a way never done before. This accessible, timely and important volume and the policy briefing and practitioner toolkit being published alongside it will help place users at the heart of court and tribunal reform. I commend this volume to all those who work in courts and tribunals and everyone interested in how users participate in hearings.

*Rt Hon Sir Ernest Ryder, Senior President of Tribunals*

# ONE

# Introduction

Jessica Jacobson

## Key messages of this volume

It is a long-established legal principle in England and Wales – expressed in statute, case law, procedure rules, practice directions and guidance – that people should be able to *participate effectively* in the court and tribunal proceedings that directly concern them. There is wide agreement among law reformers and commentators, as well as among the judiciary and legal practitioners, that participation is essential to the delivery of justice.

But what exactly does it mean for a lay person to participate effectively in judicial proceedings – whether the individual is a defendant or complainant in a criminal case, a party in a family dispute, a claimant or respondent in the Employment Tribunal, an appellant against an immigration or asylum decision, or a witness in any such setting? Why does their participation matter? What factors typically impede their participation and how can it be better supported? This book addresses these pressing, but hitherto neglected, questions in reporting on a unique study which combined cross-jurisdictional socio-legal policy analysis with close empirical inquiry.

A raft of policy initiatives over the past two decades have sought to bolster participation in judicial proceedings, and particularly that of individuals considered 'vulnerable'. Other developments in law and policy have, conversely, undermined the scope or capacity of court users to participate. These include reduced availability of publicly funded legal representation, and wide-scale court closures and the accompanying growing dependence on remote participation through live video- or audio-link and online processes. At the time this book is being completed (May 2020), the existing trend towards replacement of physical with virtual court attendance has accelerated to an extent few could have foreseen – as a result of the COVID-19 pandemic and the imperative to maintain social distancing within the justice system, as across all parts of society.[1] While it is as yet too early to assess the long-term implications for judicial proceedings of changes arising from the public health emergency, these developments make all the more urgent the need to consider what 'participation' means, why it matters and what can be done to ensure it is genuinely effective.

Judges, lawyers, court staff and other practitioners interviewed for this study – from the criminal and family courts and employment and immigration and asylum tribunals – made clear their commitment to the principle of effective participation. They spoke of participation not simply as an abstract concept, but as something that they actively mediated and facilitated, in their differing professional capacities. Courtroom observations conducted by the research team confirmed that practitioners do, by and large, make sincere efforts to help court users to participate; and that, moreover, they treat court users with courtesy, respect and kindness. And yet the observations also shed light on the profound limits to participation by individuals whose powerlessness and disadvantages are laid bare in the courtroom.

The findings of this study point to not only the facilitators of and barriers to participation, but also its multifaceted nature. It was defined in a wide range of ways by the interviewed practitioners. Across the range of court and tribunal settings, participation was variously said to be a matter of providing and eliciting information for the court; being informed; being legally represented; being protected; being managed; and being present. Its functions were described in terms of the exercise of legal rights; enabling court decision making; legitimation of court processes and outcomes; and potential therapeutic benefits.

If policy and practice are to better support participation in the future, especially at times of rapid change to the wider policy landscape, there must be a clear understanding and articulation of its many different aspects and the interplay between them. It should be recognised that all aspects are pertinent – potentially at least – to any setting, and that an over-emphasis on some at the cost of others risks undermining participation and further marginalising the individual court user. This book calls on legal professionals and practitioners, as well as policy makers and other researchers, to apply the framework for understanding participation that is set out here, and to elaborate it further as needed. We also intend the framework to be used to open up discussions with court users themselves about what they expect of judicial proceedings and what is expected of them.

## Investigating participation

Despite the significance of effective participation as a principle in English law, the concept has to date been subject to little critical analysis or empirical investigation. This volume presents the findings of a wide-ranging study, funded by the Nuffield Foundation, of participation in judicial proceedings. The research was conducted by a team based at the Institute for Crime and Justice Policy Research (ICPR) at Birkbeck, University of London, comprising the contributors to this volume (Penny Cooper, Gillian Hunter, Jessica Jacobson and Amy Kirby) and three other researchers: Bina Bhardwa, Helen Fair and Emily Setty.

The study combined a national and international policy review with extensive empirical research in a range of court and tribunal settings in England and Wales. The following questions were addressed:

- What does it mean, in both theory and practice, for lay court and tribunal users to participate effectively in court and tribunal proceedings?
- Why does participation matter?
- What factors (procedural, environmental, social, personal) impede and, conversely, facilitate participation by lay court and tribunal users – including those who are and those who are not legally represented?
- What are the implications for participation of ongoing policy developments, including cuts to legal aid and the court reform programme being implemented by HM Courts and Tribunals Service (HMCTS)?
- How might policy and practice better support participation in the future?

### Study parameters

The parameters of the study were broad. The research explored the scope and nature of participation by lay people attending oral hearings across different judicial settings – primarily, in the criminal and family courts and employment and immigration and asylum tribunals – and in different capacities: see Box 1.1. The usefulness of a generic, cross-jurisdictional approach to participation was thus a central consideration in the research.

**Box 1.1: Definitions**

**Lay court and tribunal users** include:

- **witnesses** called to give oral evidence to the court or tribunal (*excluding* expert witnesses – that is, those giving opinion evidence based on specialist knowledge);

- **parties** to oral hearings in the court or tribunal – specifically:

  - defendants in criminal cases in the Crown and magistrates' courts;
  - parties (primarily parents) in Family Court hearings;
  - claimants and respondents in Employment Tribunal hearings;
  - appellants in hearings of the First-tier Tribunal (Immigration and Asylum Chamber).

In this volume, the term '**court users**' is used as a shorthand for lay court and tribunal users; and the term '**courts**' is used as a shorthand for courts and tribunals.

Within the criminal jurisdiction, the research encompassed adult magistrates' courts, where all criminal proceedings start and most are dealt with in their entirety; and the Crown Court, which tries and sentences serious cases and hears appeals from magistrates' courts. The Family Court[2] deals with a wide variety of matters relating to families; here, the study's main focus was on Children Act cases[3] – both public law (concerning local authority applications for orders to safeguard children's welfare) and private law (concerning applications for child arrangements orders by private individuals). The Employment Tribunal (ET) hears claims against employers about such matters as unfair dismissal or discrimination; while the First-tier Tribunal (Immigration and Asylum Chamber) (IAC) handles appeals against Home Office decisions, and has UK-wide jurisdiction. These courts and tribunals make up a substantial part of the justice system in England and Wales, as made

Figure 1.1: Major first-instance courts and tribunals in England and Wales

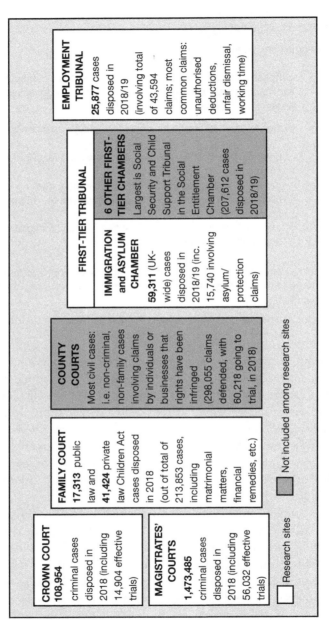

**CROWN COURT**
**108,954** criminal cases disposed in 2018 (including 14,904 effective trials)

**MAGISTRATES' COURTS**
**1,473,485** criminal cases disposed in 2018 (including 56,032 effective trials)

**FAMILY COURT**
**17,313** public law and **41,424** private law Children Act cases disposed in 2018 (out of total of 213,853 cases, including matrimonial matters, financial remedies, etc.)

**COUNTY COURTS**
Most civil cases: i.e. non-criminal, non-family cases involving claims by individuals or businesses that rights have been infringed (298,055 claims defended, with 60,218 going to trial, in 2018)

**FIRST-TIER TRIBUNAL**

**IMMIGRATION and ASYLUM CHAMBER**
**59,311** (UK-wide) cases disposed in 2018/19 (inc. 15,740 involving asylum/protection claims)

**6 OTHER FIRST-TIER CHAMBERS**
Largest is Social Security and Child Support Tribunal in the Social Entitlement Chamber (207,612 cases disposed in 2018/19)

**EMPLOYMENT TRIBUNAL**
**25,877** cases disposed in 2018/19 (involving total of 43,594 claims; most common claims: unauthorised deductions, unfair dismissal, working time)

☐ Research sites

▨ Not included among research sites

Source: Ministry of Justice (2019)[5]

6

clear by Figure 1.1. They are settings in which, every week, many thousands of legal decisions are made with potentially far-reaching consequences for ordinary people's lives.[4]

The decision to focus the research on the courts and tribunals named earlier reflected not only their reach and significance, but also – given the research team's interest in 'participation' in the broadest sense – their diversity in terms of types of disputes adjudicated, levels of formality of proceedings, extent of self-representation of parties and history of provision for vulnerable court users. This diversity, moreover, means that the research findings are likely to have applicability to other types of court and tribunal; as suggested also by the emergence of common themes from across the justice system in the policy and academic literature reviewed for this study. The selection of research sites was also informed by the advice of a project steering group and judicial reference group and practical considerations such as ease of research access.

### 'Vulnerability' and 'participation'

As will be discussed later and in subsequent chapters of this volume, much of the existing law and policy around participation in courts and tribunals has tended to address the issue through the prism of court user vulnerability. That is, the focus has been on how the minority of court users identified as vulnerable – usually understood to be on the basis that they are a child or that they are an adult with a 'disorder', 'impairment' or 'disability' – can be helped to participate in proceedings. Reflecting this, the present study was originally conceived as an examination of provision for vulnerable court users. However, as the work got under way, the research team became increasingly aware of the problematic aspects of the concept of vulnerability in the context of judicial proceedings. It is apparent that a vast array of personal and social attributes, many of which are not readily identifiable, can potentially hinder a court user's capacity to understand or engage fully with the court process. Further, many intrinsic features of the court process itself can add to an individual's 'vulnerability' and further impede participation.[6] The research team consequently decided that what was of greatest interest to them was the nature of, limits to and potential supports for *participation by all court users*, rather than the question of how court users deemed vulnerable could be better provided for.

## 'Participation' in law and legal procedure

In criminal law, there has long been a recognition that defendants should be able to participate effectively in order to exercise their right to a fair trial under Article 6 of the European Convention on Human Rights (ECHR). 'Minimum rights' of the criminally accused under Article 6.3 comprise: (a) being promptly informed 'in a language which he understands and in detail' about the charge; (b) having 'adequate time and facilities' to prepare the defence; (c) 'to defend himself in person or through legal assistance of his own choosing'; (d) 'to examine or have examined witnesses against him', as well as 'witnesses on his behalf'; and (e) to have access to interpretation if needed. European Court of Human Rights guidance (2019: 27) stipulates that Article 6 'guarantees the right of an accused to participate effectively in a criminal trial ... In general this includes, inter alia, not only his or her right to be present, but also to hear and follow the proceedings.' Among the most significant case law supporting this principle is *SC* v *UK* ([2005] 40 EHRR 10), in which the European Court of Human Rights ruled that an 11-year-old's right to a fair trial had been breached because he had had insufficient understanding of proceedings and their consequences. According to Owusu-Bempah (2018), however, there has been little legal scrutiny of the concept of defendants' effective participation since *SC* v *UK*, other than through the Law Commission's review of fitness to plead

(2016).[7] The criteria for determining fitness to plead (although criticised by the Law Commission for being out of date and inconsistently applied) support the principle of effective participation; they are generally understood in terms of capacity to understand the charge(s), decide on plea, challenge jurors, instruct a lawyer, follow proceedings and give evidence (Law Commission, 2016: 10–11).

Fair trial rights are applicable to civil as well as criminal trials,[8] but are not generally understood to extend to complainants and other witnesses in criminal cases (other than in relation to any civil law claims they might make arising out of the crime) (von Wistinghausen, 2013; Fundamental Rights Agency, 2016). Thus, support in law for witnesses' participation is largely framed in terms other than the right to a fair trial – most commonly, with reference to the need to improve the quality of witnesses' evidence. This, for example, is the main expressed aim of the 'special measures' provisions of Part II of the Youth Justice and Criminal Evidence Act 1999, whereby witnesses (but not the accused) identified as vulnerable can give evidence from behind a screen, by live video-link, with assistance from an intermediary, or with other specified forms of help. The Criminal Procedure Rules 2015 set a broader goal, in requiring the courts 'to facilitate the participation of *any person, including the defendant*' (para 3.9.(3) (b), emphasis added).[9] To this end, the Criminal Practice Directions (3D: 'Vulnerable people in the courts') require courts 'to take "every reasonable step"'.[10] These provisions thus treat witnesses and defendants – and particularly those who are vulnerable – as entitled to help to participate in proceedings, but do not elaborate on the concept of participation or reference 'effectiveness'.

In terms that are similarly generic and again link the issue to that of vulnerability, participation is emphasised by the Family Procedure Rules. Part 3A (effective from 27 November 2017) is titled 'Vulnerable persons: participation in proceedings and giving evidence', and sets out the circumstances in which a court should make a 'participation direction', which is analogous to a special measures direction in the criminal courts.[11] This provision is supplemented by Family Practice Direction 3AA, which (para 3.1) directs courts to:

consider the ability of the party or witness to –
a)  understand the proceedings, and their role in them, when in court;
b)  put their views to the court;
c)  instruct their representative/s before, during and after the hearing; and
d)  attend the hearing without significant distress.[12]

As observed by McKeever (2020), a defining feature of the 'normative model' of tribunal hearings – especially since the creation of HMCTS in 2011 merged tribunals with courts in a single service – is that litigants should be better able to participate without representation than they are in the courts. While she questions the extent to which this model is realised in practice, the aspiration to facilitate participation is, in some respects, embedded in tribunal structures and procedures that are overall less legalistic and adversarial and more informal than those of the (civil and criminal) courts. The IAC Procedure Rules state that cases should be dealt with 'fairly and justly', which is said to include 'avoiding unnecessary formality and seeking flexibility in the proceedings' and 'ensuring, so far as practicable, that the parties are able to participate fully in the proceedings' (para 2(2)(b) and (c)).[13] The ET Procedure Rules include a similar direction to that in the IAC Rules to 'deal with cases fairly and justly', including by reducing formality and seeking flexibility (para 2(b) and (c)); here, however, 'participation' is not explicitly mentioned.[14]

The *Equal Treatment Bench Book*, published by the Judicial College (2018), provides guidance to judges and magistrates working across the courts and tribunals system. Its stated purpose is 'to increase awareness and understanding of the different circumstances of people appearing in courts and tribunals. It helps enable effective communication and suggests steps which should increase participation by all parties'.[15] The guidance stresses the centrality of participation to the fair and just operation of the courts; noting in the introduction, for example, that: 'Effective communication underlies the entire legal process: ensuring that everyone involved understands and is understood. Otherwise the legal process will be impeded or derailed' (2018: 4). Included in the guidance are 'practical suggestions ... for enabling LIPs [litigants-in-person] to participate fully in the court process' (2018: 10); and consideration of the adaptations expected of courts and tribunals 'to facilitate the effective participation of witnesses, defendants and litigants' who are children or vulnerable adults (2018: 48).

In the legal, procedural and guidance documentation reviewed very briefly earlier, a variety of terminology is used: references to 'participation' in general, to 'effective participation', to help for court users to 'participate fully' and to 'effective communication'. It is clear that participation is widely treated as 'a core element of procedural and substantive justice and of legal values embedded in procedural rules' (McKeever, 2020). It is, moreover, deemed to be closely interrelated to the broader principle of access to justice. For example, Article 13.1 of the UN Convention on the Rights of Persons with Disabilities (UNCRPD), to which the UK has been a signatory since 2007, requires that persons with disabilities should have 'effective access to justice ... on an equal basis with others ... *in order to facilitate their effective role as direct and indirect participants*' (emphasis added).[16] The research reported on in this volume aims to provide insight into whether and in what ways participation does indeed contribute to the delivery of justice, and its constraints and limitations.

## The study

This study comprised two main components: a review of national and international policy pertinent to the theme of participation, and an empirical investigation of practice. The study findings and conclusions are presented over the four chapters of this volume following this introduction.

Chapter Two, by Gillian Hunter, discusses the key policy and practice reforms in England and Wales over the past 20 years and their implications – both positive and negative – for participation by lay people in judicial proceedings. Through a narrative review of research and policy literature, and reflecting some current debates about access to justice, the national policy review sets the context for subsequent chapters. It provides a brief chronology of the introduction of various special measures for supporting court users and examines how professional practice is changing in response to guidance and advice about how lay participation can be better facilitated. It explores what existing research tells us about court users' experiences of judicial proceedings, including the barriers they have faced in understanding and engaging with the judicial process. The chapter also reflects on the (potential) effects on court users of the government's ongoing courts modernisation programme and the significantly reduced availability of publicly funded legal representation. Additionally, in light of the extraordinary circumstances that prevail as this volume is being completed, some questions are posed about supporting lay participation in the courts at a time of pandemic lockdown.

Chapters Three and Four are concerned with the empirical component of the study. There were two parts to this empirical investigation, both of which were qualitative: interviews with practitioners working in and around the courts, the findings of which are presented by Amy Kirby in Chapter Three; and observations of court hearings, as described by Jessica Jacobson in Chapter Four. Both the interviews and the observations were conducted by the team of seven researchers in three cities of roughly comparable size located in Wales and two regions of England. (Where needed in order to access a sufficient number of court and tribunal hearing centres, the fieldwork extended to neighbouring areas of the cities.) Formal approval for the research was obtained by HMCTS and the Judicial Office, as well as other relevant bodies at national and local levels.[17] Further information on methodology is provided at the outset of each chapter.

The purpose of the practitioner interviews was to explore respondents' views, based on their professional experience, of the meaning of 'participation' by court users, whether and why it is important, and the factors that support and impede it. A total of 159 practitioners were interviewed, mostly one-to-one, but occasionally in small groups; they included members of the judiciary, lawyers, court staff and others. The large majority of practitioners worked predominantly or solely in the field of criminal, family, employment or immigration law, while a small number worked in other parts of the justice system, including the coronial jurisdiction, where issues of participation are pertinent.[18] As described in Chapter Three, the interview data revealed contrasting but overlapping conceptualisations among practitioners of what participation *entails*: they spoke of it as a matter of informing and eliciting information; being informed; being represented in court; being protected; being managed; and, in its weakest sense, being present. Practitioners variously explained the *importance* of participation in terms of: the exercise of legal rights; the essential part it plays in court decision making; its legitimating function; and a possible therapeutic value for court users.

The observational research was carried out with the aim of exploring how, in practice, court users participate in hearings. The research team conducted the observations over the course of 90 visits to 17 venues – spending a total of 316 hours across all the (criminal and family) court and (ET and IAC) tribunal settings. It is argued in Chapter Four that while the settings differed widely from one another, there were also many commonalities across them. Almost every case that was observed had at its heart a story of conflict, loss and disadvantage; and each court user's 'participation' in the case could be understood as a process by which they told, or had told on their behalf, their own version of that story. Practitioners in the courtroom – including judges, magistrates, lawyers, legal advisors and others – made extensive efforts to help court users to participate, and tended to treat them respectfully and sympathetically. At the same time, it was evident that the very nature of the court process, which involved the translation of court users' stories into legal questions and legal answers, was marginalising and disempowering.

The empirical data presented in Chapters Three and Four are fully anonymised: no details that could identify any of respondents or observed cases are included. Since the findings did not point to any major differences between the three sites in terms of approaches to participation, the material is presented collectively rather than by area. It is not claimed that the interview responses and observational data are representative of courts and tribunals across England and Wales. However, the breadth of the work (in terms of its jurisdictional reach and numbers of interviews and observations conducted) and its depth (arising from the qualitative approach, which involved close examination of practitioners' views and day-to-day court proceedings) provides for a unique and compelling dataset, especially when considered in the context of the wider policy analysis.

Chapter Five, by Penny Cooper, concludes the volume by making the case for a principled approach to supporting participation across the justice system. In so doing, Cooper discusses what such an approach would entail; considers what can be learnt about supporting participation from other jurisdictions and what other jurisdictions have learnt from England and Wales; and reflects on how learning can best be shared, in both national and international settings.

These issues are considered in light of current responses to the COVID-19 pandemic, which has already provided a major impetus – in England and Wales and across much of the globe – to rapidly expanded use of alternatives to face-to-face court attendance and hearings. Cooper argues that while these current developments are urgent and largely ad hoc responses to an unprecedented public health emergency, and the extent to which they will lead to sustained change is not yet known, they compel us to think in innovative and creative ways about the fundamental nature and purpose of oral hearings in the justice system.

Cooper also observes that the complex theme of lay court users' participation in judicial proceedings, and the policy goal of better supporting participation, demands further research – including research which solicits court users' accounts of their own expectations and experiences, and further international studies. She also explores how the findings of this study could, in a very immediate and practical way, enhance practitioners' and policy makers' engagement with court users.

## Notes

[1] Sections 53–57 of the Coronavirus Act 2020 expanded the availability of live video and audio links in courts and tribunals.

[2] The unified Family Court was created by the Crime and Courts Act 2013, and came into being in April 2014. It hears with almost all family proceedings in England and Wales, and its judiciary includes High Court judges, circuit judges, district judges and magistrates, sitting in a range of court settings.

[3] That is, proceedings under the Children Act 1989.

[4] It should be noted that Figure 1.1 does not provide a full picture of cases culminating in oral hearings in each jurisdiction, as comprehensive information on this is lacking.

[5] *Criminal Court Statistics Quarterly: July to September 2019* (Tables M1, M2, C1, C2), www.gov.uk/government/statistics/criminal-court-statistics-quarterly-july-to-september-2019; *Family Court Statistics Quarterly: July to September 2019* (Table 1), www.gov.uk/government/statistics/family-court-statistics-quarterly-july-to-september-2019; *Civil Justice Statistics Quarterly: July to September 2019* (Table 1.1), www.gov.uk/government/statistics/civil-justice-statistics-quarterly-july-to-september-2019; *Tribunal Statistics Quarterly: July to September 2019* (Tables S1, FIA_2, ET_2, ET_3), www.gov.uk/government/statistics/tribunal-statistics-quarterly-july-to-september-2019

[6] There are growing critiques of the concept of 'vulnerability' within other spheres of public policy. With regard to social welfare, for example, it has been argued that ' "vulnerability" is so loaded with political, moral and practical implications that it is potentially damaging to the pursuit of social justice' (Brown, 2011: 313).

[7] The recommendations of which have not been implemented.

[8] See, for example, discussion of participation in the 'civil limb' European Court of Human Rights guidance on Article 6.

[9] The Criminal Procedure Rules 2015, www.legislation.gov.uk/uksi/2015/1490/contents/made

[10] Criminal Practice Directions 2015, www.judiciary.uk/wp-content/uploads/2015/09/crim-pd-2015.pdf

[11] The Family Procedure (Amendment No. 3) Rules 2017, www.legislation.gov.uk/uksi/2017/1033/made

[12] Practice Direction 3AA – Vulnerable persons: Participation in proceedings and giving evidence, www.justice.gov.uk/courts/procedure-rules/family/practice_directions/practice-direction-3aa-vulnerable-persons-participation-in-proceedings-and-giving-evidence

[13] The Tribunal Procedure (First-tier Tribunal) (Immigration and Asylum Chamber) Rules 2014, www.legislation.gov.uk/uksi/2014/2604/article/2/made

[14] The Employment Tribunals (Constitution and Rules of Procedure) Regulations 2013, www.legislation.gov.uk/uksi/2013/1237/schedule/1/made

[15] www.judiciary.uk/publications/new-edition-of-the-equal-treatment-bench-book-launched/

[16] UNCRPD – Articles, www.un.org/development/desa/disabilities/convention-on-the-rights-of-persons-with-disabilities/convention-on-the-rights-of-persons-with-disabilities-2.html

[17] Ethical approval for the research was obtained from Birkbeck's School of Law.

[18] Coroners have responsibility for hearing inquests into deaths which were violent, unnatural, unexplained or occurred in state detention. Close family of the deceased can attend the inquest as 'interested persons', which gives them the right to question witnesses (directly or through a legal representative) and to ask to see evidence in advance of the hearing. Recent years have seen a growing policy emphasis on ensuring that bereaved family members are 'at the heart of' the coronial process (see, for example, Ministry of Justice, 2013: 4 and 2019: 9).

## References

Brown, K. (2011) ' "Vulnerability": handle with care', *Ethics and Social Welfare*, 5(3): 313–21.

European Court of Human Rights (2019) *Guide on Article 6 of the European Convention on Human Rights: Right to a Fair Trial (Criminal Limb)*, updated on 31 December 2019, Strasbourg: Council of Europe/European Court of Human Rights.

Fundamental Rights Agency (2016) *Handbook on European Law Relating to Access to Justice*, Vienna: European Union Agency for Fundamental Rights.

Judicial College (2018) *Equal Treatment Bench Book: February 2018 Edition (March 2020 Revision)*, London: Judicial College.

Law Commission (2016) *Unfitness to Plead: Summary*, London: Law Commission.

McKeever, G. (2020) 'Comparing courts and tribunals through the lens of legal participation', *Civil Justice Quarterly*, 39(3): 217–236.

Ministry of Justice (2013) *Implementing the Coroner Reforms in Part 1 of the Coroners and Justice Act 2009: Response to Consultation on Rules, Regulations, Coroner Areas and Statutory Guidance*, London: MoJ.

Ministry of Justice (2019) *Final Report: Review of Legal Aid for Inquests*, London: MoJ.

Owusu-Bempah, A. (2018) 'The interpretation and application of the right to effective participation', *International Journal of Evidence and Proof*, 22(4): 321–41.

von Wistinghausen, N. (2013) 'Victims as witnesses: views from the defence', in T. Bonacker and C. Safferling (eds) *Victims of International Crimes: An Interdisciplinary Discourse*, The Hague: TMC Asser Press, pp 165–173.

# TWO

# Policy and Practice Supporting Lay Participation

Gillian Hunter

This chapter sets the context for empirical findings discussed in Chapters Three and Four. It provides an overview of law, policy and practice intended to support and manage lay participation in courts and tribunals in England and Wales, and presents a brief account of change over the past two decades in the jurisdictions under study. This includes a description of the development and evaluation of special measures for vulnerable and intimidated court users, and the guidance available to practitioners to improve their communication with court users and support participation. In assessing the effects of these various forms of assistance and professional guidance, the limited research on lay users' experiences of court is examined. The chapter is framed by discussion of broader system issues, including reforms made to legal aid in 2012 and the courts modernisation programme in England and Wales, documenting how these factors are perceived to impact participation and access to justice. Additionally, reflecting the fact that the chapter was completed in May 2020 at the time of the UK's 'lockdown' in response to the COVID-19 pandemic, some questions are raised about supporting lay participation when physical attendance at court is largely ruled out.

## Approach

Sources published between 2000 and 2020 were used to describe the policy and practice environment in England and Wales relating to lay participation. These comprised:

- research identified through searching electronic databases – Criminal Justice Abstracts and Westlaw UK – to locate studies on effectiveness of practice and court users' experiences;
- policy and practice guidance from government (for example, HM Courts and Tribunals Service (HMCTS), Ministry of Justice (MoJ), Crown Prosecution Service (CPS)), the judiciary and professional bodies (for example, the Law Society);
- wider commentary on lay participation and access to justice, including from advocacy and reform organisations.

Multiple jurisdictions are covered – the criminal and family courts, the Employment Tribunal (ET) and the First-tier Tribunal (Immigration and Asylum Chamber) (IAC). It is impossible within the space available to report on every matter pertinent to lay participation or to discuss in detail those issues which are included. Rather, the chapter gives an overview of key aspects of policy and procedure that may assist or challenge lay participation in judicial proceedings. In the following sections, the concept of court user vulnerability and its relevance to the development of practice across the courts is examined. The evolution of special measures is tracked – as a main example of processes being adapted for lay users – from their introduction in the criminal courts to their uptake elsewhere, and the evidence for the efficacy of these measures is reviewed. This is based mainly on developments in the criminal courts, where to date most research has focused. The development of professional practice and the extent to which this is changing to accommodate and support lay participation is examined. The key structural issues considered are access to state-funded legal representation as an important provision for 'equality of arms' when disputes reach the courts, and reforms introduced to digitise court processes and increase the use of virtual hearings in lieu of physical attendance at court.

## Vulnerability

Factors shaping lay participation in the justice system extend beyond individual traits that might render a court user vulnerable so defined in narrow legal terms. Brown and colleagues (2017), for example, draw attention to the myriad ways in which vulnerability as a concept is discussed and understood, depending on disciplinary and theoretical perspective. Of note is how 'vulnerability' is deployed in different policy and practice contexts against normative standards that support narratives about 'deserving and un-deserving citizens' (Brown et al, 2017).This is especially pertinent when determining the allocation of state resources, where the focus is firmly on the individual rather than the structural processes and mechanisms that might make people 'vulnerable'.

The starting point for this review was how the 'vulnerable' court user is defined and here too it is possible to identify how the delineation of vulnerability sets out how far and for whom the courts are willing to adapt procedures to support lay participation.

Vulnerability of court participants is referred to in primary legislation concerning the criminal courts only, but has been the subject of procedure rules, practice directions and professional guidance across jurisdictions. Most recently, the Civil Justice Council (2020) consulted on the treatment of vulnerable witnesses and parties within civil proceedings, issuing a series of recommendations in order to better align assistance for vulnerable parties in civil courts with that provided in the criminal and family courts.

### Vulnerability in law

Statutory 'tests' of vulnerability are set out in the Youth Justice and Criminal Evidence Act (YJCEA) 1999: with regard to witnesses (prosecution and defence) in the criminal courts and for defendants in the Police and Justice Act 2006 (s 47) and Coroners and Justice Act 2009 (s 104). These stipulate factors that may negatively affect meaningful participation in criminal proceedings – where it is deemed proper that a person should participate[1] – and thereby undermine the right to a fair trial[2] and access to justice (Jacobson, 2017).

The Act specifies that the court can take measures to support a vulnerable witness as defined under section 16 of the YJCEA (and similarly those defined as intimidated under section 17). Such witnesses are *eligible* for support, but an application to the court must be made, including how the measure will improve the quality of evidence. Factors that *may* elicit additional support from the criminal courts for a witness to give evidence are under section 16:

- age of under 18 years;
- mental disorder (defined by the Mental Health Act 1983);
- significant impairment of intelligence or social functioning;
- physical disability or disorder.

And under section 17:

- witnesses who are 'intimidated' (as opposed to 'vulnerable') and need assistance on grounds of fear or distress about testifying.

Some of these broad categories of vulnerability – aside from age – can be difficult to identify, to confirm or to make an objective assessment about their likely impact on participation (Jacobson, 2017; Owusu-Bempah, 2018). Ultimately, validating who is vulnerable becomes a matter of judgment for the courts, although other statutory agencies – for example, the police and CPS in the case of complainants and other witnesses in the criminal courts – have important roles in identifying and alerting the courts to lay users' needs.

## Vulnerability among court users

Consistently, data on offenders' backgrounds suggest high levels of vulnerability as defined in the YJCEA, including mental health problems and learning difficulties (Jacobson et al, 2010). Studies have also highlighted higher rates of criminal victimisation among people with physical and learning disabilities and mental health problems compared to the general population, including experience of violent and sexual offences (Khalifeh et al, 2013; Pettit et al, 2013). Mr Justice Cobb,[3] in a speech to the Family Bar Association Conference in 2017, described the many forms of 'vulnerability' among parties in the Family Court, emphasising the mix of personal needs and wider circumstances that make people vulnerable in the context of judicial proceedings:

> Some exhibit their vulnerability visibly and unmistakably, others subtly, silently and discreetly. There are those whose vulnerability is defined by their age or mental incapacity. There are those who are paralysingly vulnerable because of the behaviours of others towards them, suffering intimidation and persecution. Some deliberately hide their vulnerability out of shame or fear; the spouse who bears the emotional and unhealed wounds of years of control and coercion. The cohort is populated with many others including those with learning difficulties, dyslexia, dyspraxia, behavioural disorders, with ADHD or Asperger's Syndrome, with autism, the list goes on.

Research conducted among immigration and asylum detainees underscores the importance of conceiving of vulnerability as fluid: something that can emerge over time, and which involves an interaction between an individual's experiences and pre-existing factors. It is stressed that vulnerability can relate as much to the nature of the legal system as to individuals' personal circumstances. For example, factors creating vulnerability among asylum seekers appearing before the IAC can include:

- having fled their country of origin because of war, persecution, harassment and discrimination;
- limited economic resources or social connections;
- inability to speak English;
- experiences of sexual abuse, ill-treatment and torture;
- feelings of anxiety, depression, trauma and/or suspicion of authority due to experiences.
  (See, for example, Blake, 2011; the Detention Forum's Vulnerable People Working Group, 2015; Royal College of Psychiatrists, 2016; Shaw, 2016.)

The ways in which vulnerability can be *created* or exacerbated by the justice process have also been noted in research on the criminal courts. For example, research on the Crown Court (Jacobson et al, 2015; Kirby, 2017) has highlighted the elaborate, ritualised and often archaic aspects to the contested trial which can make the process difficult, confusing and stressful. Further, it is argued that the adversarial system and rules for testing evidence in court can render all witnesses and defendants vulnerable to some extent, which can be experienced by some as a form of secondary victimisation (Wheatcroft et al, 2009).

Inequalities of power between lay participant and court, or lay claimant versus professional respondent, feature heavily in discussions of the ET (for example, Busby and McDermott, 2012). Such concerns are pertinent across the justice system, especially taking into account the increase in numbers self-representing after government cuts were made to publicly funded legal representation in 2012 (to be discussed later).

More generic barriers to participation underline court users' estrangement from the specialist knowledge, language and formality of court processes and the anxiety and stress experienced when having to enter such alien spaces to resolve disputes (McKeever, 2013). Even in tribunals, which are structured to be more accessible to the lay user than the court, differences in education, language, culture, communication skills and confidence, compounded by lack of availability or awareness of sources of information and advice about hearings, create wide disparities in how court users cope with adjudication processes (Genn et al, 2006).

## Evolution of special measures

The aspiration to improve participation and access to justice informed much of the development of specialist support for those defined as vulnerable. Closely aligned with this, however, are more instrumental concerns, including how to ensure that witnesses and parties provide their 'best evidence' (Tribunals Judiciary, 2010). With regard to the criminal courts, there has also been political pressure to 'rebalance' the system in favour of victims, including by trying to give them a greater voice in proceedings and easing their experience of attending and giving evidence in court[4] (for example, MoJ, 2013, 2014; Crown Prosecution Service, 2016).

### In the criminal courts

Adaptations to traditional court processes for vulnerable witnesses outlined in the YJCEA include provision for:

- giving evidence from behind a screen so witnesses cannot be seen by nor see the defendant – screens can also shield witnesses from the public gallery (s 23);

- giving evidence via live video-link to the courtroom from a room or building elsewhere, with a supporter if necessary (s 24);
- clearing the courtroom of public and press (s 25);
- lawyers and judges removing wigs and gowns (s 26);
- using a pre-recorded video statement as evidence-in-chief (s 27) or pre-recorded cross-examination and re-examination (s 28);
- receiving communication assistance via a witness intermediary[5] who facilitates communication for witnesses who experience communication difficulties (s 29) (see Wurtzel and Marchant (2017) for detail on the intermediary's role);
- using communication aids (s 30).

The legislative picture is complicated when trying to determine who is eligible for special measures. While the YJCEA explicitly excluded defendants from access to adaptations, subsequent legislation has extended some support to defendants. Provisions in the Police and Justice Act 2006 allow for a vulnerable defendant to give evidence by live-link, although with additional criteria to meet.[6] The Coroners and Justice Act 2009 *would* permit access to an intermediary to aid communication during testimony, but this is not yet in force (see Chapter Five). Aside from those defined through statute, there are wider obligations on the courts to make adjustments for witnesses and defendants, as stipulated in case law, Criminal Practice Directions and Criminal Procedure Rules (to be discussed later).

### Evaluating special measures in the criminal courts

Research examining special measures in the criminal courts has tended to focus on whether legislative objectives are being met, including through: identification of the need for measures and whether they are requested in time; levels of judicial agreement to measures; and their effects as perceived by court users. Resource constraints and the differential support for defendants and witnesses have also been examined.

For witnesses, the police and CPS must identify early in case preparation the need for special measures and apply to the courts. Several studies, involving case file reviews and practitioner interviews, have highlighted problems with this process, resulting in late applications or missed opportunities to apply. Commonly, this involved failure to identify need, poor information exchange between the police and CPS, and lack of detail about vulnerabilities in supporting paperwork (Burton et al, 2006; McCleod et al, 2010; Charles, 2012).

Cooper (2017), commenting on an appeal court case (*R*. v *G* [2017] EWCA Crim 617), highlighted continuing problems with how 'vulnerability' criteria are understood and applied in court, despite the concept of the 'vulnerable witness' being over 20 years old.[7] The case in question illustrates the blurred line between determinations of 'vulnerability' and 'intimidation'. Analysis of CPS data on outcomes of special measures applications in the early days (2003–2004) suggested that when vulnerability was identified and a timely application made to the courts, most were successful (Roberts et al, 2005). Reasons for refusal were most commonly noted as at 'judge's discretion' (based on matters of law), for example, where it was felt that the statutory criteria had not been met or because the application was late. A small number were rejected on pragmatic grounds, including lack of facilities at court (Roberts et al, 2005).

Research on witnesses' experiences of measures has generally found positive responses. Survey feedback from 569 vulnerable and intimidated witnesses attending criminal courts during 2003 (video recorded testimony and intermediaries were not available then) showed that those who received special measures were less likely to report feeling anxious or distressed. A third also said that they would have been unwilling to give evidence without them (Hamlyn et al, 2004). Burton and colleagues (2006) found that video-recorded evidence and the live video-link were highly regarded by witnesses and practitioners, although some practitioners had reservations about televised evidence because they thought it was less convincing than evidence given in person.

Witness intermediaries were piloted in six areas between 2004 and 2005 (Plotnikoff and Woolfson, 2007) before national roll-out in 2007. The evaluation showed that intermediaries were viewed positively by those who had used them, including for their help in identifying witnesses' communication difficulties. However, poor awareness and misunderstanding of eligibility criteria for appointing intermediaries, over-estimation of advocates' competence to question effectively, and under-estimation of witnesses' communication needs were identified as factors likely to inhibit wider uptake.

Ground rules hearings – introduced into the Criminal Practice Directions in 2013 and then the Criminal Procedure Rules in 2014 – were devised as part of intermediary training. They are a means by which the intermediary (ratified by the judge) pre-trial can inform the style and format of an advocate's questions to a witness to help understanding. These hearings are now used routinely for court users who have been identified as vulnerable or as having communication needs. Adaptations to the trial process can also be agreed in ground rules hearings; for example, how the intermediary will alert the court if the witness requires a break (Cooper et al, 2015). However, research on the conduct of hearings is limited, and there is evidence that practice varies on who is present, the extent of judicial direction on how the case will be put to the witness, and whether or not written questions are requested by the judge in advance (Cooper et al, 2015). On this last point, the practice of submitting cross-examination questions in advance for judicial vetting has become more widespread where a witness is young or vulnerable, and is not limited to hearings using intermediaries or those conducted under s28 (to be discussed later) as noted in *R* v *Zafer Dinc* [2017] EWCA Crim 1206.

Demand for intermediaries in England and Wales has grown. The latest annual report on the Witness Intermediary Scheme (MoJ, 2019a) reports that 6276 requests were made for a registered intermediary in the financial year 2018/19 (a monthly average of 523), representing a 190 per cent increase in requests since 2013/14. The majority were for child witnesses (47 per cent) followed by witnesses with learning disabilities (34 per cent), mental illness (13 per cent) and physical disabilities (6 per cent). Ninety-six per cent of requests were matched with an intermediary.

The last special measure to be introduced (s28 of the YJCEA) allows for a vulnerable witness's cross-examination and re-examination to be recorded in advance of the trial. This was piloted in three Crown Courts from 2014 and had been expanded to a further five sites by June 2019.[8]

During piloting, 194 s28 cases, mainly involving sexual offences, were dealt with. (Baverstock, 2016; Plotnikoff and Woolfson, 2016). Evaluation findings indicated continuing problems about awareness of eligibility criteria for special measures among the police and CPS, resulting in missed opportunities for pre-recording of evidence and cross-examination. There were reports of technological problems including poor visibility and sound quality of witnesses on screen. Findings suggested some positive outcomes, including practitioners' views that the experience of cross-examination was less stressful, and that questioning was more focused where ground rules hearings had been used to prepare questions. Trial lengths were shorter on average when using s28, and cross-examination took place earlier, which had benefits for witness recall (Baverstock, 2016).

In contrast to provisions for witnesses, there has been criticism of poor progress and late implementation of legislation affording special measures for defendants. This underlines the inequity of provision for vulnerable defendants compared to vulnerable witnesses, not least because the imbalance flouts compliance with rights legislation[9] and the courts' safeguarding responsibilities (e.g. Burton et al, 2006; Bradley, 2009; Tonry, 2010; Fairclough, 2016, 2018).

Jacobson and Talbot (2009), in research that reviewed court provision for adult defendants with learning disabilities, highlighted inadequate processes for identifying learning needs, including lack of specificity in defining learning difficulty and its conflation with mental illness. They also noted that defendants' exercise of their right to a fair trial and their meaningful participation was hindered by limited provision of support services before and during court hearings.

Despite the 2009 statute, vulnerable defendants still do not have access to the MoJ-registered intermediary scheme, nor rights to funding for this, with courts required to use their inherent powers to direct assistance from an intermediary for a defendant. There is no requirement for these intermediaries to be registered, meaning that they are not accredited, funded or regulated by the MoJ (Cooper and Wurtzel, 2013). More recent revisions to Criminal Practice Directions (in 2016) have further downgraded access to an intermediary for defendants, noting the measure to be 'rare' for testimony, but 'very rare' for the whole trial (Hoyano and Rafferty, 2017). It is further stated in directions that there is no presumption that a defendant should receive assistance, and even where an intermediary would improve the trial process, access is not a given. This underscores the prioritising of witnesses' access to intermediaries – as a costly resource. The guidance is laid out in *R* v *Rashid* [2017] EWCA Crim 2, whereby the rarity of a defendant having an intermediary's support throughout trial is reiterated, with the onus placed on the advocate to be able to ask a defendant questions in an appropriate and comprehensible manner.

Research conducted with a small sample of criminal lawyers identified three barriers to defendants gaining access to live-links to give evidence (the other statutory provision for vulnerable defendants). These were: lack of awareness among defence lawyers that this was available for defendants; poor identification of vulnerability and a view that it was not tactically advantageous to have defendants give evidence in this way (Fairclough, 2016).

## In the Family Court

There is no statutory definition of vulnerability in the Family Court, but there has been strong support for reforming practice in this area. The Family Justice Review[10] (2011) recommended that government and judiciary 'actively consider how children and vulnerable witnesses may be protected when giving evidence in family proceedings' (Family Justice Review Panel, 2011: 24). The judicial response to the review (Ryder, 2012)[11] suggested changes to practice directions to offer guidance on how an incapacitated adult party might be represented and how to identify and ask for special measures for vulnerable parties. In addition, these documents stressed the importance of the 'child's voice' in proceedings, whereas it was previously considered detrimental for a child to give oral evidence. This referenced the need to comply with the United Nations Convention on the Rights of the Child (1989) through judges ensuring the child's understanding of proceedings, that their wishes have been ascertained and that the court's final decision is explained to them.

The 'child's voice' is mainly represented through the Children and Family Court Advisory and Support Service (Cafcass), introduced in 2001 by the Criminal Justice and Court Services Act 2000. Cafcass advisors are trained social workers whose role is to safeguard and promote the welfare of children; give advice to the court about applications; make provision for children to be represented; and provide information and support to children and their families. Ofsted's[12] latest inspection of Cafcass (2018) rated the service as 'outstanding', noting that listening to and understanding children and acting on their views was well embedded in practice in both public and private law.

The position on children's non-participation in family proceedings was successfully challenged (*Re W (Children) (Abuse: Oral Evidence)* [2010] UKSC 12). In response, the Supreme Court concluded that there should no longer be a presumption against children giving oral evidence, but left it open for the Court to determine its position on a case-by-case basis, and to decide what practical steps should be taken to accommodate children giving evidence.

Sir James Munby (President of the Family Division from 2013 to 2018) has vigorously highlighted the Family Court's shortcomings in accommodating children's voices and views when considering their 'best interests', and has extended this criticism to provision for all parties who are vulnerable in some way (see, for example, Munby, 2016). He declared the Family Court to be 'shamefully behind' the criminal courts in this regard and set up the Vulnerable Witnesses and Children's Working Group (VWCWG) to review guidelines on involving children in proceedings, address the wider needs of vulnerable people in the Family Court and establish how best to adapt provisions and developments from the criminal courts to the Family Division, including through revising Family Procedure Rules and practice directions.

The resulting report from the VWCWG (Judiciary of England and Wales, 2015) noted the high prevalence of vulnerability among parties in the Family Court. It also highlighted ongoing concerns about the lack of resources for provision of intermediaries and government reforms that made most private law cases ineligible for legal aid, thus increasing numbers of litigants in person (LiPs) in the Family Court. These funding changes had also made it more likely for abuse complainants to be cross-examined in court by their alleged abusers;[13] something which was reported to be happening all too frequently and which received attention[14] from lawyers' professional associations, the charity Women's Aid and commentators in the media who were incredulous that such practice was being allowed to persist.

For example, data collected over three months during 2015, from 89 per cent of Family Court centres in England and Wales, identified 124 hearings where there was actual or potential cross-examination of a vulnerable or intimidated witness by a LiP accused of domestic abuse (Corbett and Summerfield, 2017). Qualitative interviews with 15 family judges explored management of such cases and identified the use of screens, remote video-links or judicial intervention to relay questions from the LiP to the witness. This last technique, however, raised concerns among judges about maintaining impartiality in proceedings and they called for clearer guidance on appropriate case management practices. Latterly, legislation included in the Domestic Offences Bill (Home Office, 2019–21)[15] prohibits perpetrators of domestic and other forms of abuse from cross-examining their victims in person in the Family Court and will also prevent victims from having to cross-examine their abusers. This additionally gives the court discretion to prevent cross-examination in person where it would diminish the quality of the witness's evidence or cause the witness significant distress.

Family Procedure Rule 3A and accompanying Practice Direction 3AA took effect in November 2017, underlining the court's duty to be aware, and take account, of a range of factors that might impact on a court user's ability to participate effectively in proceedings. These include:

- actual or perceived intimidation by another party, witness or their wider family or associates;
- a mental disorder or significant impairment of intelligence or social functioning;
- a physical disability or disorder;
- the age, level of maturity, and ethnic, social, cultural and religious background and domestic circumstances;
- any issues arising in proceedings, including concerns in relation to abuse.

Nevertheless, the courts' ability to support participation appears to be tempered. Commentators have highlighted the absence in the amended rules of powers to ensure public funding for certain measures. For example, MoJ guidance to family courts stressed that there was no statutory requirement for HMCTS to fund an intermediary or intermediary assessment in family proceedings.[16] Thus, while there is the option for specialist support, its use continues to be constrained (Cooper, 2018).

### In the Employment Tribunal

In general, tribunals are intended to be much less formal than the courts and to operate in ways that should facilitate lay participation. For example, Sir Andrew Leggatt's review of tribunals (2001) suggested that lay users should be able to present their case without the need for expert legal representation, through support from external advice services and with the assistance of tribunal staff and judiciary who have expertise in tribunal jurisdictions.

It has been argued that the ET can exercise a relatively high level of discretion to accommodate vulnerability. Cooper and Arnold (2017: 5), for example, explain that the ET 'can and does adjust procedures to remove barriers to effective participation of witnesses and parties at oral hearings'. Case management discussions are used to determine what adjustments are needed for vulnerable and intimated parties and reasonable adjustments can then be made to questioning, language, giving evidence and provision of support and intermediaries.

The Employment Tribunal (Constitution and Rules Procedure) Regulations 2004 confer wide procedural discretion through provisions, including:

- so far as practicable, ensuring that parties are on an equal footing and that the case is dealt with fairly: regulation 3(1) and (2)(a) and (c);

- powers to manage proceedings that mean the judge may at any time, either on application of a party, or on their own initiative, make an order in relation to any matter which appears to be appropriate (for example, these may concern the manner in which the proceedings are to be conducted);
- the judge can seek to avoid formality in proceedings, not be bound by any enactment or rule of law relating to the admissibility of evidence in proceedings: rule 14(2);
- the judge or tribunal shall make such inquiries of persons appearing and of the witnesses as considered appropriate and shall otherwise conduct the hearing in the manner she considers most appropriate for the clarification of issues and generally for the just handling of the proceedings: rule 14(3).

The case law examples cited in the following paragraphs illustrate how procedural discretion is used to ensure parties have a fair hearing and can participate. These stress that it is up to the ET to investigate and make decisions based upon evidence and circumstances of the case and parties, and to draw upon expert opinion as required regarding the need for adaptations. However, it is also contingent on the parties' acceptance of adjustments, and the implications for fairness to both sides need to be factored into assessments and any adjustments made.

In accounting for intimidation and distress, *Duffy* v *George* [2013] EWCA Civ 908 demonstrates the court's powers to allow parties to give evidence in the absence of one another. Case law relating to procedural adjustments for disability or ill health among parties include *JW Rackham* v *NHS Professionals Ltd* [2015] UKEAT/0110/15/LA, which concerned a claimant with Asperger's Syndrome (Cooper and Arnold, 2017). Here, the ET obtained a GP's report and sought expert advice to determine the procedural adjustments required. Adjustments to the hearing, including to cross-examination, were agreed by the parties and endorsed by the claimant's GP.

The following examples, however, suggest a lack of consistency in how thorough the ET is expected to be in assessing the need for adjustments to ensure fairness. In *Hak* v *St Christopher's Fellowship* [2015] UKEAT 0446/14/DA, the claimant was a non-native English speaker making a claim about unfair treatment and racial discrimination at work. He requested an interpreter, but none was found and when asked whether he was happy to proceed, he said 'yes'. After losing the case, he appealed, but this was dismissed on grounds that he said he had been happy to proceed, so there was no unfairness or procedural irregularity. In *Galo* v *Bombardier Aerospace UK* [2016] NICA 25, the Northern Ireland Court of Appeal held that the tribunal had not provided a fair trial to a claimant with Asperger's Syndrome because it failed to make reasonable adjustments for his disability and medical circumstances when he was a LiP. The court adjudged a more active approach was required, stating that inquiries should have been made about any necessary procedural adjustments in light of his disability. It criticised the tribunal for failing to obtain a medical report or arrange for a doctor to attend the hearing. It was also stated that the tribunal should have taken note of the *Equal Treatment Bench Book* (ETBB) that provides guidance for all judges on addressing the difficulties experienced by vulnerable litigants.

The ETBB 2018 published by the Judicial College advises that ground rules hearings should be conducted to consider adjustments for participation and that expert evidence might be needed to assist decision making. Matters which can be considered at such a hearing when a person is 'vulnerable' include:

- approach to questioning and cross-examination – how it is controlled, and tone, language and duration of questioning;
- a full explanation of court procedures for an applicant with a disability or LIP and advice on availability of pro-bono assistance and voluntary sector help;
- the need for extra time for those with learning disabilities to ensure they have understood;
- language and vocabulary;

- whether the respondent's counsel should offer cross-examination and questions in writing to assist the claimant.

### In the Immigration and Asylum Chamber

Guidance for IAC judiciary encourages the use of discretion to respond to the needs of vulnerable appellants to ensure they receive a fair hearing. For example, a Practice Direction issued in 2008 for first and upper tribunal (child and sensitive witnesses)[17] allowed children and vulnerable adults, as defined in the Safeguarding and Vulnerable Groups Act 2006, and 'sensitive' witnesses, whose quality of evidence might be diminished due to fear or distress, to give evidence via telephone, video-link or other means and to be supported if required by a skilled individual. The direction also urges judges to consider the need for calling a witness where this might be prejudicial to their welfare.

Further guidance (Joint Presidential Guidance for Tribunals Judiciary, Note 2) was issued in 2010 encouraging judges to be proactive, emphasising they should use their discretion to determine what adjustments might be needed for vulnerable appellants. The guidance is premised upon the notion that effective communication and comprehension is essential to the legal process, and that vulnerable appellants may require measures, adaptations or procedures to enable participation. It is acknowledged that without identifying or accounting for vulnerability, the quality of evidence may be compromised. Judges are guided to account for vulnerability before, during and after the hearing, when making decisions and weighing up the evidence. A range of factors are listed as potentially creating vulnerability, which may vary in terms of nature, extent and impact, and may be hidden or emerge over time. These factors are for the judge to assess and may relate to:

- mental health;
- social or learning difficulties;

- religious beliefs or practices;
- sexual orientation;
- ethnic, social and cultural background;
- domestic or employment circumstances;
- physical disability or impairment.

Vulnerability may relate to extraneous factors, including experiences of detention or torture. Judges are directed to identify vulnerabilities at a case management meeting, or at the beginning of the substantive hearing, to seek expert evidence where necessary, to take into account the needs and wishes of the vulnerable person, to consider what adjustments are required, and to anticipate behavioural difficulties or challenges that may arise in the hearing.

Measures and discretionary actions by the judge may include seeking agreement on key areas of dispute pre-hearing; allowing a representative or supporting adult to identify concerns about well-being; restricting public or family members' access to the hearing to ensure evidence can be given freely; speaking clearly and jargon-free; curtailing aggressive cross-examination; ensuring questioning is tailored to age and maturity; ensuring the appellant has understood and is allowed breaks; and adjourning the case if vulnerability emerges in the course of the hearing, in order to seek expert advice about its impact.

The guidance states that vulnerable appellants may require more time to understand and think about questions and may be easily influenced. Inconsistencies and contradictions may indicate a lack of understanding and/or power imbalances. Factors underlying vulnerability may affect comprehension, articulation and so forth, and so should be taken into account when assessing evidence and making decisions.

A Court of Appeal case – *UK – AM (Afghanistan) v Secretary of State for the Home Department* [2017] EWCA Civ 1123 – concerning an asylum claim by a 17-year-old male, illustrates how practice directions and guidance about accommodating vulnerable appellants in the IAC are upheld. The appeal was granted on the grounds that the tribunal had failed to follow expert advice about the ground rules that were needed during the hearing to account for the appellant's learning difficulty, but also that the Joint Presidential Guidance Notes (2010) stressing the importance of the best interests of the child had been ignored.

## Guidance for practitioners and judges

Guidance for practitioners addresses 'professional culture' in courts and tribunals in relation to the participation of court users.

The Advocate's Gateway[18] (TAG, founded in 2013) hosts resources, including 'toolkits' that offer guidance on communicating with young and vulnerable court users. There are toolkits written for the criminal, family and civil courts and those that focus on questioning people with specific communication needs, such as autism. The toolkits detail evidenced advice on question format, language to use or avoid and the importance of body language, and they provide links to source materials and examples of good and bad practice for eliciting testimony. Data from Google Analytics on 'traffic' to the TAG website between March 2019 and February 2020 show in total 18,755 'visits' were made to the ten most viewed toolkits on TAG.

There is some evidence from the criminal courts that such guidance is having a positive effect. Research commissioned by the Bar Standards Board and the Solicitors Regulation Authority (Hunter et al, 2018) comprised interviews with 46 circuit judges and four High Court judges across England and Wales about their perceptions of the quality of criminal advocacy. While many respondents were critical of advocacy, an area of practice that was said to be improving was skills in questioning vulnerable witnesses, and TAG was sometimes name-checked in these discussions.

Guidance for judges found in the ETBB (Judicial College, 2018) emphasises judicial responsibility for ensuring fair and equal treatment for court users. It includes sections on special measures and seeks to raise awareness of the potential effects of a wide range of physical and mental disabilities and ethnic, cultural, religious and socio-economic factors on court users' capacity to understand and engage in court processes. It offers guidance on identifying and accommodating these various needs to support more effective participation. However, the extent to which the guidance is applied is unknown.

As is clear from previous sections, much of how the courts accommodate lay participation is determined by practice directions and procedure rules, by appellate decisions and through professional convention. In the criminal courts, for example, practice regarding vulnerability among witnesses and defendants has evolved through Criminal Practice Directions which emphasise requirements to take 'every reasonable step' to facilitate participation of witnesses and defendants to give their best evidence, and also to enable defendants' understanding of proceedings so they can engage fully with their defence. The Practice Directions also underline judicial responsibility for controlling cross-examination of a vulnerable witness or defendant (including preventing over-rigorous or repetitive questioning) and the option of departing from traditional forms of cross-examination if required.

Henderson (2016: 181), discussing criminal trial management, describes the attitudes of judges and advocates – rather than legislation or government policy – as 'the single most important factor in achieving any sort of change'. Her interviews with judges, advocates and intermediaries show that while judges recognise the need to manage trials dealing with vulnerable witnesses and defendants, some remain reticent about doing so, perceiving intervention to threaten their neutral role. This echoed concerns raised by a Judicial Working Group (2013) convened to assess how best to accommodate LiPs. The group sought further training for judges to better prepare them for managing LiPs, and amendments to Practice Directions to allow for a more inquisitorial approach in cases where at least one party is unrepresented. Indeed, an updated section in the ETBB offers practical guidance on supporting LiPs while 'holding the confidence of both sides' (2018: 30).

The tribunal process is intended to be more inquisitorial than adversarial (McKeever, 2020). Thomas (2013) describes an 'active enabling approach' to hearing evidence from lay participants, which can be achieved by creating the right atmosphere – not overly formal – and assisting the appellant to bring out the relevant issues in the case; something that is especially important when dealing with unrepresented parties. Indeed, claims as to the inquisitorial nature of tribunals and their ability to manage unrepresented parties have been deployed by government in defence of cuts to funding for legal advice and representation – arguments that Thomas (2013) asserts are over-blown. He notes that while there is a move away from traditional adversarial approaches, this varies and depends on the individual judge's approach and experience in drawing out evidence; further, procedures in some tribunals (he cites both the IAC and ET here) remain largely adversarial.

While lay participants may not experience tribunals as informal in tone (Genn et al, 2006; McKeever, 2013), interviews with tribunal users identify factors which encourage lay participation, including help to understand the process and what is required, recognition that low levels of prior knowledge are likely, and support with setting out their case. While judicial input is key, so too is the role of tribunal staff and others who offer advice and moderate user expectations before a hearing (McKeever, 2013).

This highlights the importance of judicial practice in supporting lay users, but also of the role played by other practitioners; it is professional understandings of and attitudes to lay participation that are the subject of the empirical research discussed in the next chapter of this volume. Judicial discretion is frequently invoked in rules and directions about accommodating vulnerable court users and LiPs in courts and tribunals. In proposed court reforms (to be discussed later), judicial discretion is cited as central to decision making about what types of hearing can be heard by telephone, via video or in person.[19]

One recent observational study of judicial discretion in IAC hearings (Gill et al, 2017) suggests a range of dynamics are at play and that judges use their discretion in ways that variously ameliorate or exacerbate the impact of vulnerability, or otherwise convey their indifference. Analysis of 290 IAC cases showed that helpful behaviours were less common than indifferent or exacerbating behaviours and that factors including gender of judge (female), appellant age (under 18 and over 50), day of the week (helpful discretionary actions declined over the course of the week) and appellant gender (male) were associated with more helpful behaviours. The authors note that there may be some ways judges seek to help that are less observable, and court users, judges and legal professionals may differ in their perceptions of what kinds of behaviours are more or less helpful.

## Equality of arms

The Legal Aid, Sentencing and Punishment of Offenders Act 2012 (LASPO) came into force in 2013. The legislation was intended to reduce the stated £2 billion annual costs of publicly funded legal representation as part of government plans to reduce the fiscal deficit (MoJ, 2010). LASPO removed funding for legal advice and representation for areas of law, including most employment law, non-asylum immigration cases and most private family law cases. For criminal cases, means testing[20] to determine eligibility for legal aid has been in place in the magistrates' court since 2006 and in the Crown Court since 2010 and is set out in LASPO,[21] although thresholds for legal aid are currently under review (MoJ, 2019b). In brief, it is available to all defendants under 18 years of age and adults with a disposable household income of under £12,475. An income of up to £22,325 allows for funding – if the additional interest of justice test is met – for cases in both magistrates' and Crown courts, and between £22,325 and £37,500 for legal aid in the Crown Court, although this might cover only partial costs. Further, funding will only be granted for cases in a magistrates' court where it is deemed 'in the interest of justice' for the defendant to be represented. Guidance from the Legal Aid Agency (2018) to improve consistency of decision making in staff assessments about the interests of justice outlines the following key factors:

- if there is high risk to liberty, livelihood or serious damage to reputation if proceedings go against the defendant;
- whether proceedings involve consideration of a substantial question of law;
- difficulty for the defendant in understanding and presenting their case;
- if the case involves expert cross-examination of a prosecution witness.

The guidance stresses the principle of 'equality of arms' whereby a defendant must have an effective opportunity to present their case to the court and not be placed at a substantial disadvantage in relation to the prosecution. This emphasises a case's legal complexity rather than concerns about equality of arms between lay court user and legal practitioner.

A narrative review of international research on LiPs in the family and civil courts (since 1990), undertaken to assess the *likely* impacts of LASPO reforms (Williams, 2011), found that LiPs tended to be younger and have lower levels of income and education than those who were represented. An earlier study on these same courts found that a significant minority were vulnerable, defined as being a victim of violence or having substance misuse or mental health problems (Moorhead and Sefton, 2005). LiPs were reported to have difficulties understanding evidential requirements or identifying legally relevant facts and could find the court process overwhelming. The support they required to navigate hearings created extra work for practitioners, but also raised questions about what help could be offered while maintaining impartiality. Williams (2011) stressed the lack of research on case outcomes for LiPs compared to those with legal representation, but contended that the weight of available evidence suggested these were poorer for LiPs.

Litigants bringing certain types of cases to court – including the IAC and Family Court – are required to pay court fees in addition to, where necessary, funding their own legal representation.[22] Two Justice Committee inquiries (2015; 2016) have found that court charges subvert access to justice for lay users, raising crucial questions about how government efforts to reduce public expenditure are balanced against efforts to preserve legal rights and access to justice.

Criminal Court fees for defendants of between £150 and £1,200 were introduced in April 2015, including a higher fee for those convicted after a not guilty plea. These were found to have perverse effects, including incentivising guilty pleas among those wishing to avoid the risk of paying the higher charge if later found guilty. Further, doubts were raised about whether monies owed could be successfully collected, given the limited financial means of many defendants. The fees were scrapped by December 2015. Between 2013 and 2017, claimants were charged for making a claim to the ET (Pyper et al, 2017). The inquiry into court and tribunal fees (2016) found that their introduction was associated with a substantial fall in cases being brought and there were concerns about the impact of fees on those of low means and pregnant women, and the resultant 'inequality of arms' between individuals and small businesses on the one hand and the state and major companies on the other. There was also concern that discrimination claims in particular were being deterred by the potentially substantial proportion of any award that the fees represented. In July 2017, the Supreme Court ruled that ET fees were unlawful under UK and EU law as they prevented access to justice (*R (on the application of Unison) (Appellant)* v *Lord Chancellor* [2017] UKSC 51). This was supported by evidence that would-be claimants often cited fees as their reason for not pursuing a claim.

### Impacts of legal aid reforms

Assessments of the effects of reforms to legal aid have indicated that any savings accrued to the public purse were outweighed by costs to the courts of managing increasing numbers of cases where one or both parties were unrepresented (National Audit Office, 2014; Law Society, 2017). A review by the Law Society of the impact of civil legal aid reforms cited evidence of their 'corrosive impact on access to justice' (2017: 2), collating a range of data to highlight the consequences: the increased numbers of vulnerable people in non-criminal cases who no longer had access to legal aid, continuing barriers for those who were eligible because of significant gaps in availability of legal advice and services, and the wider negative impacts on society of unresolved disputes.

In 2019, the President of the Family Division, Sir Andrew McFarlane, launched a review of the Family Court, noting the burden on the court of the growing number of LiPs in private law disputes. He also emphasised the difficulties faced by the judiciary who had to manage often 'emotionally charged' LiPs.[23] Routine data collated from the Family Court for the period July to September 2019 (MoJ, 2019c) showed that the proportion of disposals where neither applicant nor respondent had legal representation was 39 per cent: an increase of 25 per cent since 2013.

The increasing presence of LiPs in the courts throws into sharp relief the problem of overly complex courtroom language and the need for court procedures to be made clearer to lay people in order that they can participate effectively (JUSTICE, 2019). Research carried out by the Law for Life

Advice Project (2014) identified information needs of LiPs that were not being properly addressed, including with regard to the role of the court, court processes, legal language and the law. They recommended that all new court materials or those that require updating should be made suitable for LiPs and suggested that bespoke 'how to' guides should be produced, including on case preparation. Building professional capacity in designing and writing materials for lay participants was noted as fundamental to supporting LiPs.

*Court users' experiences of self-representing*

On the basis of research involving interviews and observations in family and civil courts in Northern Ireland – where procedures are similar to those in England and Wales – McKeever and colleagues (2018) identify three main barriers to participation: a dearth of pre-hearing information and advice for LiPs about how to self-represent; linked to this, a lack of awareness among LiPs of their knowledge deficits; and understandable difficulties in separating emotion from legal argument.

Trinder and colleagues (2014) conducted 151 case studies across five family courts during four weeks in 2013. Each comprised observation, interviews with parties and professionals involved and review of case files. Cases were sampled to include different hearing types and those involving represented and unrepresented parties. While highlighting commonalities with LiPs before LASPO, a crucial difference was the increasing numbers who were unrepresented because of inability to pay rather than by choice. Of the LiPs in their study, most had difficulties with court procedures and the legal issues involved in their cases; noted even for those with higher levels of education or professional experience. Approximately half were vulnerable in some way, making self-representation even more difficult. Issues faced by the courts included refusal by some LiPs to engage with proceedings, and – infrequent – aggressive or disruptive behaviour.

Lee and Tkacukova (2017) surveyed nearly 200 LiPs at Birmingham Civil Justice Centre during four weeks in 2016, half of whom were attending the Family Court. Just under two thirds said they had no qualifications or had left school prior to A-levels and over half received state benefits. The authors use these data to highlight potential vulnerability and limited capacity to fund legal advice or representation or to self-represent effectively. For the subset of respondents trying to resolve private family law matters, most reported having undertaken no advance preparation for their hearing.

The numbers of defendants self-representing in magistrates' courts is unknown, but the view among magistrates and lawyers interviewed[24] for a small study (Transform Justice, 2016) is that their number is increasing. Interviewees noted three reasons for this: ineligibility for legal aid or difficulties proving eligibility; lack of awareness of legal rights or of the importance of seeking legal advice; and poor organisation associated with defendants' often chaotic lives. Self-representation was described as impeding defendants' effective participation throughout the court process and the achievement of just outcomes. The main problems were said to be:

- limited ability to understand charges, and to assess the strength of the case against them in deciding how to plea;
- lack of understanding of the difference between defence and mitigation;
- anxiety about self-representing;
- unreliable systems for sending or receiving paperwork, exclusion from digital systems;
- lack of understanding of the rules of evidence;
- lack of experience in conducting cross-examination.

Concern was expressed by interviewees about the limited opportunity for identifying vulnerability among self-representing defendants, as needs and requirements for adaptations to support participation tend to be raised with the court on a defendant's behalf by their lawyer.

LiPs in the Crown Court are rarer, although recent figures show an increase since 2010 in those self-representing at first hearing.[25] Such cases are also said to be more time consuming for judiciary and court staff who have to adjust practice to accommodate defendants' lack of understanding (Thompson and Becker, 2019).

Kirk and colleagues (2015) have challenged government claims of ET litigants being too quick to raise applications, or bringing weak or vexatious claims, as a rationale for funding cuts and ET charges. Their study of over 150 workers seeking redress for work-related grievances between 2012 and 2014 found that significant barriers existed prior to the introduction of fees.

Busby and McDermott (2012) interviewed ten non-unionised employees who could not afford legal advice and had used the Citizens Advice Bureau (CAB) for support with their dispute. The study showed how the formality of the ET process was intimidating to claimants. The authors suggested that while the CAB could help rectify some power imbalances by explaining processes and supporting claimants with completing forms, a lack of claimant representation can produce inequality as employers tend to be represented. Similar findings were noted in a survey of 500 low-paid, non-unionised employees (Pollert, 2010). This study uncovered stories of powerlessness among claimants and resistance and obfuscation among employers, which meant that cases were often dropped as they became too stressful or difficult to pursue. Pollert (2010: 74) argued that, at all stages, claimants' experiences suggested that detailed, specialist evidence and cross-examination would have been needed to mount a serious challenge; elements that were beyond the means and capacity of many of the claimants. Both the Pollert (2010) and Busby and McDermott (2012) studies highlight imbalances of power as jeopardising access to justice for ET claimants, especially employees who lack financial means and legal or union representation.

Describing a 'crisis', the Bach Commission[26] (2017) outlined three main issues affecting 'everyday' access to justice post LASPO: the reduction in scope of legal aid and 'stringent' eligibility criteria to receive funding; a shrinking advice and information sector; and reduced numbers of legal practitioners willing to carry out legally aided work because of its limited availability, low fees and the increased bureaucracy that must be negotiated in order to obtain funding. The Commission argued that problems with access to justice have become so widespread – the report cites numerous examples collected as evidence – that there is a need for a 'Right to Justice Act' to codify the right to receive funded legal assistance, including early advice and legal representation across jurisdictions, and a Justice Commission to monitor and enforce such rights.

The government's current review of legal support (MoJ, 2019c) proffers actions to address concerns, linked into wider court reforms. These include simplifying application processes and raising awareness about access to and eligibility for aid, promoting methods of earlier resolution and enhancing support for LiPs, including by increasing funding for more face-to-face legal support.

## Court reform programme and access to justice

The government court reform programme was launched in 2016 by the Ministry of Justice and Senior Judiciary with the stated aim of improving the accessibility and efficiency of the justice system (MoJ, 2016). It was announced as a £1 billion programme of work comprising 50 different projects to bring new technologies and modern ways of working to the courts and tribunals.[27] The National Audit Office (2018) has since questioned the government's ability to deliver reforms, citing scale and costs of the technological and cultural change that is being proposed. Other commentators focus more specifically on the effects of various reforms on lay users of the justice system.[28]

Court users are certainly central to the rhetoric of reform with targets to 'simplify' procedures and to design systems for users rather than professionals (MoJ, 2016; HMCTS, 2019). Key components involve replacing many paper processes with online forms and procedures and increasing the use of remote attendance (via use of video and telephone) to replace physical attendance at court. Criticism of proposals question government intentions, highlighting cost and efficiency savings rather than needs of court users as the greater stimuli. The following discussion reviews the reaction to reforms and their potential effects on lay experiences of justice, highlighting also the extraordinary circumstances of conducting court business at the time of COVID-19.

### Remote court attendance

Use of video-enabled participation (live and pre-recorded) is established and largely well-regarded as a special measure to protect and reduce anxiety and stress among vulnerable and intimidated court users in the criminal and family courts. Beyond this, use of video technology in the criminal courts has been significantly expanded as part of the reform process. For example, defendants frequently appear from police stations or prison for first, or interim or sentencing hearings (but not, to date, for trials). Here, it has the benefit of reducing costs of prison processing and transportation of prisoners, often for long distances to attend short hearings. In the Family Court, piloting is underway of live video hearings dealing with applications for injunctions by victims of domestic abuse who can appear from their solicitors' offices (HMCTS, 2019). However, there is limited research on the effects of virtual hearings on the justice process, including how lay participants engage with the court and vice versa, and crucially how appearing virtually as opposed to being physically present may affect outcomes. Research conducted by Gibbs (2017) on practitioners' experiences of, and views about, remote attendance in the criminal courts, and evidence given by various individuals and organisations to the House of Commons Justice Committee (2019) about proposed extensions to video use, have underlined potential deficits to justice associated with remote hearings. The key points are summarised here.

Technical problems with establishing remote links, and maintaining good quality audio and video, are commonly reported (including during the piloting of the only full video hearings that have been independently evaluated thus far[29]). In addition to the obvious ways in which such glitches will impede ability to communicate, vulnerabilities among court users such as learning needs are thought likely to create additional challenges for communicating remotely (see Chapter Three). This includes the limited opportunities to identify vulnerability in the first instance when a party is not physically present in court. Video hearings have been deemed unsuitable for court users with additional language needs or LiPs and are said to create barriers to communication between a party and their lawyer, and also to negatively affect engagement with the court, which could influence outcome. Research on the use of secure video-links from police station to court for first hearings found that the rate of guilty pleas and custodial sentences were higher in the two pilot sites than in traditional comparator courts (Fielding et al, 2020).

Remote administration of justice is being hastily organised in response to COVID-19 (see Chapter Five) and caution about changes to the hearing procedure has arguably been set aside to ensure compliance with social distancing rules while trying to keep at least some of the show on the road. Efforts to document the issues arising, especially the experiences of lay participants in this impromptu, emergency pilot, will add to the currently limited evidence base.

## *Online forms and processes*

Increasingly, online form-filling is the norm in many aspects of life. Susskind (2019), a strong proponent of 'online courts' and advisor on the court reform programme, argues digital processes will improve access to justice by making minor conflicts easier and less expensive to resolve, thus freeing up costly court time for more complex legal work. While noting the first iteration of online processes is largely devoted to the more straightforward work of the lower courts, including, for example, resolving small-scale civil disputes, he envisions that advances in technology could radically transform how justice is delivered. His description of these future systems seems less fantastical in light of the emergency response to COVID-19:

> All users might be visible, arrayed perhaps like participants in the TV quiz show, University Challenge ... More sophisticated still would be systems that arrange all or many of those linked in a way that resembles the appearance of a court. Using immersive telepresence technologies, participants might in fact feel they are all gathered together in one place. (2019: 59)

In the here and now, there is evidence of user satisfaction with some initial online court resources.[30] However, an obvious concern is the level of access to IT and of digital literacy among court users and the impact of this upon access to justice. An independent report on digital exclusion (JUSTICE, 2018) cites research data on internet access among the general population to show that those most lacking IT access, and basic digital skills, are concentrated in more vulnerable groups – largely the same 'groups' that are over-represented among court users. Digital literacy potentially creates further challenges for those who are self-representing, particularly in the context of reduced availability of legal advice and information services. Creating an accessible online system requires careful design, including investment in developing appropriate guidance for lay users, but also enhancing public legal education more generally (Susskind, 2019). While there are various proposed mechanisms to support the use of digital resources, these are currently in planning and largely untested. The Single Justice Procedure offers online administration of justice by a single magistrate for low-level cases that would result in a financial penalty. While arguably convenient, concerns have been raised about whether online systems permit proper consideration of the consequences of pleading guilty.

### Court closures

HMCTS has closed 127 courts since reforms were introduced (NAO, 2019), making it more difficult for people to attend a local court. Despite proposals to increase virtual hearings, in-person hearings will continue to be recommended for many court users with vulnerabilities and for LiPs, albeit it remains to be seen whether the responses to the COVID-19 pandemic will have a sustained impact in this regard.

HMCTS has defined as 'reasonable' a journey that involves leaving home by 7.30 am and returning no later than 7.30 pm, including a four-hour round trip on public transport. Already there is evidence for why such calculations do not translate well to real life[31] and there have been calls for the government to commission independent research into the effects of court closures on lay participants. A single local analysis of the impact of the closure of two of three courts in Suffolk (Adisa, 2018) found this had increased incidence of non-appearance of lay participants in the areas furthest from the remaining court and had disrupted informal relationships that had been built between court staff and defence advocates working on behalf of their clients. Closing ill-adapted or under-used court buildings might be less controversial if alternative 'justice spaces' were available. The law reform organisation JUSTICE recommends combining remote access with more imaginative approaches to physical venues, such as the use of 'pop-up-courts' in appropriate community venues (JUSTICE, 2019). The emphasis on staying local during the pandemic lockdown might create greater impetus in future for enhancing aspects of local infrastructure to provide this function.

## Conclusion

This chapter has touched on some of the factors that influence lay participation in justice processes. It highlights to what extent and for whom the courts have been willing to adapt, and where systems and structures continue to inhibit or deny support. It notes the importance of professional competence and judicial discretion in creating cultural change to better accommodate lay users and cites current debates about the impact of court reforms on access to justice. While funds – or lack thereof – are at the forefront of much policy discussion, user experiences of the courts point also to ways in which lay participation can be better understood and professional practice duly enhanced – issues that are considered more fully in the chapters that follow.

## Notes

[1] A defendant may be deemed 'unfit to plead' if he or she is considered unable to: understand charge(s); decide upon plea; be able to challenge jurors; instruct lawyers; follow proceedings; and give evidence in his or her own defence. Witness competence to give evidence at trial (s 53 of the YJCEA 1999) states the witness should be able to understand questions put to him or her and give answers that can be understood.

[2] As enshrined in Article 6 of the European Convention on Human Rights.

[3] High Court Justice in the Family Division since 2013.

[4] For example, through provision for Victim Personal Statements, special measures and separate waiting areas at court for victims/witnesses.

[5] Registered intermediaries are trained, accredited and regulated by the Ministry of Justice. Intermediaries within this scheme support two-way communication with vulnerable victims and witnesses. Some work is also undertaken in family proceedings. Non-registered RIs are not accredited, but are trained to undertake this work.

[6] No automatic eligibility for live-link for defendants under the age of 18. They must be proved to have compromised ability to participate effectively due to level of intellectual or social functioning, but also that the live-link will allow more effective participation. There is a higher threshold for adult defendants in that it is not available to defendants with physical disabilities or to intimidated defendants.

[7] First mention of 'vulnerable witness' was in 'Speaking up for justice' (Home Office, 1998), which gave rise to special measures' provisions in the YJCEA (1999).

[8] www.icca.ac.uk/further-rowith-effect-from-3-june-2019-s-28-of-the-youth-justice-and-criminal-evidence-act-1999

[9] The Human Rights Act 1998; The Disability Discrimination Act 2005; The Equality Act 2010.

[10] The Review Panel took evidence from over 700 individuals and organisations involved in family justice.

[11] The launch of a single Family Court for England and Wales was intended to set groundwork for a modernisation programme. This focused on changing the culture of the court through strong judicial governance and evidence-based practice.

[12] The Office for Standards in Education, Children's Services and Skills. Inspection of Cafcass as a national organisation (2018), available from: https://reports.ofsted.gov.uk/provider/12/1027080

[13] The exceptional case funding scheme requires evidence of domestic abuse such as a criminal conviction or civil injunction; however, this applies only to the party who has experienced abuse and not the perpetrator.

[14] www.theguardian.com/society/2018/may/30/domestic-abusers-still-able-to-cross-examine-victims-in-court; www. resolution.org.uk/news/resolution-the-law-society-and-womens-aid-issue-joint-call-to-government-to-urgently-ban-cross-examination-of-victims-by-their-abusers-in-the-family-courts/

[15] The Bill had its first reading in March 2020.

[16] https://assets.publishing.service.gov.uk/government/uploads/system/uploads/attachment_data/file/681275/guidance-courts-on-payment-certain-mmeasures-family-proceedings.pdf

[17] www.judiciary.uk/wp-content/uploads/JCO/Documents/Practice+Directions/Tribunals/Childvulnerableadultandsensitivewitnesses.pdf

[18] The Advocate's Gateway aims to promote high ethical standards when questioning people who are vulnerable in justice settings.

[19] https://assets.publishing.service.gov.uk/government/uploads/system/uploads/attachment_data/file/775594/Public_Accounts_Committee_Recommendation_2_31_Jan_2019.pdf

[20] www.gov.uk/guidance/criminal-legal-aid-means-testing#overview

21 Includes calculating 'disposable household income', taking account of claimant's family circumstances, living costs and assets.

22 www.gov.uk/court-fees-what-they-are

23 www.theguardian.com/law/2019/jul/03/family-courts-running-up-a-down-escalator-due-to-increase-in-cases

24 Interviews were conducted with ten prosecutors from the Independent Bar, seven magistrates and four District Judges, and an online survey interview was completed by 42 prosecutors.

25 www.theguardian.com/law/2019/nov/24/legal-aid-cuts-prompt-rise-in-unrepresented-defendants

26 Founded in 2015 to develop realistic but radical proposals with cross-party appeal for re-establishing the right to justice. The commission compiled written and oral evidence from over 100 academics and individuals working in the criminal justice system and related organisations.

27 www.gov.uk/guidance/hmcts-reform-programme-projects-explained

28 See Transform Justice for useful synopsis of key research and commentary: www.transformjustice.org.uk/bedtime-reading-list-on-digital-court-reform-and-court-closures/

29 First-tier Tribunal (Tax) (Rossner and McCurdy, 2018).

30 For example, HMCTS (2019) reports positive feedback on the online applications for divorce.

31 www.civillitigationbrief.com/2019/05/14/court-reform-view-from-the-district-judges-we-question-whether-there-has-been-meaningful-as-opposed-to-token-consultation-with-all-levels-of-the-judiciary/

## References

Adisa, O. (2018) 'Access to justice: assessing the impact of the magistrates' court closures in Suffolk', a research report, University of Suffolk.

The Bach Commission (2017) *The Right to Justice*, London: Fabian Society.

Baverstock, J. (2016) *Process Evaluation of Pre-recorded Cross-examination Pilot (s. 28)*, London: Ministry of Justice.

Blake, J. (2011) 'Current problems in asylum and protection law: the UK judicial perspective', paper presented at the Ninth World Conference of the International Association of Refugee Law Judges, 7 September, Slovenia.

Bradley, K. (2009) *The Bradley Report: Lord Bradley's Report of People with Mental Health Problems or Learning Disabilities in the CJS*, London: Department of Health.

Brown, K., Ecclestone, K. and Emmel, N. (2017) 'The many faces of vulnerability', *Social Policy and Society*, 16(3): 497–510.

Burton, M., Evans, R. and Sanders, A. (2006) *Are Special Measures for Vulnerable and Intimidated Witnesses Working? Evidence from the Criminal Justice Agencies*, London: Home Office.

Busby, N. and McDermont, M. (2012) 'Workers, marginalised voices and the employment tribunal system: some preliminary findings', *Industrial Law Journal*, 41(2): 166–83.

Charles, C. (2012) *Special Measures for Vulnerable and Intimidated Witnesses: Research Exploring the Decisions and Actions Taken by Prosecutors in a Sample of CPS Case Files*, London: Crown Prosecution Service.

Civil Justice Council (2020) *Vulnerable Witnesses in Civil Proceedings: Current Position and Recommendations for Change*, London: Civil Justice Council.

Cooper, P. (2018) 'Participation of vulnerable people: don't expect fireworks', *Family Law Journal*, 48 (Jan): 3.

Cooper, P. and Arnold, J. (2017) 'Listening without prejudice? Procedural adjustments in the employment tribunal', ELA briefing, March, 5–7.

Cooper, P., Marchant, R. and Backen, P. (2015) 'Getting to grips with ground rules hearings: a checklist for judges, advocates and intermediaries to promote the fair treatment of vulnerable people in court', *Criminal Law Review*, 6: 420–35.

Cooper, P. and Wurtzel, D. (2013) 'A day late and a dollar short: in search of an intermediary scheme for vulnerable defendants in England and Wales', *Criminal Law Review*, 1: 4–22.

Corbett, N.E. and Summerfield, A. (2017) *Alleged Perpetrators of Abuse as Litigants in Person in Private Family Law: The Cross-Examination of Intimidated and Vulnerable Witnesses*, London: Ministry of Justice.

Criminal Practice Directions I: General matters – 3D: Vulnerable People in the Courts; 3E: Ground rules hearings to plan the questioning of a vulnerable witness or defendant; 3F: Intermediaries; 3G: Vulnerable defendants.

Criminal Procedure Rules and Criminal Practice Directions, October 2015 edition, amended April 2016, especially Criminal Procedure Rules, 3.9: Case preparation and progression; 3.11: Conduct of a trial or an appeal.

Crown Prosecution Service (2016) *Speaking to Witnesses at Court: CPS Guidance*, London: CPS.

The Detention Forum (2015) 'Rethinking "vulnerability" in detention: a crisis of harm', available from: http://detentionforum.org.uk/2015/07/09/rethinking-vulnerability-in-detention-a-crisis-of-harm/

Fairclough, S. (2016) '"It doesn't happen … and I've never thought it was necessary for it to happen": barriers to vulnerable defendants giving evidence by live link in crown court trials', *International Journal of Evidence and Proof*, 24(8): 1–19.

Fairclough, S. (2018) 'Speaking up for injustice: reconsidering the provision of special measures through the lens of equality', *Criminal Law Review*, 1: 4–19.

Family Justice Review Panel (2011) *Family Justice Review: Final Report*, London: Ministry of Justice and Department for Education.

Fielding, N., Braun, S., Hieke, G. and Mainwaring, C. (2020) 'Video enabled justice evaluation', Sussex Police and Crime Commissioner and University of Surrey, available from: http://spccweb.thco.co.uk/media/4851/vej-final-report-ver-11b.pdf

Genn, H., Lever, B., Gray, L., Balmer, N. and National Centre for Social Research (2006) *Tribunals for Diverse Users*, DCA Research Series 1/06, London: DCA.

Gibbs, P. (2017) *Defendants on Video – Conveyor Belt Justice or Revolution of Access?*, London: Transform Justice.

Gill, N., Rotter, R., Burridge, A. and Allsopp, J. (2017) 'The limits of procedural discretion: unequal treatment and vulnerability in Britain's asylum appeals', *Social and Legal Studies*, 27(1): 49–78.

Hamlyn, B., Phelps, A., Turtle, J. and Sattar, G. (2004) *Are Special Measures Working? Evidence from Surveys of Vulnerable and Intimidated Witnesses*, London: Home Office.

Henderson, S. (2016) 'Taking control of cross-examination: judges, advocates and intermediaries discuss judicial management of the cross-examination of vulnerable people', *Criminal Law Review*, 3: 181–205.

Her Majesty's Courts and Tribunals Service (2019) 'Reform update: summer 2019', available from: https://assets.publishing.service.gov.uk/government/uploads/system/uploads/attachment_data/file/806959/HMCTS_Reform_Update_Summer_19.pdf

House of Commons Justice Committee (2015) *Inquiry into Criminal Courts Charge. Second Report of 2015/16*, London: House of Commons.

House of Commons Justice Committee (2016) *Inquiry into Courts and Tribunals Fees: Second Report of 2016/17*, London: House of Commons.

House of Commons Justice Committee (2019) *Inquiry into Courts and Tribunals Reforms: Second Report of 2019*, London: House of Commons.

Hoyano, L. and Rafferty, A. (2017) 'Rationing defence intermediaries under the April 2016 Criminal Practice Direction', *Criminal Law Review*, 2: 93–105.

Hunter, G., Jacobson, J. and Kirby, A. (2018) *Judicial Perceptions of the Quality of Criminal Advocacy*, London: Solicitors Regulation Authority and Bar Standards Board.

Jacobson, J. (2017) 'Introduction', in P. Cooper and H. Norton (eds) *Vulnerable People and the Criminal Justice System: A Guide to Law and Practice*, Oxford: Oxford University Press, pp 1–21.

Jacobson, J., Bhardwa, B., Gyateng, T., Hunter, G. and Hough, M. (2010) Punishing Disadvantage: A Profile of Children in Custody, London: Prison Reform Trust.

Jacobson, J., Hunter, G. and Kirby, A. (2015) *Inside Crown Court: Personal Experiences and Questions of Legitimacy*, Bristol: Policy Press.

Jacobson, J. and Talbot, J. (2009) *Vulnerable Defendants in the Criminal Courts: A Review of Provision for Adults and Children*, London: Prison Reform Trust.

Judicial College (2018) *Equal Treatment Bench Book: February 2018 Edition (March 2020 Revision)*, London: Judicial College.

Judicial Working Group on Litigants in Person (2013) *Judiciary of England and Wales*, available from: www.judiciary.uk/wp-content/uploads/JCO/Documents/Reports/lip_2013.pdf

Judiciary of England and Wales (2015) *Report of the Vulnerable Witnesses and Children Working Group*, available from: www.judiciary.uk/wp-content/uploads/2015/03/vwcwg-report-march-2015.pdf

JUSTICE (2018) *Preventing Digital Exclusion from Online Justice: A Report of JUSTICE*, available from: https://justice.org.uk/wp-content/uploads/2018/06/Preventing-Digital-Exclusion-from-Online-Justice.pdf

JUSTICE (2019) *Understanding Courts: A Report by JUSTICE*, London: JUSTICE, available from: https://justice.org.uk/wp-content/uploads/2019/01/Understanding-Courts.pdf

Khalifeh, H., Howard, L., Osborn D., Moran, P. and Johnson, S. (2013) 'Violence against people with disability in England and wales: findings from a National Cross-Sectional Survey', *PLoS ONE*, 8(2): e55952.

Kirby, A. (2017) 'Effectively engaging victims, witnesses and defendants in the criminal courts: a question of "court culture"?' *Criminal Law Review*, 12: 949–68.

Kirk, E., McDermont, M. and Busby, N. (2015) *Employment Tribunal Claims – Debunking the Myths*, Bristol: University of Bristol.

Law for Life (2014) 'Meeting the information needs of litigants in person', June, available from: www.lawforlife.org.uk/wp-content/uploads/Meeting-the-information-needs-of-litigants-in-person.pdf

The Law Society (2017) 'Access denied? LASPO four years on: a Law Society review', Law Society of England and Wales, available from: www.lawsociety.org.uk/support-services/research-trends/laspo-4-years-on/

Lee, R. and Tkacukova, T. (2017) 'A study of litigants in person in Birmingham Justice Centre', Birmingham: Centre for Professional Legal Education, available from: http://epapers.bham.ac.uk/3014/1/cepler_working_paper_2_2017.pdf

Legal Aid Agency (2018) 'Interests of justice: guidance on the consideration of defence representation orders', available from: https://assets.publishing.service.gov.uk/government/uploads/system/uploads/attachment_data/file/858654/Interests_of_justice_desktop_aid_2018_v2_.pdf

Leggatt, A. (2001) *Tribunals for Users: One System, One Service*, London: The Stationery Office.

Marks, A. (2016) 'What is a court? A report by JUSTICE', available from: https://justice.org.uk/wp-content/uploads/2016/05/JUSTICE-What-is-a-Court-Report-2016.pdf

McKeever, G. (2013) 'A ladder of legal participation for tribunal users', *Public Law*, 7: 575–98.

McKeever, G. (2020) 'Comparing courts and tribunals through the lens of legal participation', *Civil Justice Quarterly*, 39(3): 217–36.

McKeever, G., Royal-Dawson, L., Kirk, E. and McCord, J. (2018) *Litigants in Person in Northern Ireland: Barriers to Legal Participation*, Belfast: Ulster University.

Ministry of Justice (2010) 'Proposals for the reform of legal aid in England and Wales', available from: https://assets.publishing.service.gov.uk/government/uploads/system/uploads/attachment_data/file/228970/7967.pdf

Ministry of Justice (2011) 'Achieving best evidence in criminal proceedings: guidance on interviewing victims and witnesses, and guidance on using special measures', available from: www.cps.gov.uk/sites/default/files/documents/legal_guidance/best_evidence_in_criminal_proceedings.pdf

Ministry of Justice (2013) 'Transforming the CJS: a strategy and action plan for the criminal justice system', available from: https://assets.publishing.service.gov.uk/government/uploads/system/uploads/attachment_data/file/209659/transforming-cjs-2013.pdf

Ministry of Justice (2014) 'Report on review of ways to reduce the distress of victims in trials of sexual violence', available from: https://assets.publishing.service.gov.uk/government/uploads/system/uploads/attachment_data/file/299341/report-on-review-of-ways-to-reduce-distress-of-victims-in-trials-of-sexual-violence.pdf

Ministry of Justice (2016) 'Transforming our justice system: by the Lord Chancellor, the Lord Chief Justice and the Senior President of Tribunals', available from: https://assets.publishing.service.gov.uk/government/uploads/system/uploads/attachment_data/file/553261/joint-vision-statement.pdf

Ministry of Justice (2019a) 'The witness intermediary scheme: annual report 2018/19', available from: https://assets.publishing.service. gov.uk/government/uploads/system/uploads/attachment_data/ file/887122/witness-inter-scheme-annual-report.pdf

Ministry of Justice (2019b) 'Family Court statistics quarterly, England and Wales, July to September 2019', available from: https://assets. publishing.service.gov.uk/government/uploads/system/uploads/ attachment_data/file/857335/FCSQ_July_to_September_2019_ 2.pdf

Ministry of Justice (2019c) 'Legal support: the way ahead. An action plan to deliver better support to people experiencing legal problems', available from: https://assets.publishing.service.gov. uk/government/uploads/system/uploads/attachment_data/file/ 777036/legal-support-the-way-ahead.pdf

Moorehead, R. and Sefton, M. (2005) *Litigants in Person: Unrepresented Litigants in First Instance Proceedings*, DCA Research Series, 2/05, London: DCA.

Munby, J. (2016) Address of the President Sir James Munby at the annual dinner of the Family Law Bar Association in Middle Temple Hall on 26 February 2016.

National Audit Office (2014) 'Implementing reforms to civil legal aid', available from: www.nao.org.uk/wp-content/uploads/2014/ 11/Implementing-reforms-to-civil-legal-aid1.pdf

National Audit Office (2018) 'Early progress in transforming courts and tribunals', available from: www.nao.org.uk/wp-content/uploads/ 2018/05/Early-progess-in-transforming-courts-and-tribunals.pdf

National Audit Office (2019) 'Transforming courts and tribunals: A progress update', available from: www.nao.org.uk/wp-content/ uploads/2019/09/Transforming-Courts-and-Tribunals.pdf

Owusu-Bempah, A. (2018) 'The interpretation and application of the right to effective participation', *International Journal of Evidence and Proof*, 22(4): 321–41.

Pettit, B., Greenhead, S., Khalifeh, H., Drennan, V., Hart, J., Hogg, J., Borschmann, R., Mamo, E. and Moran, P. (2013) 'At risk yet dismissed: the criminal victimisation of people with mental health problems', available from: www.mind.org.uk/media-a/4121/at-risk-yet-dismissed-report.pdf

Plotnikoff, J. and Woolfson, R. (2007) *The 'Go-Between': Evaluation of Intermediary Pathfinder Projects*, London: Ministry of Justice.

Plotnikoff, J. and Woolfson, R. (2016) 'Worth waiting for: the benefits of section 28 pre-trial cross-examination', *Archbold Review*, 8 September, Issue 8: 6–9.

Pollert, A. (2010) 'The lived experience of isolation for vulnerable workers facing workplace grievances in 21st-century Britain', *Economic and Industrial Democracy*, 31(1): 62–92.

Pyper, D., McGuiness, F. and Brown, J. (2017) 'House of Commons Library briefing paper no. 7081: employment tribunal fees', London: House of Commons Library.

Roberts, P., Cooper, D. and Judge S. (2005) 'Monitoring success, accounting for failure: the outcome of prosecutors' applications for special measures directions under the Youth Justice and Criminal Evidence Act 1999', *International Journal of Evidence and Proof*, 9(4): 269–90.

Rossner, M. and McCurdy, M. (2018) *Implementing Video Hearings (Party-to-State): A Process Evaluation*, London: Ministry of Justice.

Royal College of Psychiatrists (2016) *Consultation Response to Immigration and Asylum Appeals on Proposals to Expedite Appeals by Immigration Detainees*, London: Royal College of Psychiatrists.

Ryder, E. (2012) 'Judicial proposals for the modernisation of Family Justice: Mr Justice Ryder', Judiciary of England and Wales, available from: www.judiciary.uk/wp-content/uploads/JCO/Documents/Reports/ryderj_recommendations_final.pdf

Shaw, S. (2016) *Review into the Welfare in Detention of Vulnerable Persons: A Report to the Home Office by Stephen Shaw*, London: HM Stationery Office.

Susskind, R. (2019) *Online Courts and the Future of Justice*, Oxford: Oxford University Press.

Thomas, R. (2013) 'From "adversarial v inquisitorial" to "active, enabling, and investigative": developments in UK', in R. Thomas, L. Jacobs and S. Baglay (eds) *The Nature of Inquisitorial Processes in Administrative Regimes: Global Perspectives*, Farnham: Ashgate Publishing, pp 51–70.

Thomson, J. and Becker, J. (2019) *Unrepresented Defendants: Perceived Effects on the Crown Court in England and Wales – Practitioners' Perspectives*, London: Ministry of Justice.

Tonry, M. (2010) 'Rebalancing the criminal justice system in favour of the victim: the costly consequences of populist rhetoric', in A. Bottoms and J. Roberts (eds) *Hearing the Victim: Adversarial Justice, Crime Victims*, Abingdon: Routledge, pp 72–103.

Transform Justice (2016) 'Justice denied? The experience of litigants in person in the criminal courts', available from: www.transformjustice.org.uk/wp-content/uploads/2016/04/TJ-APRIL_Singles.pdf

Trinder, L., Hunter, R., Hitchings, E., Miles, J., Moorhead, R., Smith, L., Sefton, M., Hinchly, V., Bader, K. and Pearce, J. (2014) *Litigants in Person on Family Law Cases*, London: Ministry of Justice.

Tribunals Judiciary (2008) 'Practice Direction First Tier and Upper Tribunal: Child, vulnerable adult and sensitive witnesses', London: Tribunals Judiciary, available from: www.judiciary.uk/wp-content/uploads/JCO/Documents/Practice+Directions/Tribunals/Childvulnerableadultandsensitivewitnesses.pdf

Tribunals Judiciary (2010) 'Joint Presidential Guidance Note no 2 of 2010: Child, vulnerable adult and sensitive appellant guidance', London: Tribunals Judiciary, available from: www.judiciary.uk/wp-content/uploads/2014/07/ChildWitnessGuidance.pdf

Wheatcroft, J., Wagstaff, G. and Moran, A. (2009) 'Re-victimising the victim? How rape victims experience the UK legal system', *Victims and Offenders*, 4(3): 265–84.

Williams, K. (2011) *Litigants in Person: A Literature Review*, Research Summary, 2/11, London: Ministry of Justice.

Wurtzel, D. and Marchant, R. (2017) 'Intermediaries', in P. Cooper and H. Norton (eds) *Vulnerable People and the Criminal Justice System: A Guide to Law and Practice*, Oxford: Oxford University Press.

# THREE

# Conceptualising Participation: Practitioner Accounts

Amy Kirby

## Introduction

This chapter and the one that follows present the findings of the empirical component of the study. This chapter focuses on the interviews conducted with 159 practitioners working in and around a number of court and tribunal settings: predominantly the criminal courts (both Crown and magistrates'), Family Court, Employment Tribunal (ET) and Immigration and Asylum Chamber (IAC). As will be discussed, the interview findings point to a range of ways in which the practitioners understood the meaning and functions of participation by lay witnesses and parties – henceforth 'court users' – in oral hearings held as part of judicial proceedings. From these accounts, it is possible to discern ten overlapping and interlinked conceptualisations of what participation entails and why it matters. The discussion here thus reflects practitioners' own definitions and understandings of participation rather than those presented in the wider policy and academic literature, which are described elsewhere in this volume.

Practitioner accounts provide insight into the meanings and functions of participation from the perspectives of those immersed in the day-to-day realities of the courts, and generate knowledge about how participation is mediated by those who directly interact with court users. This is an important undertaking as it has a bearing on how, and the extent to which, participation is achieved in practice. The final part of the chapter examines what practitioners had to say about barriers to and facilitators of participation, which advances thinking about how participation can be better supported in future.

## Interviews with practitioners: rationale and methodological approach

The practitioners interviewed for the study included judges, lawyers, magistrates, court staff and others who regularly attend court and tribunal hearings in a professional capacity, or provide support to witnesses or parties attending court. The introduction to this volume briefly set out some of the ways in which participation as a legal principle is articulated in law and procedural and practice guidance. The aim of the interviews was to examine how participation, and the part it plays in the delivery of justice, is conceptualised by those who have regular contact with court users, or – in various ways – have some part to play in shaping the court environment.

Following selection of the judicial settings and three geographic sites (one Welsh and two English cities and their surrounding areas) in which the research was to be conducted (see Chapter One), formal approval for the interviews with practitioners was obtained from national bodies where required: the Judicial Office with regard to judges and magistrates; HM Courts and Tribunals Service for court staff; Cafcass (the Children and Family Court Advisory and Support Service) and Cafcass Cymru for Cafcass officers; and HM Prisons and Probation Service for probation officers.

Research access was additionally negotiated nationally and locally with relevant agencies and services. The research team adopted a purposive, convenience approach to sampling (see Bryman, 2016), whereby target numbers of respondents within each practitioner category were agreed, and recruitment was undertaken through local professional contacts and networks.[1]

In total, 159 practitioners were interviewed, the large majority of whom worked in the fields of criminal, family, employment and immigration law. A small number worked in the coronial jurisdiction, in other areas of justice or cross-jurisdictionally. The practitioners were drawn from various backgrounds, which are categorised as follows:

- Judiciary: circuit judges, district judges, magistrates, employment and tribunal judges and one coroner.
- Lawyers: solicitors and barristers across all the specified jurisdictions, some of whom were involved in pro bono services.
- Court staff: legal advisors to magistrates (in both the criminal and family jurisdictions) and ushers.
- Voluntary sector practitioners: paid staff and volunteers from a range of services working with court users, including the Witness Service, Personal Support Unit,[2] Coroners' Courts Support Service and Trade Unions.[3] Intermediaries are also included in this category.[4]
- Statutory sector practitioners: this is a broad category encompassing professionals who attend court as part of their role with statutory services such as probation, social services, Cafcass, and criminal justice liaison and diversion services. A small number of Home Office Presentation Officers (HOPOs), who represent the Home Office in IAC hearings, are included in this category.

The breakdown of respondents by jurisdiction and role is set out in Table 3.1. The interviews with this diverse range of practitioners enabled the research team to examine how participation is understood from multiple vantage points, including

**Table 3.1: Breakdown of respondents by jurisdiction and role**

| Primary jurisdiction | Number | Percentage | Role | Number | Percentage |
|---|---|---|---|---|---|
| Crime | 63 | 40 | Judiciary | 55 | 35 |
| Family | 46 | 29 | Lawyer | 27 | 17 |
| Employment | 19 | 12 | Court staff | 13 | 8 |
| Immigration and Asylum | 15 | 9 | Voluntary sector | 39 | 24 |
| Coronial | 7 | 4 | Statutory sector | 25 | 16 |
| Other* | 9 | 6 | | | |
| **Total** | **159** | **100** | **Total** | **159** | **100** |

* This group comprises those who had no primary jurisdiction or worked in other parts of the justice system.

those of practitioners with varying levels of interaction with, and relations to, court users. The table shows that some jurisdictions and roles were overrepresented in the sample. For example, two fifths of respondents were from the criminal jurisdiction; however, this should be seen in the context of the criminal courts having the highest volume of cases of the jurisdictions under study (see Figure 1.1 in Chapter One). The small number of respondents from the coronial jurisdiction reflects the exploratory nature of this part of the study. Members of the judiciary accounted for over one third of the sample, which can be seen as a strength of the study given that scant existing research has incorporated such a cross-section (in terms of both jurisdiction and status) of judicial perspectives on court users and participation. While the following discussion of findings draws some comparisons between jurisdictions and roles, the varying levels of representation pose limits on the extent to which this can be done.

The practitioner interviews lasted around 45 minutes on average and were conducted face-to-face or via telephone in accordance with respondents' preferences. A small number of group interviews were held, to suit the respondents' convenience, but most were one-to-one. The interviews were semi-structured and guided by an interview schedule which was oriented around three main themes: what respondents considered to be 'effective participation'; whether and on what grounds they believed participation by court users to be important; and what they perceived to be the main barriers to and (actual and potential) facilitators of participation. With respondents' permission, interviews were audio-recorded and transcribed by an external transcription company. A thematic approach to analysis of the transcripts was adopted, involving the iterative development and refinement of a coding framework structured around respondents' conceptualisations of participation and key barriers and facilitators.

## What is participation?

Respondents across all jurisdictions and roles tended to speak of court users' participation in judicial proceedings as essential to the delivery of justice. In so doing, they did not draw upon ready-made or precise definitions of participation, but rather articulated the concept in a wide range of ways. Through close analysis of the interview transcripts, the research team identified several contrasting conceptualisations of what court user participation entails, and the functions of participation, as set out in Box 3.1.

I will now examine each of the six perspectives on 'what participation entails' that emerged from the data, with discussion of practitioners' perspectives on 'functions' to follow in the next section of this chapter. In advance of that, it is important to note three general points. First, what are described here as practitioners' contrasting perspectives on participation and why it matters are not clear-cut or discrete. They are, rather, closely overlapping ways of talking about participation from which the research team have identified certain key features. Secondly, respondents varied widely in terms of which, and how many, of the conceptualisations they tended to articulate in their answers to the interview questions. Thirdly, there were salient areas of both difference and similarity in these articulations between jurisdictions and roles – demonstrating that while participation must be understood as a multifaceted phenomenon, it can be usefully examined and applied cross-jurisdictionally.[5]

---

**Box 3.1: Conceptualisations of participation**

Practitioners variously described **what participation entails** in terms of:

- the provision and/or elicitation of information for the court;
- being informed about proceedings;
- having legal representation;
- protection of well-being;
- the management of the court user, such that disruption to proceedings is avoided;
- presence at proceedings.

Practitioners variously described the **functions of participation** in terms of:

- the exercise of legal rights;
- enabling court decision making;
- legitimation of court processes and outcomes;
- potential therapeutic benefits.

---

### *Participation entails: providing and eliciting information*

A large majority of practitioners described participation by court users as a matter of *providing information*, by giving evidence or submitting statements to the court; or *eliciting information*, for example, by asking questions of other parties or witnesses. The 'information-provider' (see Edwards, 2004) or 'information-elicitor' role of lay participation was articulated by respondents in each practitioner group and across all the five jurisdictions. Box 3.2 provides some short examples of the numerous comments on this theme.

Some respondents spoke of participation *only* in terms of – and thus as equating to – provision of information. For example, when asked to describe what participation means, a Witness Service volunteer replied: "I assume you mean participating in the fact of giving evidence, because that's the only time they [witnesses/complainants] are participating." However, many others spoke of the provision and elicitation of information as one of several aspects of participation; for example, in most of the Box 3.2 quotations the respondents also referred to participation as a matter of being informed.[6]

---

**Box 3.2: Providing and eliciting information**

'They've got to be able to express themselves, I mean, they've got to be able to say what they want to say in a court setting. They've got to know what ... they should be saying and what documents they either should be producing, or are 'allowed' to produce.' (Judge; immigration)

'It is making sure that they can give the best evidence that they can. Because it seems to me that they need to understand, obviously, what's happening in the courtroom. But I think the main thrust is towards making sure that whatever they're there to do as a witness of fact, they can communicate that.' (Barrister; family)

'At a simple level, if someone has been involved in a road traffic accident, and they're also an important eyewitness to what occurred, the judge needs to ensure that that person gives a coherent account of what occurred. Not feeling under pressure. Not feeling obliged to answer at 100 miles an hour, etcetera.' (Judge; other)

'For a witness to be able to participate, they just need to listen and answer the questions that they're asked.' (Barrister; coroners)

'Well, to be able to participate, really, you need to be well enough to read documents, take it all in, work out how to structure your arguments and take part in asking questions of witnesses, work out who to call as witnesses and which documents to ask for.' (Judge; employment)

---

## Participation entails: being informed

Indeed, references to court users *being informed* as a core component of participation were commonplace, and cross-cut professional and jurisdictional boundaries. While more than half of all respondents spoke in these terms, the lawyers were the most inclined to do so (maybe because they regard keeping clients informed as an essential aspect of their professional role). Respondents emphasised the importance of court users *understanding* the judicial process and outcomes – as neatly summarised by an intermediary who practised in the criminal courts:[7]

'The most important part of effective participation is having an understanding. That's having an understanding of the case that's against them. Having an understanding of what everybody is saying about them and what the whole trial process is. I don't feel that anybody can participate effectively if they don't have a full understanding.'

Practitioners spoke of court users' need to be informed about a number of interlinking matters, including the essential functions and nature of the justice system, and specific legal conventions and procedures:

'For me, [participation] really means being able to understand what's going on. I don't mean that in the most basic sense. I think in Coroners' Courts with inquests, you're talking about an inquisitorial process. There are lots of rules in the Coroner's court that lay people are not going to understand and appreciate.' (Solicitor; coroners)

Some said that fundamental to being informed is an understanding of courtroom language, which can pose particular difficulties for laypeople (as has been widely documented elsewhere[8] and will be considered also in Chapter Four):

'For a court user, they need to have a basic understanding of what's going to happen, which most people don't. They've got to be able to understand the language that's used. Basically, what's happening and how it impacts upon them, whether that's as a defendant or a witness or whoever. Because, I think, going into a court for someone who's never been in a court, is probably like going somewhere where they speak a foreign language and you don't speak that language ... It is very alien.' (Solicitor; crime)

Another necessary feature of informed participation was said to be that court users understand their own role within the judicial process, including what is expected of them and any limits to this:

'Lay clients won't always understand necessarily what they should do. For example, simple things like evidential matters. They won't necessarily know what documents or what evidence they should be collecting if they don't have a lawyer to advise them on that. Then, although they may actually in practice go to court and be in the hearing, they're not really participating effectively if they aren't aware of what they should be putting before the court.' (Barrister; immigration)

### Participation entails: being represented

A sizeable minority of respondents – more than one quarter – closely associated court user participation with *legal representation*. For example, when asked to describe what participation means, an usher in the criminal courts responded: "I think, a lot of the time, especially with criminal cases, [participation] will be through the representative, rather than through the defendant." For these respondents, participation is problematic only where a party is unrepresented (or, perhaps, represented poorly); conversely, a party who is represented is, by definition, deemed to participate, even if they are doing so indirectly via their lawyer.[9]

As discussed in Chapter Two, access to publicly funded legal representation varies widely depending on the type of case and lay party concerned. In line with this, it was possible to discern notable differences between jurisdictions in the extent to which practitioners associated participation with representation. Most notably, those practising in the ET – where legal representation is relatively uncommon – were less inclined to speak in these terms than practitioners from other jurisdictions:

'Well it's still the case that the vast majority of defendants are represented ... Principally, you are relying upon their representative to have explained procedures, processes ... As I say, because most people are represented, you are really focusing on their representative rather than on the defendant themselves.' (Judge; crime)

'[Court users] have to tell me their story. And, it is my job to make sure they can ... It's much easier if they've got legal representation.' (Judge; immigration)

'Without the benefit of having a legal advocate, I see parents floundering in court proceedings, not understanding the very basics of even attending at court.' (Cafcass officer; family)

That the relationship between representation and participation is not entirely straightforward was alluded to by several practitioners, who pointed to the possibility that an advocate (or supporter) can get in the way of a party's active engagement with proceedings. A probation officer commented: "[Defendants] don't really get much to participate in actual court unless they're *not* represented. Everything that they do at court tends to be via the intermediary or a solicitor."

## *Participation entails: being protected*

Around a quarter of respondents, including representatives from all jurisdictions, spoke of participation as being dependent upon the *protection of the court user's well-being*. From this perspective, court users can participate effectively only if they feel safe and reasonably comfortable within the court environment and are protected from intimidation or excessive fear or distress. A legal advisor in the criminal courts described participation in the following terms:

> 'getting the best quality evidence and experience from that particular witness, to present their best before the court, unhindered by, maybe, being too stressed, for example … I think the court should do its utmost to try and make it more palatable for people to come to court and give off their best.'

Some respondents were concerned with the impact on court users of the formalities of the court environment or the (usually) adversarial nature of proceedings. Others, speaking mostly about victims and witnesses in the criminal courts, or parties in the Family Court, spoke more about court users' needs for protection from fear or intimidation. Also under the general theme of 'protection' were comments made about the importance of understanding and addressing court users' physical, intellectual or mental health needs which have a bearing on their participation. In light of this, practitioners spoke frequently about adjustments to the court process (see Chapter Two for more detail on these) which can help lay users to participate in a protected manner:

> 'We, as a bench … [need to] make sure that [witnesses] aren't put under pressure with the questioning from either the defence advocate, or, indeed, the defendant put [under] undue pressure by repeated questioning from the prosecution.' (Magistrate; crime)

'It's important that [lay parties] do participate, and it's important that the court makes whatever arrangements are necessary in order to enable them to do so. That goes for people with mental health difficulties, as well as the ordinary man in the street.' (Judge; family)

Importantly, a number of practitioners argued that 'being protected' in some instances requires that the party or other individual does *not* participate in proceedings, particularly when it comes to children who are the subject of Family Court proceedings. Such children may sometimes meet the judge presiding over their case in chambers, but direct participation in proceedings was said to be rare, on the grounds that it is potentially harmful. Speaking about the potential role of the child where there are allegations of abuse, a Cafcass officer said:

'By and large, it'd be emotionally quite damaging for the child to give evidence ... It depends what other evidence the judge has against the potential perpetrator, and the after effect, the impact, that it would have on the child in terms of family relations; whether the child can emotionally deal with the magnitude of giving evidence against the perpetrator. So yes, there is an option there, but it's carefully considered.'

### Participation entails: being managed

Some respondents conceived participation as something to be *managed* by practitioners so as to avoid disruption of the court process or otherwise inappropriate behaviour. Participation was spoken of in these terms by around one fifth of respondents – largely court staff and members of the judiciary, perhaps reflecting the fact that they hold primary responsibility for ensuring the smooth running of proceedings. Underlying the notion that lay participation necessitates management were some concerns about possible 'over-participation' by court users who may be inclined to provide too much, or inappropriate, information:

'I think it's then more about how lay people are handled. For instance, to be told in advance that they should answer the questions put to them, and even though they might have other things that they know, to be told that [these things] aren't necessarily relevant, would help.' (Magistrate; crime)

'I do feel [that participation is] very important, but I think the court users' understanding of participating is not necessarily the same as the tribunal's understanding, because they're not legally trained. They don't necessarily focus on relevant issues, they simply want to tell you everything. Sometimes, it's not necessary.' (Judge; immigration)

As the preceding quotations illustrate, 'over-participation' was often deemed to be borne out of a lack of understanding of the court process. Accordingly, the need for 'managed' participation was sometimes referred to in discussions of litigants in person (LiPs). Management of court users for the sake of saving court time was another issue raised, as by a magistrate in the criminal courts: 'There's always this balance between people feeling they've had a fair hearing and it needing to be managed ... especially because these days we are generally quite short of time.' Other practitioners spoke of the need to contain the heightened emotions that are often an inherent feature of involvement in judicial proceedings:

'They want to participate and sometimes the only difficulty is to make sure to keep them on the point, because they can get very emotional.' (Judge; other)

'I've also sat in one [hearing] where people have been kicking off, and a coroner has actually had to say, "Look, I've got two police officers here, giving evidence. I've got no qualms in getting you removed from my court." It's a balance, I think.' (Support service; coroners)

Understandings of participation as something to be managed were often expressed with reference to court users whose participation is 'obligatory' (see Owusu-Bempah, 2017) rather than voluntarily entered into, such as defendants in the criminal courts. This was also the case with regard to the final conceptualisation of what participation entails: namely, that it is about presence.

### Participation entails: being present

Participation was described by a minority of practitioners as essentially a matter of *being present* at the court or tribunal hearing:

'If they don't [participate the case] will be heard in their absence and it would more likely go against them than for them. It's in their benefit to participate with the court.' (Court usher; crime)

'To actually be able to get there in terms of actually being able to access the building for whatever reasons, and also being able to get there in terms of that their needs are being met ... So it's actually being able to be there and be part of it.' (Intermediary; family)

'It's still important for them to physically be in court and see what is happening, and understand what is happening ... In fact, you participate by turning up.' (Barrister; immigration)

If not made explicit (as in the last of the previous quotations), most comments about presence implied that this should be physical rather than via remote means such as video-link. Some respondents conceived of a court user's presence as having an active dimension – on the basis that attendance at a hearing enables the individual to provide information to the court or be otherwise directly involved in proceedings. There is thus an overlap with the other understandings of participation as discussed earlier. For example, when describing what participation means, a family solicitor commented:

> '[If] they're not present at the hearing, they don't participate effectively ... If they're there, you can always gain instructions from them ... The problem arises when they don't engage with you before the hearing or after the hearing, because then that puts you on the back foot at the hearing. Or, if they've completely disengaged with you and they don't turn up at the hearing, they can't participate at all.'

Other comments focused on passive or minimal participation through presence, with reference to circumstances in which a court user is legally obliged to attend proceedings:

> 'Defendants don't have any choice than to engage in the judicial role because they are the people on trial for alleged criminal offences. So when you say to what extent they should engage, if they plead guilty then they've engaged to the extent that they're going to be sentenced.' (Legal advisor; crime)

> 'Participation is almost a strange term to use because ... the legal process is not about, if you like, bringing people together in some form of communicative exercise ... To some extent the participants, many of them, may be unwilling participants, but they are essential and some

of them have no choice. For example, the defendant has no choice ... He's compelled. Witnesses are summonsed.' (Witness Service; crime)

In comments such as those just quoted, the meaning of participation was articulated in a weak sense: in terms of *mere* presence or legal obligation. Notions of the 'managed' court user likewise tend to imply a weaker form of participation than most perceptions of the participating court user as one who provides or elicits information, or is informed, represented or protected. This highlights how practitioners' conceptions of participation may influence the extent to which participation is achieved in practice.

## Why does participation matter?

This section of the chapter focuses on respondents' understandings of the *functions* of participation. As noted earlier, there were four main aspects to this. First, respondents spoke of participation as being, in and of itself, the exercise of one's legal rights; secondly, they described it as that which enables the court to make its decisions; thirdly, participation was said to have the function of legitimating the judicial process and outcomes; and, finally, there were references to the potential therapeutic value of participation. While the first of these understandings is of participation as an end in itself, the other three conceive of participation as having an instrumental value: that it is the means to achieving certain ends. These ends were understood to be, respectively, decision making, legitimacy and therapeutic benefits to the court user.

### *Participation is the exercise of legal rights*

More than half of the respondents across jurisdictions and professional groups spoke of the act of participation in terms of the exercise of legal rights, including the right to a fair trial:

'[Participation] is a fundamental principle of our justice, isn't it? I know we've got human rights legislation in place, but I think that any person who is facing a crime has their absolute right to be heard and participate in that hearing.' (Legal advisor; crime)

Correspondingly, participation was said to imbue the court process with what some described as 'fairness':

'[Participation] is essential, absolutely essential, yes. It goes to the basic tenet of justice must be seen to be done. If you're made aware that someone doesn't have the ability to follow the proceedings, whether it be because they don't speak the language, whether they have some disability, whether they have a lack of ability to concentrate on matters or understand matters, then all those factors need to be taken into consideration in order to ensure that they have a fair trial ... under Article 6 of the European Convention of Human Rights.' (Judge; family)

As this quotation indicates, the notion that participation ensures a fair hearing also encompasses ideas about 'equality of arms'. This was frequently commented upon with reference to the disadvantages faced by court users arising from such factors as language difficulties, emotional or mental health needs, or absence of legal representation. This was seen as especially pertinent in the context of the IAC,[1] where appellants are challenging the state (and with potentially life or death consequences):

'Where you have court proceedings where one side is always the government, the government comes to proceedings fully armed, or is capable of coming to the proceedings fully armed ... So we have to do our best to make sure that there's an equality of arms within court proceedings. Where one side has that built in advantage, it does mean that it is the other side that you're looking after, but doing so in a neutral way ... It's very important they're able to participate because without the participation, they don't have the chance to present their [case].' (Judge; immigration)

Although respondents often spoke passionately of participation as the exercise of legal rights, several also referred to the need to manage the lay user's expectations of what this entails. For example, they referred to the problems that can arise when a court user equates exercising their legal rights with achieving their desired outcome:

'The British justice system is not a search for the truth. That's not what it is, that's never been what it's about ... It's, "Have we got enough evidence to convict this person?" That's what it is and that's a very different thing. People generally think it's a search for the truth. They come and say that. I think they're disappointed by that.' (Solicitor; crime)

'The old phrase: "I want my day in court." Why? was always my question. Why? What do you think you're really going to achieve? From your point of view, from anybody else's point of view, do you really want to put yourself through that? And how will you feel if it doesn't go the way you want it to?' (Support service; family)

### Participation enables decision making

Many respondents spoke of participation as having the essential function of allowing the judicial process to reach an outcome:

'The whole system will not work unless all the parties are participating and fulfilling their role properly ... I don't think you're going to get justice if they're not. Quite simply. Because if you can't get witnesses into court and get them understanding what's going on, you've got nobody to give evidence; if a defendant isn't participating, he may, for example, plead not guilty when he should be pleading guilty ... or the person may plead guilty when he's not guilty.' (Judge; crime)

As described in the previous section, most practitioners conceived of participation in terms of (among other things) the provision and elicitation of information. Comments on this theme often included references to the court's need for the information in order to do its essential work of decision making:

'The question, I suppose, you pose to yourself, as a judge, in any particular case is, "What's going to help these parties give their best evidence so that you can reach the best decision and they can leave more confident that what they've experienced is justice?"' (Judge; employment)

'I think it's important that [lay participants] are as engaged as they can be. As the professionals ... We want to hear what they've got to say. We want them to give their best evidence. Particularly with family cases, we want to make sure that we've got all of the available information, so that the right decisions are being made in relation to the child who's at the centre of it.' (Legal advisor; family)

Decision making was said to be facilitated through participation by which court users were able to demonstrate their credibility or individuality. In this sense, participation was understood to have a 'humanising' quality. This was said to involve, for example, a jury being able to see and hear the testimony of witnesses before determining the verdict, a judge being able to directly interact with a litigant or defendant before reaching a decision or a legal practitioner meeting a child subject to

Family Court proceedings before representing their interests. Direct interaction with court users was said to be central to this:

> 'I'm always surprised and taken aback by the number of cases that I will read on paper, and then when I actually get people into court and I hear them give evidence, my impression of them, my view of the case, can completely change. You need oral evidence and you need to put people in the best position to give it. If there is any view that this can become a paper exercise, that we can get rid of the adversarial system, I'm afraid I'm completely against that. My experience is that you've got to hear the evidence.' (Judge; family)

> '[Early in my judicial career], I sat with a judge, and one of the first things he told me about sentencing was: "Never send anybody to prison unless you can look them in the eye when you do it." It was a salutary lesson, and of course it's not very easy to look someone in the eye on a video link. I understand all the cost pressures, and all the rest of it, but in my view he or she should be in court, where you see them and they see you.' (Judge; other)

The last respondent quoted was not alone in raising concerns about the implications for participation (and thereby for court decision making) of the use of video-link technology; others, however, had contrasting views on remote attendance, as will be further discussed later.

### Participation legitimates the judicial process and outcomes

Legitimacy is a complex and contested concept; however, broadly speaking, prominent scholars on the subject[10] argue that in order for institutions to make and maintain a 'valid' claim to hold authority (see Bottoms and Tankebe, 2012), they need to be perceived as legitimate in the eyes of the citizens that they serve. This is conceived both in terms of the presence of shared normative standards, or beliefs, between the authority and individual citizen *and* the extent to which the individual expresses consent for the authority – for example, by cooperating with it. Although they did not speak explicitly in these terms, almost half the respondents – and particularly members of the judiciary and court staff – indicated that they associated participation by court users with the users' perceptions of the court's authority as legitimate:

> '[Participation] makes all the difference in the world. You have court users participating, walking away from the court believing the case has been heard fairly whether they're the defendant or whether they're the participants in family cases. It's very, very necessary that people have an understanding and a belief they've had their chance in court to either present the case, to defend the case or to simply explain why the situation has arisen.' (Magistrate; crime)

Many respondents loosely articulated the principles of procedural justice theory, whereby 'procedurally just' treatment of court users helps to secure legitimacy.[11] Tyler (2007) identified four aspects to procedural justice in a court setting: having a voice in the process; neutrality in decision making; respectful treatment; and trust. In particular, the importance of the court user's voice within (the legal constraints of) the system was emphasised by a number of respondents, including a criminal solicitor: "Being able to participate is what makes it inherently fair because you've had your turn, you've had your voice heard, you've had fair play." Crucially, it was also said that what matters to court users is not simply that they have a voice, but that their voice is *listened to* by those administering justice:

> 'I think participation means being able to participate in every sense of the word and *feel* that you've had the

opportunity to do that as well ... Everybody needs to have the opportunity to feel that they've been listened to. That's the fairness of it, and because the decisions that are made are so important to people's lives and the children's lives.' (Solicitor; family)

Some respondents placed special weight on respectful treatment, such as an employment judge who referred to: "A bit of dialogue, a calmness of manner, measured tone, courtesy, offering breaks, that's all part of fairness. It's a process." This he described as "procedural fairness", which he distinguished from "just a substantive fairness". Others emphasised the importance of fair and equal treatment and, in line with procedural justice theory, suggested that perceptions of a fair *process* can even outweigh considerations of outcome:

'Issues like equal treatment should be as important if not more important, frankly, than getting it right because that really deals with how, when somebody leaves the courtroom, they should feel that they've had a fair hearing. There should be no doubt in their mind that everything they wanted to say has been said. They shouldn't have been cut off. They shouldn't feel as though their evidence has been curtailed unfairly, that they've been bullied or cajoled.' (Judge; immigration)

'I think in the employment tribunals, to show that people have participated effectively, we want the two people walking away to feel like ... they've been heard, and that whatever the outcome, they can accept it because they were able to fully participate in that process.' (Solicitor; employment)

Where the process is not perceived as fair, it was also suggested, an individual might be less inclined to comply or engage with the legal system in future:

'If [court users] didn't feel that their contribution was listened to and welcomed, they wouldn't be willing to repeat the experience if they were involved in another case ... If somebody has something that they feel is relevant and might make a difference to the final outcome but their voice isn't heard or their thoughts are not represented in any way, then that again could lead to frustration and, perhaps more importantly, a lack of faith in the court system.' (Magistrate; crime)

The impact that perceptions of legitimacy can have on future cooperation and compliance with authorities has been a central concern of legitimacy scholars, who argue that those with a strong belief in the legitimacy of authorities and institutions are more likely to cooperate or comply with authorities in any future interactions (Tyler, 2007).

### Participation provides (potential) therapeutic benefits

It has been shown that some respondents deemed participation to have a legitimating function, in that they assumed that the effectively participating court user was more likely to view the court process and outcome as fair. Closely overlapping with this perspective is the assumption that the court user who participates effectively (also) stands to benefit *as an individual*: that, in other words, participation potentially has therapeutic benefits. In the context of the legal system, 'therapeutic' can be understood to mean interactions that contribute to the court user's well-being or are rehabilitative. As with 'legitimacy', respondents did not explicitly talk of 'therapeutic' functions, but a small number did speak in broad terms about individuals feeling 'empowered' or otherwise benefiting from participation:

'[Lay users] have to participate because otherwise it's very disempowering. They have to be part of it, they can't be, sort of, dished out things.' (Judge; immigration)

'It's not the pieces of paper that make this scenario work, it's the users themselves. So we are only providers of the tools, or the supports, to try and make that happen in as amicable a way as possible, but we are not the final resolution of the matter, because we will end; they will go on and they'd have to keep dealing with that issue.' (Legal advisor; family)

Such perspectives accord with 'therapeutic jurisprudence' models of justice, which are concerned with the consequences for well-being of involvement in formal legal processes (see, for example, Wexler, 2000). Reflecting, in part, an emphasis in both on the importance of the individual's 'voice' in judicial proceedings, there is a clear complementarity between procedural justice theory and therapeutic justice approaches (Kaiser and Holtfreter, 2016). The latter, however, are often focused on particular types of court or groups of court users.[12] In this study, the therapeutic benefits of participation were sometimes discussed in general terms, regardless of jurisdiction or the nature of the individual's role in proceedings; at other times, they were spoken of in relation to specific lay users or types of hearing. For example, it was suggested that a sentencing court's consideration of a Victim Personal Statement[13] provides for a form of participation that is therapeutic for victims of crime:

'For the complainant it's a step towards feeling, "I'm in charge on this occasion. I've been able to do it" ... Especially if they've been the subject [of] sexual abuse, it gives them some closure, it gives them a sense of empowerment that they've actually been able to tell the [defendant] to their face what it's meant to them. I think it's very important from their point of view.' (Judge; crime)

The potentially therapeutic benefits of participation were also described with reference to convicted offenders who, post-sentence, are required to report back periodically to the court on their progress on drug treatment:

'It's really good to see how the magistrates – and they enjoy it – interact with the defendant at the same level. Some of the defendants will say "It's the first time I've ever been given any positive feedback, ever." To receive it from an authority figure is quite powerful, so encouraging participation in that way, I think, is really good.' (Legal advisor; crime)

## Barriers to and facilitators of participation

In addition to exploring practitioners' understandings of participation as a concept, the research interviews probed respondents' views on barriers to, and facilitators of, participation. The respondents often spoke at length and in detail about the range of intersecting factors that can limit participation, several of which were alluded to in the quotations set out in the preceding discussion. Many of the barriers identified by respondents have been examined in prior research (see Chapter Two), and were noted also through the observational research (to be reported in Chapter Four) – and will therefore not be examined in detail here.

In brief, however, the barriers to participation described by practitioners fell into three broad categories. The first of these were barriers said to arise from court users' needs and vulnerabilities – including mental health problems, learning disabilities and communication needs, language barriers – and other associated forms of social disadvantage or cultural difference. Secondly, respondents spoke about what might be termed the 'old' barriers to participation: long-standing structural and cultural features of the justice system which impede court users' engagement with it – such as its intimidating formality and architectural design,[14] the complexities of legal language and processes,[15] legal constraints on participation and limits to 'story-telling',[16] and endemic delays and inefficiencies.[17] Thirdly, respondents referenced what can be characterised as 'new' barriers to participation: that is, factors impacting court users which arise from recent policy developments. As described in detail in Chapter Two, these include reduced public funding for legal representation, which has led to increased numbers of LiPs across much of the justice system, and reforms introduced under the HMCTS courts modernisation programme.[18] In relation to the latter, many respondents had particular concerns about LiPs and some spoke at length about the large-scale court closures which have been seen in recent years. A related development under the courts modernisation programme is the expansion in use of remote methods of court attendance, particularly video-link. Since the time that the interviews took place, the COVID-19 pandemic has vastly (and unexpectedly) accelerated this development – in light of which, it is interesting to look in a little more depth at respondents' comments on this theme.

### *Remote court attendance*

Respondents had mixed and often nuanced views on the value and limits of virtual or remote participation. Their reservations tended to centre around two main issues. First, there were concerns about the perceived loss of interaction and the potential impact on participation. Some referred to the absence of body language, non-verbal cues or "human cues" (judge; employment) in video-enabled or telephone hearings; others commented that remote hearings prevented practitioners appreciating the "full picture" (magistrate; crime) of the case or individual concerned. Some alluded to the risk that court users may not be able to understand or fully engage with hearings attended remotely, which was said to be a particular issue for individuals with additional needs, such as those lacking literacy or technological skills, unrepresented parties, or those receiving the assistance of an interpreter. Court user participation via video-link was sometimes described as highly constrained – such as in circumstances when the audio is muted because the court user is perceived to be disruptive (a clear illustration of 'managed' participation), or when the court user appearing by video-link is "present in the hearing but not [participating]" (barrister; crime).

A second set of reservations concerned the practical difficulties involved in video-enabled or other forms of remote participation. Those with experience of using video technology described a number of "glitches" (magistrate; crime), such as difficulties connecting, problems with sound quality and not all parties being present at the allotted time. Others raised concerns about maintaining a secure connection or the potential impact on confidentiality, such as when video consultations between defendants in custody and lawyers take place while a prison officer is sitting in the video-link room. A range of participatory and practical considerations led one immigration judge to comment:

> 'I spend a long time and put a lot of effort into making people be as at ease as they can … It can be small bits of your body language that helps them feel at ease. I take pride, I take professional pride in letting people give their best evidence. You cannot do that over a screen. You cannot. Humanity is required to let people give their best evidence and you cannot do that over the screen … Quite apart from the fact that I don't believe it'll ever work … I just don't believe that the technology this side of five years is going to be good enough.'

However, positive comments were also made about remote hearings. Some respondents said that such hearings *enable* participation by court users who are otherwise unable, or would find it extremely difficult, to participate. There was support for the use of video-link as a special measure for vulnerable or intimidated court users, which facilitates 'protected' participation. An intermediary with experience of practising in the criminal courts described her experience of helping a defendant on the autism spectrum give evidence:

> 'He struggled to speak in front of multiple people, and he also found it difficult to give eye contact ... I supported the recommendation that he should leave the courtroom and go and give evidence via live link, because basically the difference was he [otherwise] couldn't do it. He felt like he could not do it if he had to do it in a courtroom, sitting in the witness box, but he felt like he could do it if it was over video link and I was sat next to him.'

A small number of respondents commented that video-enabled participation helps to create a less formal environment in which direct interaction between practitioners and court users is made easier. The use of remote hearings was also spoken of positively in cases in which court users would have to travel very long distances, including from abroad, to give evidence or for those with medical conditions which make travel to court difficult. Remote attendance was said to be of value in "simple and straightforward" (judge; employment) cases, such as bail or case management hearings. For example, reference was made to regular use of telephone hearings for preliminary matters in the ET, and several criminal practitioners said that remote attendance from prison is useful when defendants might otherwise have to travel long distances to court in a prison van, or risk losing their current cell to another incoming prisoner.

### Practitioners as facilitators

Perhaps one of the most salient findings from this study is that, when respondents were asked about how the participation of court users can be facilitated, they often spoke about the part that they themselves or other practitioners have to play in this. In other words, assisting or supporting participation – to the extent that this is possible, within the various constraints referred to earlier – was seen by many to be central to the role of practitioners in the courtroom. (The other main source of support for participation was said to be the availability of special measures or adjustments for vulnerable court users, as discussed elsewhere in this volume, which were widely described in positive terms.)

This focus on facilitating participation was evident not only in comments from respondents in explicit support roles, such as intermediaries and representatives of agencies such as the Witness Service and Cafcass. Many other practitioners, including court staff and members of the judiciary, appeared to regard the provision of assistance with participation as integral to their work:

'I will, if appropriate, give a little chat to a witness and say, 'Look, this is what's going to happen. This is what cross-examination is. It's not going to be a punch-up. It's not like TV.' All of that, again, just to settle them down …There's an awful lot that's probably going on in the back of my brain thinking about, "How can I just ensure that this person has the best opportunity to do whatever they're here to do?"' (Judge; employment)

'I always check what clients are aware of, and what they aren't aware of. If there are any gaps in that information, I try and fill that gap, and to make them feel comfortable about that because if they're unaware, or uncertain, or have difficulty understanding what's going on, that clearly means that they don't feel comfortable doing it.' (Barrister; immigration)

There may have been an element of 'interviewer effect' (see Bryman, 2016) in respondents' descriptions of their own endeavours to support court user participation. However, many spoke not only of the assistance they provide, but also that offered by their peers, and of how practitioners work together to support participation:

> 'Our clerks are very professional and friendly with the people that they encounter. We try and keep it as friendly as possible ... We don't always manage it, but we try and write [our judgments] in accessible English, not like a Chancery pleading out of Dickens ... That level of courtesy, I would hope, is not unique to us by any stretch. I think that's something you should do in all first-instance courts and tribunals.' (Judge; employment)

> 'I had a gentleman that was elderly and hard of hearing, so again, I would have addressed that with the solicitors, who then raised it with the bench, who then accepted that the individual wouldn't have to stay standing and made sure that things were fully explained during that process. The solicitor was able to turn around and explain what was happening.' (Liaison and diversion worker; crime)

Several respondents, including legal advisors themselves, said that providing help to LiPs was an important part of the legal advisor role, especially with the growth in numbers of unrepresented parties in the courts. This was described by one magistrate in the criminal courts as a "positive duty" of the role, and in the following manner by another respondent:

> 'If they're not offered the duty solicitor or it doesn't fall within the ambit of the scheme, then the legal advisors will ultimately explain to them what the procedure is. I know that lots of legal advisors ... will explain, "Well it's not my job to tell you to plead guilty or not guilty, but if I explain the law and procedure to you, you can

make your own decision on it" ... It's changed our roles significantly, I think, because you're more involved with [LiPs].' (Legal advisor; family)

Some practitioners were said to go "over and above" (magistrate; crime) or "out of their way" (solicitor; employment) in their efforts to facilitate participation and to act as a bridge between an otherwise complex, intimidating system and the individual appearing within it:

'I can spend as much time with [bereaved family members] as I like. That will be around explaining what the court is about, having advice sheets for them ... meeting them, talking over what the purpose is, talking about their role in helping the coroner, so that they feel as comfortable as possible when it comes to actually being physically in the court. I think there's a lot of information available, but there's a lot of human contact as well.' (Solicitor; coroners)

It was also suggested that the emphasis on inclusion and supporting court users is something of a recent trend. A judge in the criminal courts commented, "We've tended to have gone from the aloof, stuffy sort of judge approach to a more inclusive approach, a more sort of user-friendly approach, if you like," while a trade union representative (with experience of the ET) said:

'A few years back there would have been some judges who were a little old fashioned, is a polite way to put it, [laughter] and yes, maybe not quite as sensitive to diversity issues as they might have been. Genuinely, I think that's changed. There's been a lot of training put in for the tribunals, for judges and lay members, to make sure that people are aware.'

The efforts made to bridge the, sometimes substantial, gap between the system and individual court users are evidently not without personal cost to the practitioners. In interview, respondents were asked if their or their colleagues' well-being was affected by their work. In response, many spoke of the impact on themselves or their peers of the most serious or distressing cases, and particularly of hearing evidence about physical or sexual abuse or other trauma:[19]

> 'I know that there is a fear, and there is some evidence, that some judges who have had a constant diet of very serious sexual offences cases have felt that it has affected them psychologically and have had to take time off work.' (Judge; crime)

> 'If you are dealing with and speaking to people who have been through significant trauma, I mean you're speaking to people sometimes who are describing details of torture and it's very severe ... I'm not a psychologist, but I imagine it is going to affect people.' (Barrister; immigration)

Respondents also spoke of the impact of other aspects of their role, and interactions with lay users, on their well-being. Some referred to the emotional or psychological repercussions – particularly for members of the judiciary – of making life-changing decisions about individuals. There was also discussion of difficult working conditions within the courts and tribunals, associated with high caseloads or regular interaction with highly distressed or agitated court users:

> 'Particularly in care cases when you've had maybe a protracted hearing: you've had parents who've got their own vulnerabilities but that, sadly, aren't able to provide good enough parenting. So you're then looking at a decision to remove that child permanently from their care.

That's an enormous decision for magistrates and one which does affect them and does affect the legal advisor giving that advice, I think. It's always countered by the fact that that is the job that you signed up for and the job that you have to do. I think it would be wrong to say that it has no effect on you.' (Legal advisor; family)

'In the cases I deal with, because of the pressure on funding, I very, very rarely have a solicitor with me at court ... So, not only do I have to deal with the legal arguments and the court and everything else, but I'm also having to do all the hand-holding with the clients, which can be incredibly stressful. I had a case ... where I found [my client] huddled in a corner, in enormous distress after he'd given evidence. I had to call a halt to proceedings, and I had to get someone from my solicitors' office to come down and help take him to a psychiatric hospital ... Obviously you go home from work, and you can't just forget about that.' (Barrister; employment)

## Conclusion

This chapter has examined how court user participation is understood by practitioners immersed in the 'social world' (see Rock, 1993) of courts and tribunals. The study findings point to the multifaceted nature of participation. Participation was variously said to be a matter of providing and eliciting information for the court; being informed; being legally represented; being protected; being managed; and being present. Its functions were described in terms of the exercise of legal rights; enabling court decision making; legitimation of court processes and outcomes; and potential therapeutic benefits. Practitioners' conceptualisations of what participation entails, and why it matters, are interlinked and overlapping. An important finding of this research is that participation was described in similar terms, albeit to various degrees, by respondents in different professional groups and from different jurisdictions – demonstrating the value of adopting a cross-jurisdictional approach to researching this phenomenon and considering the policy implications. This chapter has highlighted the various barriers, both 'old' and 'new', to participation and has shown that its facilitation is widely regarded as integral to the role of practitioners in the courtroom. Nevertheless, as will be illustrated in the chapter that follows, there appears to be a gap between practitioners' understandings of participation and its empirical realities.

## Notes

[1] Additional assistance with recruitment was provided by a steering group and judicial reference group established for the project, and – with regard to the fieldwork conducted in Wales – by the Commission on Justice in Wales, which was set up by the Welsh Government and was undertaking a review of the justice system in Wales (2019) which coincided with the fieldwork for this project.

[2] Since the time of the research, the Personal Support Unit, which provides assistance to litigants-in-person, has been renamed Support Through Court.

[3] Specifically, trade union officials with experience of supporting ET claimants.

[4] Intermediaries facilitate communication in court, whether on a statutory basis (acting as Registered Intermediaries for witnesses in criminal cases) or as part of a non-statutory service (assisting defendants in criminal cases or parties or witnesses in the Family Court).

[5] For an analysis of the conceptual distinction between courts and tribunals through the lens of participation, see McKeever (2020). In this article, McKeever argues that, contrary to the assumption that tribunals are more likely to be participatory than the courts, there exists a spectrum of adjudication whereby some courts and tribunals are more participatory than others.

[6] This corresponds with Kirby's (2019) conceptualisation of participation as concerning the degree to which a lay user understands and expresses themselves within proceedings.

[7] In all instances where a respondent practised in more than one jurisdiction, as was the case for this interviewee, only the primary jurisdiction is referenced.

[8] See, for example, Jacobson et al (2015), JUSTICE (2019) and McKeever (2020).

[9] For a critical analysis of the extent to which legal representation acts as a 'proxy' form of participation, see Owusu-Bempah (2018). Similarly, McKeever (2020) describes the ways in which representation can both facilitate, and act as a barrier to, participation.

[10] Such as Beetham (1991) and Jackson et al (2015).

[11] And corresponding with McKeever's assertion that 'participation is an intrinsic part of procedural justice' (2020).

[12] For example, therapeutic jurisprudence has informed the development of specialist courts such as drug or domestic violence courts (Bowen and Whitehead, 2016), and has influenced developments in coroners' courts in some jurisdictions (Freckelton, 2007).

[13] A Victim Personal Statement is a victim's account of how they have been affected by the offence; where the offender is convicted, the statement may be read out in court at the sentencing hearing – sometimes by the victim themselves (www.gov.uk/government/publications/victim-personal-statement).

[14] See, for example, Carlen (1976), Mulcahy (2013), Kirby (2017) and Mulcahy and Rowden (2019).

[15] See, for example, Jacobson et al (2015), JUSTICE (2019) and McKeever (2020).

[16] See, for example, Rock (1993), Fielding (2006) and Jacobson et al (2015).

[17] See, for example, Church (1982), Duff and Leverick (2002) and Jacobson et al (2015).

[18] See, for example, National Audit Office (2014), Law Society (2017), Ministry of Justice (2018), National Audit Office (2018) and Ministry of Justice (2019).

[19] For a recent review of the impact of 'vicarious' or 'secondary trauma' on practitioner well-being, see James (2020).

## References

Beetham, D. (1991) *The Legitimation of Power* (1st edn), Basingstoke: Palgrave Macmillan.

Bottoms, A. and Tankebe, J. (2012) 'Beyond procedural justice: a dialogic approach to legitimacy in criminal justice', *Journal of Criminal Law and Criminology*, 102(1): 119–70.

Bowen, P. and Whitehead, S. (2016) *Problem-Solving Courts: An Evidence Review*, London: Centre for Justice Innovation.

Bryman, A. (2016) *Social Research Methods* (5th edn), Oxford: Oxford University Press.

Carlen, P. (1976) *Magistrates' Justice*, London: Martin Robertson.

Church, T.W., Jr (1982) 'The "old and the new" conventional wisdom of court delay', *Justice System Journal*, 7(3): 395–412.

The Commission on Justice in Wales (2019) *Justice in Wales for the People of Wales Report*, Cardiff: The Commission on Justice in Wales.

Duff, P. and Leverick, F. (2002) 'Court culture and adjournments in criminal cases: a tale of four courts', *Criminal Law Review*, 1: 39–52.

Edwards, I. (2004) 'An ambiguous participant: the crime victim and criminal justice decision-making', *British Journal of Criminology*, 44(6): 967–92.

Fielding, N. (2006) *Courting Violence: Offences against the Person Cases in Court*, Oxford: Oxford University Press.

Freckelton, I. (2007) 'Death investigation, the coroner and therapeutic jurisprudence', *Journal of Law and Medicine*, 15(2): 242–53.

Jackson, J., Hough, M., Bradford, B. and Kuha, J. (2015) 'Empirical legitimacy as two connected psychological states', in G. Meško and J. Tankebe (eds) *Trust and Legitimacy in Criminal Justice: European Perspectives*, Cham: Springer International, pp 137–60.

Jacobson, J., Hunter, G. and Kirby, A. (2015) *Inside Crown Court: Personal Experiences and Questions of Legitimacy*, Bristol: Policy Press.

James, C. (2020) 'Towards a trauma-informed legal practice: a review', *Psychiatry, Psychology and Law*, 27(2), available from: www.tandfonline.com/doi/full/10.1080/13218719.2020.1719377

JUSTICE (2019) *Understanding Courts: A Report by JUSTICE*, London: JUSTICE.

Kaiser, K. and Holtfreter, K. (2016) 'An integrated theory of specialized court programs: using procedural justice and therapeutic jurisprudence to promote offender compliance and rehabilitation', *Criminal Justice and Behavior*, 43(1): 45–62.

Kirby, A. (2017) 'Effectively engaging victims, witnesses and defendants in the criminal courts: a question of "court culture"?', *Criminal Law Review*, 12: 949–68.

Kirby, A. (2019) 'Engaging with legitimacy: an examination of lay participation in the criminal courts', PhD thesis, University of Surrey, available from: http://epubs.surrey.ac.uk/851936/

The Law Society (2017) 'Access denied? LASPO four years on: a Law Society review', Law Society of England and Wales, available from: www.lawsociety.org.uk/support-services/research-trends/laspo-4-years-on/

McKeever, G. (2020) 'Comparing courts and tribunals through the lens of legal participation', *Civil Justice Quarterly*, 39(3): 217–36.

Ministry of Justice (2018) *Fit for the Future: Transforming the Court and Tribunal Estate*, London: MoJ.

Ministry of Justice (2019) *Response to 'Fit for the Future: Transforming the Court and Tribunal Estate' Consultation*, London: MoJ.

Mulcahy, L. (2013) 'Putting the defendant in their place: why do we still use the dock in criminal proceedings?', *British Journal of Criminology*, 53(6): 1139–56.

Mulcahy, L. and Rowden, E. (2019) *The Democratic Courthouse: A Modern History of Design, Due Process and Dignity*, London: Routledge.

National Audit Office (2014) *Implementing Reforms to Civil Legal Aid*, London: NAO.

National Audit Office (2018) *HM Courts and Tribunals Service: Early Progress in Transforming Courts and Tribunals*, London: NAO.

Owusu-Bempah, A. (2017) *Defendant Participation in the Criminal Process*, London: Routledge.

Owusu-Bempah, A. (2018) 'The interpretation and application of the right to effective participation', *International Journal of Evidence and Proof*, available from: https://doi.org/10.1177/1365712718780800

Rock, P. (1993) *The Social World of an English Crown Court*, Oxford: Oxford University Press.

Tyler, T.R. (2007) 'Procedural justice and the courts', *Court Review*, 44(1–2): 26–31.

Wexler, D.B. (2000) *Therapeutic Jurisprudence: An Overview*, 17(1): 125–34.

# FOUR

# Observed Realities of Participation

Jessica Jacobson

## Introduction

The preceding chapters of this volume have discussed policy and practitioner perspectives on the legal principle that lay people should participate effectively in the judicial proceedings that concern them. This chapter is concerned with participation in practice, as observed by the research team across the range of courts and tribunals that are the focus of the study. After a short methodological note on the conduct of the observations, the chapter reports on differences between the variety of judicial settings, in terms of the institutional parameters of lay participation. This is followed by consideration of the commonalities across the settings. Here, it is argued that at the heart of almost every case observed by the researchers was a story of conflict, loss and disadvantage; and each lay court user's 'participation' in the case could be understood as a process by which they told, or had told on their behalf, their own version of that story. The final part of the chapter describes how judicial proceedings did not simply entail the *telling* of the court users' stories, but also their *translation* into legal questions and legal answers – and how this was a process which often had the effect of silencing and marginalising court users.

## Observing court proceedings

The research team conducted a total of 316 hours' observation over the course of 90 visits to 17 venues covering the Crown Court, magistrates' courts, Family Court Employment Tribunal (ET) and First-tier Tribunal (Immigration and Asylum Chamber) (IAC). The venues were located across the three cities – one in Wales, two in England – and surrounding areas which had been selected as the main fieldwork sites (see Chapter One). During the visits, the researchers observed a total of 339 hearings in full or part, at which a total of 430 lay court users (witnesses or parties) were in attendance (see Box 4.1 for more details).

---

**Box 4.1: Observations and court users**

**Crown Court**

- 70 hours' observations over 20 visits to three centres;
- 69 hearings observed with 77 lay court users attending: 72 defendants (three unrepresented); five witnesses;
- characteristics of the 77 court users, as recorded by observers:*
  - ○ 70 male; seven female;
  - ○ 62 white; thirteen BAME; two ethnicity unknown;
  - ○ 58 British nationality; six non-British nationality; 13 nationality unknown.

**Magistrates' courts**

- 97 hours' observations over 24 visits to three courts;
- 180 hearings observed with 187 lay court users attending: 184 defendants (24 unrepresented); three witnesses;
- characteristics of the 187 court users, as recorded by observers:*
  - ○ 152 male; 32 female;

- ○ 147 white; 39 BAME; one ethnicity unknown;
- ○ 160 British nationality; 18 non-British nationality; nine nationality unknown.

## Family Court

- 59 hours' observations over 18 visits to three hearing centres;
- 34 hearings (12 public law; 22 private law) observed with 64 lay court users attending: 59 parties (24 unrepresented); five witnesses/intervenors;
- characteristics of the 64 court users, as recorded by observers:*
  - ○ 29 male; 35 female;
  - ○ 52 white; 11 BAME; one ethnicity unknown;
  - ○ 52 British nationality; four non-British nationality; eight nationality unknown.

## Employment Tribunal

- 49 hours' observations over 13 visits to four hearing centres;
- 17 hearings observed with 35 lay court users attending: 17 claimants (14 unrepresented); three respondents (one unrepresented); 15 witnesses;
- characteristics of the 35 court users, as recorded by observers:*
  - ○ 23 male; 12 female;
  - ○ 30 white; four BAME; one ethnicity unknown;
  - ○ 31 British nationality; four non-British nationality.

## Immigration and Asylum Tribunal

- 41 hours' observations over 13 visits to four hearing centres;
- 39 hearings observed with 67 lay court users attending: 42 appellants (five unrepresented); four sponsors; 21 witnesses;
- characteristics of the 67 court users, as recorded by observers:*
  - ○ 34 male; 33 female;
  - ○ Nationalities: Afghani (eight), Indian (eight), Nigerian (six), British (five), Iraqi (four), Nepali (three), Rwandan (three), Bangladeshi (two), Chinese (two), Ghanaian (two), Ukrainian (two), US (two), Burundi (one), Dominican Republic (1), Iranian (1), Irish (1), Kenyan (1), Pakistani (1), Somali (1), Sri Lankan (1), Venezuelan (1), unknown (11).

---

* Gender, ethnicity and nationality were assessed on the basis of observed characteristics when they were not explicitly referred to in court.

In conducting the observations, the researchers usually sat in the public gallery of the court or tribunal room, or were sometimes directed by court staff to sit in sections designated for press or officials. Specific types of case or hearing were not targeted, but the researchers sought to attend a range of proceedings while concentrating as far as possible on those at which lay people were present and – where applicable – likely to give evidence. The researchers took detailed contemporaneous notes of proceedings (mostly by hand and subsequently typed up), guided by a template. The template prompted the recording of lay participants' backgrounds, characteristics, demeanour and interaction with the court during proceedings. Also recorded were substantive issues addressed in the hearing; the courtroom's physical lay-out and environment; the way practitioners presented and expressed themselves; presence or absence of legal representation, interpreters and supporters of the parties; and features of the case, such as adjustments for vulnerability.

The reported observations are necessarily subjective. They comprise a series of snapshots of proceedings, based on what was said in open court during the observations, and the researchers' interpretation of the behaviours of the (lay and professional) participants. Participants' views or background information on the cases were not collected (although occasionally practitioners provided unsolicited information[1]), and the researchers were very often unaware of the case outcomes. Nevertheless, the advantage of observation as a research method lies in the richness of the data which derive from an activity that 'goes beyond just seeing' to include also 'hearing and listening to, not just talk, but *soundscapes*', and maintains 'a sensitivity to physical environments and material things' (Atkinson, 2015: 40). Further, the researchers' use of a detailed template ensured that the observations were conducted as consistently and systematically as possible.[2]

As noted in Chapter One, this volume is being completed at a time of rapid expansion in the use of remote methods for court attendance, in response to the COVID-19 pandemic. The observational research provided only limited insight into the implications for participation of remote court attendance, since this was a feature of very few of the observed cases: just 15 of the defendants, and one witness, appeared by video-link in the observed criminal cases, while one party in the Family Court was meant to appear by video-link, but withdrew at the start of the hearing. However, brief consideration is given to this issue in the final section of the chapter, on 'Translation and disconnection'.

## Institutional parameters of participation

It was immediately clear to the observers that the role of the lay court user in judicial proceedings varies greatly according to the jurisdiction to which the case belongs, the type of hearing within that jurisdiction and the court user's role or legal status. These intersect with a number of other factors setting the parameters of court users' participation, including:

- the kinds of parties (for example, individuals, corporate entities, the state) involved;
- the extent to which court users have elected to take part (such as ET claimants) or have no choice (as with defendants in criminal proceedings);
- the stake court users have in the outcome (which could be as significant as their liberty, access to their children or right to stay in the country; or could be minimal, as for witnesses with no sense of personal involvement in the case);
- whether parties are legally represented;
- rules of evidence;
- the degree of adversarialism of the process;[3]
- size, elaborateness and physical lay-out of venue in which the hearing is held.

The accounts in Box 4.2 illustrate the range of institutional factors which can shape a court user's participation. Each of these six hearings involved a lay party who had a different formal status and role: a bailed defendant on trial; a detained defendant pleading guilty and being sentenced; a parent in a contact dispute with his ex-partner; a parent in contested care proceedings; a migrant appealing against a refused asylum claim; and an ex-employee claiming unfair dismissal. Some of the cases additionally involved laypeople as witnesses, such as the two company employees who attended the ET hearing. The summaries also give some sense of the varied personal and social circumstances in relation to which the individuals found themselves caught up in judicial proceedings, and with which the court had to grapple in determining the outcome.

---

### Box 4.2: Summaries of observed hearings

#### Case 1: Defendant giving evidence in sexual offence trial in Crown Court

Having been charged with sexually assaulting a much younger, female relative-by-marriage, the 58-year-old (bailed) defendant was appearing for trial in the Crown Court. The courtroom was ornate and imposing, with extensive wooden panelling, purple drapes, arched windows and a domed ceiling; it was one of many such courtrooms in a vast, Grade I-listed courthouse.

The defendant responded in a confident manner when taken through his evidence-in-chief by his defence counsel, and then during cross-examination when repeatedly pressed about his relationship with the complainant and the language he used (such as "Hello, Sexy") in exchanges with her on social media: "... None whatsoever ... I would *never* do that ... A complete fabrication ..." At the end of the day, with the trial due to continue the next, he left the courtroom with two family members who had been sitting in the public gallery.

#### Case 2: Defendant sentenced for theft in magistrates' court

The defendant was brought to the magistrates' court from police custody, charged with five counts of theft of clothing, food and some other items from various shops. He sat quietly in the glass-screened dock in the large, modern courtroom, as his defence solicitor agreed with the prosecution that, due to his severe drug habit, he had "an awful criminal record; I'd go so far as to say horrendous". The defendant spoke from the dock at the outset of proceedings to give his guilty plea, and at the end to confirm he understood his sentence (five short, concurrent custodial terms) and the arrangements for paying compensation. During a break in proceedings, he shared a joke with the two dock officers, at which all three laughed.

### Case 3: Applicant father at interim hearing in the Family Court

A father had applied for contact with his 6-year-old daughter; she was living with his ex-partner, who did not attend the hearing. It took place in a small room that had the appearance of a personal office more than a courtroom, in which the District Judge (DJ) sat at a slightly raised, long desk, facing two advocates' benches. The room looked newly refurbished, in contrast to other parts of the court building: a civil justice centre situated in a side street, the shabby entrance to which could be easily overlooked from the outside.

The father, representing himself, spoke emotionally but eloquently about his daughter. At the end of the hearing, the DJ said that although she was currently unable to reach a decision – while another case involving the applicant and a different child and ex-partner was pending – she was pleased that the hearing had gone ahead as it had been "helpful … to discuss it with everyone able to contribute". The father said "thank you", gathered up his papers into a plastic folder and left the courtroom.

### Case 4: Respondent mother in contested care proceedings in the Family Court

In a large, modern courtroom, brightly lit through a floor-to-ceiling window taking up most of one wall, three long advocates' benches were populated by eight professionals: all women, all formally dressed. They included Cafcass (Children and Family Court Advisory and Support Service) officers, a local authority social worker and lawyers for all parties. The mother sat on her own on a fourth bench, until – some way into the hearing – the judge asked her to move forward.

A 'surveillance operative' was sworn in as a witness for the local authority and gave minutely detailed evidence about his and two colleagues' observations of the mother's movements on a day on which she had had permitted contact with her toddler son (currently in foster care). At issue was whether she had taken her son to visit her ex-partner who was believed to pose a risk to the boy. She later gave evidence herself and was cross-examined by the local authority lawyer who repeatedly accused her of lying. After the judge then ruled against her – stating the threshold was met for a care order – she continued to sit in silence for a few minutes, before abruptly getting up and leaving the courtroom without speaking to anyone.

### Case 5: Appellant in asylum case in the IAC

An Iraqi Kurd who had been in the UK for the past ten years was appealing against a Home Office decision to refuse his protection claim. The hearing centre in which the case was heard was a characterless office block in a business park on the outskirts of a small provincial city.

In the small courtroom, the discussion between the Home Office Presenting Officer (HOPO), the appellant (through an interpreter), his lawyer and the judge covered various contested issues, including the appellant's lack of contact with family in Iraq; whether and how he might access identity documents from the Iraqi authorities; and his hand-to-mouth existence in the UK, dependent on the charity of a friend and the local Kurdish community. At the end of the hearing, after the judge said he was reserving his decision, the appellant anxiously pressed into his lawyer's hands a bundle of photocopied news reports on the deaths of people returned to Iraq, but both the lawyer and judge told him these were not relevant to the case.

### Case 6: Claimant in unfair dismissal hearing in the ET

The unrepresented claimant was arguing that she had been unfairly dismissed by the large company for which she had worked for 26 years, latterly in a supervisory role. The hearing was held in a narrow, L-shaped courtroom on the second floor of a purpose-built, recently opened civil justice centre.

On day one of what was scheduled to be a two-day hearing, the claimant gave evidence and was cross-examined by the respondent company's barrister. The claimant then cross-examined two ex-colleagues appearing as witnesses for the company. Saying to the claimant that he "wanted to be fair because you are unrepresented", the judge offered explanations for technical terms that were being used; reworded as questions some comments she made to the witnesses ("I'm being [the claimant] for a minute," the judge said, before posing the questions); and checked with her that she had covered everything she needed to.

The diversity of modes and circumstances of participation reflected in the Box 4.2 summaries – which, across the full sample of observed cases, was multiplied many times over – does not render meaningless a generic concept of participation. Cross-cutting the jurisdictional and other divides, many commonalities to the hearings, and to the part played by laypeople within them, were noted. In line with the qualitative approach taken to the study as a whole, common features of the observed cases were not quantified. However, the snapshots of proceedings can be combined to create an overall picture of court user participation – to be presented over the remainder of this chapter.

## Observed commonalities: stories of conflict, loss and disadvantage

Formal court and tribunal proceedings – including those in all the settings examined for this study – generally have as their immediate function the adjudication of disputes; albeit the performance of this function can be understood as of a much broader, 'symbolic' process whereby the 'rules' of wider society are stated, considered and refined (Steele, 1984: 202). The hearings observed by the researchers variously involved the adjudication of disputes between individuals, individuals and the state, or individuals and corporate entities. The *stage* of the adjudication process likewise varied widely – with many cases being at early, preparatory stages; others at a core decision-making stage; and others in a post-adjudication phase. But at issue in every case was a set of claims, and usually counter-claims, about harmful, unlawful, unfair or otherwise inappropriate behaviours or practices by one or more of the parties. Thus, what all hearings had in common was that they addressed situations in which the law had entered people's lives because 'the fabric of ordinary interactions [was] ruptured' (Ewick and Silbey, 1998: 77); or, to put it another way, they concerned circumstances and events gone wrong. It was also clear that the vast majority of cases involved individuals who were in need or disadvantaged in some way. Accordingly, almost every case had at its heart *a story of conflict, loss and disadvantage*; and each lay court user's 'participation' in the case could be understood as a process by which they told, or had told on their behalf, their own version of that story.

## Conflict

In the court hearings observed for this study, the researchers saw the law being 'performed' so as to 'represent and replay social conflict and violence, turning history into dramatic narrative, fictionalizing social trauma, transforming it into the system of social representations, exchanges, surrogacies that make up the law' (Peters, 2008: 185). The final section of this chapter discusses the implications of this 'transformation' – or what is referred to here as 'translation' – of conflict, and associated violence and trauma, into legal questions and answers. But what is the nature of the conflict itself?

In the observed cases, the conflict underlying the claims and counter-claims being tested in court tended to be complex, multifaceted and entrenched. The ET's formal description of itself as 'an independent tribunal which makes decisions in legal disputes around employment law'[4] gives little sense of the scope of human drama and trauma that the disputes here frequently incorporate. One claimant, on day 11 of what was scheduled as a 15-day hearing of her claim of unfair dismissal as a school head, gave evidence about what she described as an 'agenda' among many of the school's governors and staff to force her out of her post. This, she said, followed disputes among staff, governors and the local authority about how the school was run, and child protection concerns she herself had raised. For their part, two witnesses appearing on behalf of the local authority described a long-running process involving disciplinary proceedings against the claimant, suspension and two appeals. Elsewhere, at a preliminary hearing, an ET judge argued that judicial mediation 'behind kind, closed doors' – a form of alternative dispute resolution – was the best option for addressing a claim of race discrimination. Both sides ultimately agreed to this, but not before the self-represented claimant, a Polish national, had insistently set out his case. When asked by the judge what he wanted, he said: "I want someone like you to listen to my story about what happened; I want them to apologise; I want justice." He described his former employment as a garage technician in which, he said, he had been subjected to racist comments (repeatedly dismissed as "banter"), accusations that his Polish qualification was fake and more general poor treatment – after several months of which he quit the job. The employer had thereafter instituted civil proceedings, claiming he had been overpaid and had taken annual leave without entitlement.

Many of the observed IAC hearings were appeals against Home Office decisions to refuse protection (or asylum) claims. In such cases, appellants' arguments typically centred on their experiences of actual or threatened extreme violence and persecution, often in the context of globalised conflicts and civil strife. For the observer, there was a marked incongruity between the usually muted ambience and anonymous setting of the tribunal and the discussion of places and unfolding humanitarian disasters that are otherwise familiar from international news reports. These hearings included that of a young Kurdish Iraqi man who, speaking through an interpreter, spoke of his father having been killed fighting for the Peshmerga (Kurdish militia), the demolition of his hometown by militant groups and threats he had personally received from ISIS. He had travelled to the UK, he said, in "a sealed vehicle, like a lorry, no windows; we couldn't see anything" and another vehicle "like a fridge-freezer lorry". The Home Office disputed his claim that his father had been a Peshmerga, and proposed his relocation to an area of Iraqi Kurdistan reported to be 'stable' and 'virtually violence free'. Another IAC appellant was a member of Afghanistan's marginalised Hazara community; he said he had been persecuted and imprisoned by the Afghan authorities following a legal dispute, and his brother had been killed. A woman from Rwanda told the IAC that her prior political activities would put her at risk if she was to return to the country. Through an interpreter, she said: "There's no peace in my country. My husband is in jail, one of my children is in jail ... I don't have a job; they've taken my business; they've frozen my accounts." The Home Office argued, in response, that she was fleeing tax evasion charges, not persecution, in her home country.

The non-asylum hearings that were observed in the IAC did not address the kinds of extreme circumstances that were at the heart of asylum claims, but most nevertheless brought complex personal struggles and conflicts into view. Cases revolved around evidence put forward by appellants about family pressures and tensions, severe financial needs and health problems of many kinds. (As will be discussed later under the heading 'Loss and disadvantage', these were recurring themes across all the judicial settings visited.) At issue in several cases were Home Office allegations of sham marriages for immigration purposes, and of cheating (for example, through use of proxies) in the English language test required for visa extensions[5] – allegations strenuously denied by the appellants.

In the Family Court, the playing out of especially bitter and protracted conflicts was observed. In private law cases, these were typically disputes between estranged parents over contact or residence arrangements for their children. Allegations of serious domestic violence frequently formed part of these cases – demonstrating also the close interconnectedness between different parts of the justice system. Not only in family cases, but also in the course of ET and IAC hearings, references to criminal convictions or allegations were noted; and some of the observed defendants in the criminal courts were simultaneously embroiled in immigration or family proceedings.

## Loss and disadvantage

The researchers found that the disputes adjudicated in courts and tribunals usually had their roots in, or at least had emerged in the context of, circumstances of loss and disadvantage. These circumstances encompassed very much more than the individual-level 'vulnerabilities' that are the main focus of special measures and other such provision for court users (discussed elsewhere in this volume). Among the wide array of court users' individual, socio-cultural and structural needs were those arising from: mental health problems; learning and behavioural difficulties; substance misuse; physical illness and disability; family and relationship breakdown; childhood trauma; bereavement; poverty; homelessness; prior offending or imprisonment; and prior experiences of discrimination, persecution and other forms of victimisation. For the most part, different forms of need and loss converged in individuals' lives, producing 'multiple layers of disadvantage' as have elsewhere been documented with regard to children in custody (Jacobson et al, 2010).

Multi-layered disadvantage was especially apparent with regard to the defendants appearing in many of the observed criminal cases. In case after case in the magistrates' courts, defendants charged with offences such as assault, theft and criminal damage were said to have profound, intersecting needs, including mental health and drug or alcohol problems, and chaotic and disorderly ways of living. In many cases of interpersonal offending, particularly violence, it was apparent that the contexts of the (alleged) offending encompassed victims and witnesses with comparable needs to those of the defendants.

Cases in which defendants were already in custody or another form of detention when charged with the offence provide a vivid illustration of the emergence of criminal proceedings from circumstances of loss and disadvantage. In these instances, the current case originated at a point at which the defendants had already lost their liberty. Among defendants observed in this situation was a woman being sentenced for assaulting a nurse in the psychiatric hospital where she was detained. In the same magistrates' court, a man pleaded not guilty over video-link from the prison where he was serving a prior sentence; he was charged with assaulting a prison officer whom he was said to have spat at. Elsewhere, another serving prisoner faced a charge of common assault on a prison officer – the offence having allegedly occurred when the officer entered his cell after he had failed a drugs test. He had originally been sentenced to imprisonment for public protection (IPP), and at the time of his court appearance had been in prison for more than ten years beyond the original 27-month minimum term he had received.[6] While at court, he initially refused to leave the cells in the basement of the building or to talk to his solicitor. In the courtroom, the district judge and defence advocate discussed the case: "He's a very difficult person as you've probably picked up this morning," the lawyer commented, adding: "I've failed to establish any rapport with this gentleman, which is unusual for me." The judge sympathised with the lawyer and observed that the defendant "knows he's playing the system … Game-playing: that's all it is."

In the course of care proceedings in the Family Court, as in criminal cases, concentrations of deep-seated needs and disadvantage in individual lives were laid bare. A circuit judge in one hearing centre dealt in quick succession with two such cases. In each case, the mother opposed the local authority's application for a care order with regard to a baby; in each case, also, many older siblings of the baby had already been removed from the mother's care. The local authorities had brought to the court's attention wide-ranging concerns about each mother's drug abuse and poor mental health, as well as domestic violence, emotional abuse and neglect of the children, and other problems (including a past allegation of sexual abuse) in the respective extended families.

Whether in criminal or family courts or in tribunals, the researchers found that court users' backgrounds of loss and disadvantage were usually integral to the substantive matter being considered in the proceedings: forming part of, for example, pleas in mitigation in the criminal courts that pointed to defendants' reduced culpability on grounds of mental ill health; arguments in the Family Court that parents lacked the ability to care properly for their children; claims of disability discrimination in the ET; and appeals against deportation to life-threatening situations in the IAC. Beyond this, the court process itself often had the effect of throwing court users' losses and disadvantages into ever sharper relief. It was apparent across the fieldwork settings that social, psychological, cognitive, emotional and other needs and vulnerabilities not only impeded court users' capacity to engage effectively with court proceedings, but were also heightened or exacerbated by the fact and nature of the individuals' involvement in those proceedings. (Discussion on 'Translation and disconnection', later, returns to this theme.) Thus, as has been previously suggested with regard specifically to the criminal courts, 'the courtroom is host not only to "vulnerable people", but also "vulnerable moments"' (Jacobson, 2018: 225).

If the disputes adjudicated in court had often arisen in *circumstances* of loss and disadvantage, it was also clear that the *outcomes* of the cases could consolidate or give rise to further disadvantage. Of course, the court and tribunal cases also offered the hope – and sometimes the reality – of redress for harms experienced and losses already incurred. For example, claimants in the ET could secure financial compensation or get their old jobs back; victims in the criminal courts could see offenders held to account for wrong-doing; and some parents in the Family Court stood to renew contact with or care for their children. Often, however, prospective losses were likely to outweigh any prospective gains.

For most of the court users (excluding those appearing as witnesses with little or no personal interest in the case), what was at stake in the proceedings was of great significance in their lives.[7] In the criminal courts, many defendants faced losing their liberty, should they be remanded or sentenced to custody. (Or, in the case of the defendant on an IPP sentence referred to earlier, a conviction would even further diminish the likelihood of release on parole at an undefined point in the future.) Defendants also faced other potential losses: restrictions on their freedom resulting from community penalties; financial loss if they were fined; and reputational damage. The last of these was of particular relevance in one hearing in which – in sharp contrast to the other observed court users – the defendant was exceptionally privileged: this was the high profile Crown Court trial of a celebrity charged with assault. In the Family Court, the stakes could be higher still: a life with or without one's children. A mother who was appealing against a previous decision by magistrates that she could have no direct contact with her two teenage sons – currently living with their father and his new wife – pleaded with the judge: "Give us a chance to be a family. Give me a chance to be with my children." But despite her claims as to the cruel behaviour of her ex-husband ("an imbecile" who had done "a hatchet job to get me and my family out of his life"), she lost the case: the judge determined that the existing (no contact) arrangements should continue, and passed an order preventing her from making further applications without permission from the court "because I am satisfied that both parties need a break from litigation".

In the IAC, it was their lives in the UK (and associated family ties and relative stability or safety) that appellants were striving to hold on to. This was a life which, one young woman from

India explained in appealing a Home Office decision to refuse her leave to remain, encompassed her marriage, house, recent birth of her baby and job for a clothing company. A Ukrainian husband and wife, who had been detained following their failure to comply with previous removal orders, applied for bail and appealed against the deportation. The wife became distressed and started crying when giving evidence and talking about the practical, domestic matters she needed to deal with – including arranging care for her cat, which had been left alone in their flat since their detention. Her husband responded scornfully when asked if he would appeal the removal decision when he was back in Ukraine, asserting that this would be like 'appealing to God when dead'. In an out-of-country appeal against refusal of leave to remain, by an elderly woman in Venezuela, the appellant's daughter acted as her 'sponsor' and gave evidence at the tribunal. She sobbed as she described her mother's deteriorating health following a series of strokes, and spoke of the inadequacies of the available health care in Venezuela. When asked how she would care for her mother in the UK, she replied: "Physical, emotional – I will look after her in every sense."

## Telling the stories of conflict, loss and disadvantage

Thus far, this chapter has highlighted the commonalities across the cases observed in a wide range of judicial settings. It has been argued that these cases – whatever their diverse origins, nature and functions – concerned circumstances and events gone wrong; and that accordingly all cases had at their heart a story of conflict, loss and disadvantage. Most proceedings entailed the telling of competing versions of the story by the parties to the case and the assessment by the court or tribunal of which of the versions had the greater credibility or pertinence to the matters at hand. It was on this basis that the outcome of the case could be determined: whether this was a decision to continue or cease proceedings; to grant or dismiss a claim, appeal or application; to convict or acquit a defendant; or to pass one sentence or another on a convicted offender. The essence of a court user's participation can thus be understood to be the telling of their story – whether directly or through a representative – and the challenging of the other party's version of the story. This chapter now moves on to examine the scope of, and limits to, participation in this sense. The focus here is on the ways in which practitioners in the courtroom were observed to support and facilitate court users' participation.

## *Supporting and facilitating participation*

Courts and tribunals operate in a highly pressured environment. It was evident during the observations that court lists were overloaded, paperwork was often missing and failures in technical equipment were common. Thus, it appears that the 'structured mayhem' observed some years before in research on the Crown Court (Jacobson et al, 2015) remains a feature of the courts and tribunals system. This is notwithstanding the endeavours by HMCTS, in the intervening period, to improve efficiency through the courts modernisation programme (discussed in Chapter Two of this volume). The findings of the observations and practitioner interviews (see Chapter Three) point to a range of factors relating to the reforms and accompanying austerity measures which undermine the effective operation of the courts – including court closures and the resultant increased workload of remaining courts and staff cutbacks. The increasing numbers of litigants-in-person (LiPs) in the courts, largely reflecting reduced availability of legal aid, pose their own challenges to the smooth and timely running of court business, on account of their particular needs for support and assistance during the court process.

Against this backdrop, the researchers repeatedly noted immense efforts made by practitioners in the courtroom – including judges, magistrates, lawyers, legal advisors and others – to help court users to participate in proceedings. As noted in Chapter Three, practitioners frequently spoke about the facilitation of court user participation as a significant part of their own and their peers' roles; and the observations of hearings provided ample evidence that this task of facilitation was indeed taken seriously and effectively carried out. This encompassed the assistance and support that practitioners proffered to the most obviously vulnerable or needy court users and to those who were LiPs; and, more generally, practitioners' humanising, sympathetic responses to the difficulties and pain revealed by the stories recounted in the courtroom.

A note of caution should, however, be added to this positive account of practitioner efforts to facilitate participation. It is possible that there was some degree of 'observer effect' which encouraged practitioners to treat court users with special care during the observed hearings. The visibility of the research team varied between settings and locations: in the criminal courts, there tended to be little interest in its presence, whereas court staff, the judiciary and sometimes lawyers were more aware of the researchers and the nature of their work in the tribunals and Family Court, where observers (unconnected to cases) are uncommon.[8] In one IAC hearing, the judge was so positively disposed towards the research that she asked the researchers, in a follow-up email, if they could provide "any feedback from the perspective of the appellant/witnesses".

### Responsiveness to vulnerabilities and need

Use of formal 'special measures' or other adjustments to help vulnerable court users to give evidence was extremely rare in the observed family and criminal cases – and did not feature in any of the observed tribunal hearings.[9] In three of the observed family hearings, a screen was put in place to separate victims of domestic violence from the perpetrators.

In the criminal hearings, one defendant had an intermediary, while another was accompanied by a support worker who sat with her in the dock, and a vulnerable witness in one case appeared by video-link. In two Crown Court cases, a judge expressed scepticism about applications for an intermediary. In one of these, the judge said with some obvious reluctance that he would accept a CPS request for an intermediary for a 13-year-old complainant, adding that many such applications were unnecessary and undermining of advocates' skills in questioning vulnerable witnesses. He commented also that he found many intermediary reports to be "a cut and paste job".

Overall, however, it is likely that the observed limited recourse to formal adjustments in the criminal courts was largely a function of the type of hearings that the researchers attended – very predominantly plea hearings and sentencing proceedings, rather than trials – and did not reflect a general reluctance on the part of the courts to make use of the available provisions. Across the courts and tribunals, the researchers found that judges and others displayed awareness of court users' needs, a willingness to make ad hoc accommodations and a general sensitivity to what are referred to earlier as 'vulnerable moments', when court users displayed heightened distress, anxiety or anger.

This may be indicative of a generalised shift in judicial proceedings towards greater responsiveness to vulnerability.[10] The researchers noted, for example, encouragement of defendants, witnesses and parties to sit down and take breaks where they appeared to be under particular physical or mental strain; the dimming of lights in an ET hearing to help a claimant feel more at ease; a judge's calm reasoning with and securing of an apology from (rather than pursuit of a contempt of court charge against) a defendant who had lost his temper and told him to "go fuck yourself"; and the provision of careful explanations of the court process to witnesses who were evidently discomfited – including a 16-year-old boy with mental health problems who was giving evidence to the IAC in support of his parents' appeal. In a Crown Court trial, a defence barrister took the opportunity of a break in proceedings to tell the judge that his client had been having heart palpitations, at which the judge asked the defendant about his health and added: "giving evidence in the Crown Court, whatever the circumstances, is very stressful ... If you feel unwell, please say so." Also in the Crown Court, a 70-year-old woman pleaded guilty to charges of defrauding and stealing from a woman in her care. She sobbed loudly throughout, and received solicitous attention from both the court interpreter and a dock officer – the latter holding her by the arm to support her. After the judge passed a suspended custodial sentence, she continued to sob in obvious relief, while also – on leaving the courtroom – hugging and kissing two bemused-looking lawyers in attendance. In the IAC, judges were accommodating when appellants had young children with them – for example, permitting one woman to bring her baby into the courtroom.

### Assisting litigants-in-person

As shown in Box 4.1, three out of the 72 defendants observed in the Crown Court were unrepresented, as were 24 of 184 defendants in magistrates' courts, 24 of 49 parties in the Family Court, five of 42 IAC appellants, and 14 of 17 claimants and one of three respondents in the ET.[11] LiPs were occasionally accompanied by representatives of voluntary organisations or personal acquaintances who provided support. Most obtained significant help in the courtroom from judges and legal advisors, sometimes including encouragement to obtain legal representation or, if that was not possible, advice from local pro bono or voluntary legal services.

Many judges took considerable care to explain procedures to LiPs. Some offered encouragement, like a Family Court judge who said to a father about the medical records he had supplied to the court: "You've assisted yourself greatly by doing that so promptly." They also offered reassurance ("Don't worry about that; we're taking it from square one," one ET judge told a claimant who had apologetically said he had never been in a court before) and practical guidance (another ET judge lent her own highlighters to a claimant, saying that the best way of preparing for his questioning of the respondent was to read through the latter's statement closely, and mark up those passages he disagreed with). Some judges, in an apparent effort to ensure equality of arms between represented and unrepresented parties, provided assistance that arguably amounted to a departure from the traditional judicial role of a neutral arbiter: like the ET judge quoted in Case 6 in Box 4.2, who reworded some of the claimant's questions and posed them to witnesses himself. The judge who lent the claimant her highlighters also, similarly, rephrased some of his questions: "This is the thing: you're not really asking questions – you're making statements. The question that *should* be asked there is: 'Do you remember him asking you …?'"

A Crown Court case in which there was notable judicial intervention – in the form of strong encouragement to negotiate the basis for a guilty plea – concerned an unrepresented defendant charged with cultivation of cannabis in his home. Having heard the defendant's plea of not guilty, and inquired about the basis of his defence and his personal circumstances, the judge referred to the sentencing options and suggested the defendant discuss his plea with the prosecution advocate, who "will be fair". After a short adjournment, the defendant pleaded guilty and the judge sentenced him to a low-level community order, with some personal guidance ("It's not my role to give you lifestyle advice, but heed this. Cannabis is not good …") into the bargain.

In a private law family case in which both mother and father were unrepresented, the legal advisor explained to them how the proceedings would run and said: "If you feel lost, do ask me." The father was serving a community order for violence against the mother, who had a restraining order against him; he was seeking to extend the limited contact he currently had with his sons. When it was time for him to question the Cafcass officer, the legal advisor stated some ground rules, including that he should allow her to finish answering one question before asking the next. Following this guidance, the father proceeded to challenge the evidence that had been presented by Cafcass in a careful and serious manner. In discussing the detail of contact arrangements, he said, "It works out now that I see them for about 3 hours per month after living with them for five years. This is very hard."

## Humanising and sympathetic responses

Courteous and respectful treatment of court users was the norm across the range of court and tribunal settings, suggestive of a broad orientation (albeit this was likely to be implicit rather than explicit) of professional culture around the values of procedural justice.[12] Moreover, a great many practitioners dealt with court users in a manner that extended beyond courtesy and respect to kindness and sympathy, and an acknowledgment of the deeply personal and often highly emotive character of what was being addressed in the courtroom.

Humanising responses to court users' 'stories' were especially evident in the Family Court, where many of the rawest accounts of individual failings and interpersonal conflict were heard – as illustrated by the examples in Box 4.3 from public law cases. Perhaps with the aim of making proceedings feel less daunting and more congenial, parents in the Family Court were often referred to by judges and other practitioners as "Mum" and "Dad". This sometimes sounded incongruous in the context, and occasionally confusing – such as when one maternal grandmother was being questioned as a witness, and was asked with regard to her daughter: "How often do you see Mum?" "Did you see Mum in hospital?"

## Box 4.3: Efforts to humanise care proceedings in the Family Court

### Case 1

A mother was treated gently by lawyers, judge and Cafcass guardian[13] throughout a final hearing in care proceedings concerning her daughter. The mother, whose health problems included schizophrenia, cried when the judge asked her towards the end of the hearing if she had anything further to say, and she replied that she knew she was not a "100 per cent" good mother. The judge – who had earlier commented that the child was "delightful", which was a credit to the mother – told her in a kindly way that no mother is 100 per cent good.

### Case 2

A social worker, while firmly making the case for a care order for a young child on the grounds of multiple, deep-seated problems in the home – referred to the "lovely baby ... Beautiful smile."

### Case 3

In a complex case involving an application for an interim care order for a 14-year-old girl because her parents were unable to control her behaviour and she was putting herself at risk, the judge was at pains to express his sympathy for the father who was, the judge said, "as worried and upset as anybody I've seen in this court for a very long time".

### Case 4

The judge congratulated a father on the "brave decision" he had made not to oppose a care order, and said warmly to two grandmothers who were involved in the case: "I don't know what we'd do without grandmothers like you."

### Case 5

After a hearing which had dealt with an interim care order for newborn twins, there was a discussion among the parents, social workers and other lawyers in the lobby outside the courtroom. The lawyer for the Cafcass guardian asked the parents if she could see a photo of the babies: "I like to see what my clients look like." The father showed some pictures on his phone, and all the practitioners made appreciative comments: "Aww, so cute!"

## Translation and disconnection

The findings set out in the previous section illustrate some of the ways in which practitioners help to ensure that court users' stories of conflict, loss and disadvantage are told in the courtroom. But of course, the telling of the stories is not the main goal of the judicial process – even if many practitioners assert, in line with procedural justice theory, that having a 'voice' is critical to a lay person's experience of justice (see Chapter Three). In the end, the court or tribunal must make a decision about the matters before it, and this must be a decision based in law; as legal philosopher Neil MacCormick states, 'Whatever question or problem is in our mind, if we pose it as a legal question or problem, we seek a solution or answer in terms of a proposition that seems sound as a matter of law, at least arguably sound, though preferably conclusive' (2005: 14). Posing a question or problem 'as a legal question or problem' necessarily entails a process of translation: during the legal proceedings, 'the real-life problem must be first translated, or transposed, into the language the law recognizes; only then – recognized by law – it may be solved, with these solutions resulting in real-life consequences' (Smejkalová, 2017: 65).

As the researchers observed court users' stories being translated into legal questions and legal answers, it became apparent that this process of translation was also a process which marginalised the individuals. Court language, concepts and structures had the combined effect of silencing court users, underlining the disparities between their social worlds and the social world of the courtroom, and ultimately disconnecting them from their own proceedings.

### *Complexity*

Although some judges, lawyers and others sought to explain terminology and processes to court users (and especially LiPs), there was a notable tendency among many practitioners to default to jargon and complex language.[14] In the first case described in Box 4.3, where the judge was sympathetic and supportive towards an evidently vulnerable and distressed mother, this did not prevent references by lawyers to the "threshold document" being "not agreed, not opposed"; the child being "avoidant"; and the need to "progress contact in a dynamic way". In the second of the Box 4.3 cases, lawyers used traditional phrases such as "my learned friend" and (more than once, when turning away from the judicial bench to consult with their client), "I'll just turn my back." In this latter case, the maternal grandmother gave evidence; visibly shaking with nerves and tearful, she provided detailed responses to most questions, but occasionally struggled to understand: asking, for example, "What's 'abstinent'?" when being questioned about her daughter's drug use.

Formal and elaborate styles of language were generally more common in the Crown Court than in the other venues in which observations were conducted, exemplified by the following exchange between judge and defence counsel following the defendant's evidence-in-chief:

Defence counsel: "If I trespassed in that way, please forgive me."
Judge: "You have my forgiveness ... You are forgiven, you are forgiven ... [It was] an excess of enthusiasm."

Formality of language could combine with the complexity of issues or concepts under discussion to make it more difficult for lay parties to understand what was being said. Unusually, a Crown Court judge apologised to a defendant in a pre-trial hearing for the fact that much of what had been discussed would have been "quite incomprehensible", and explained that the defence and prosecution had had to make various arrangements in preparation for the trial. After sentencing an unrepresented defendant for two driving offences, a magistrate asked him if he had understood everything that had happened, to which the defendant replied, "All me head's fuzzy." The magistrate told him to see probation, who would explain everything.

Sentencing an offender with long-term addiction problems to a drug-related offence, a Crown Court judge spoke rapidly: "... totality ... cycle of addiction ... balancing aggravating and mitigating factors ... considerable licence period ..." The judge then asked the defendant if he had understood, who simply said "Yes." When another Crown Court judge passed sentence on a woman in her early 30s who had pleaded guilty to a serious assault, there was an extended discussion between the judge, probation officer and defence advocate about the defendant's accommodation, since both defendant and victim had been living in the same hostel. The judge eventually decided to make a restraining order (additional to the sentence) preventing the defendant from going within 100 yards of the hostel. It was agreed that she should present as homeless to the local authority and that her friend, who was at court, should collect her belongings from the hostel. When passing sentence, the judge spoke in a brisk but kindly way. He said that the defendant had "come to this court effectively a lady of good character" and the offence had been committed "out of your vulnerability and dependence on alcohol"; but it was clear she understood little of what was said. At the end, she twice asked from the dock: "Where will I stay? ... Can I go back to [the hostel]?" The judge could not hear the question; after it was relayed by the barrister, he reiterated that she was not to go within 100 yards of the hostel.

## Silencing of court users

Most of the talking in the observed court hearings was done by the professionals in the room. Whether and to what extent lay court users communicated directly with the court or tribunal depended on a range of factors, including their role in proceedings, the type of hearing and case, and whether or not they were represented. Paradoxically, while participation is often assumed to depend on, or even to take the form of, being represented (see, for example, discussion of this in Chapter Three), it appeared that legal representation could also have the effect of undermining or even silencing the lay party's voice. While all court users were silent by the point at which the court made its adjudication, parties who were represented tended, by definition, to be silenced at an earlier stage in the court process than LiPs.[15]

In a private law case in the Family Court, magistrates considered a (represented) father's application for contact with his young daughter at the same time as the mother's application for a non-molestation order against the father. When the magistrate requested a Scott Schedule (setting out the issues under dispute), the mother's lawyer responded: "Ma'am, I think that's a sensible way forward – I can see the logic in your reasoning", and the father interrupted: "A what? Sorry – can I talk?" The magistrate said to him: "Well, you've got your representative." (Later, the magistrates decided to grant the mother's request for a non-molestation order, and went on to discuss dates for further consideration of the contact application; but the father put his head in hands, then leaned back in his chair, and said: "Just leave it. I'm not going to bother anymore.") A similar exchange took place in an IAC case – summarised as Case 5 in Box 4.2. After the judge stated that he was reserving his decision on the asylum appeal and the appellant would hear within two weeks, the appellant asked if he could speak, but was told by the judge to go through his lawyer. It was at this point that the appellant tried in vain to get both the judge and his lawyer to look at some news reports on the deaths of people returned to Iraq.

Represented parties could be silenced in other ways. In a different IAC hearing centre, another case involved a represented Iraqi appellant. Responding via an interpreter to questions from the HOPO, he spoke at length, with expressive tones and hand gestures. The HOPO complained to the judge that he was providing very long answers to short questions, leading the judge to say: "You are giving very long answers … I already have that information … only answer the questions you are asked." In a magistrates' court, the mounting distress of a defendant who felt her lawyer was not making her voice heard was evident. She was being sentenced for shoplifting various items from a supermarket, and had appeared at court from the prison at which she was already serving a sentence for assault. Crying in the dock during a break in proceedings, she repeatedly told her lawyer that she was getting help at her current prison for her drug problem and wanted to go back there so she could continue with the programme; the lawyer said there was little he could do about this, and she should relax and not worry. The defendant continued to cry and said the lawyer was not listening to her; he said the same of her. When the magistrate passed sentence shortly afterwards, nothing further was said about whether she would be returning to the same prison.

While LiPs were necessarily required to be more actively involved in proceedings than represented parties (and, as discussed earlier, were often given significant assistance), some nevertheless struggled to communicate. Particular difficulties could arise when both parties were unrepresented and each vied with the other to be heard. In one chaotic ET hearing, the complainant and respondent kept speaking over each other, with the former in particular finding it difficult to express himself; it also emerged that he had not brought the relevant documents to the tribunal. The atmosphere in one private law family case became very heated, with the two parents – both unrepresented – repeatedly interrupting and making accusations towards each other; until the judge lost patience and shouted at them: "Quiet! Stop interrupting! It's my turn!"

As noted at the outset of this chapter, there were too few observations of remote attendance to reach general conclusions about the implications for court users' engagement with proceedings. Of those cases involving remote attendance that were observed (in all but two of which defendants in prison or a police station were appearing in a criminal court by video-link), most proceeded without an obvious impact on participation, but some were problematic. The latter included a pre-trial hearing in the Crown Court, which provided an example of direct and literal silencing of a court user. The defendant, who was in prison, interrupted proceedings several times to assert that forensic evidence had been "planted" on him. Losing patience, the judge asked for the sound feed from the prison to be turned off. Similarly, the judge in another Crown Court pre-trial hearing threatened to turn off the sound as the defendant demanded over video-link: "Where's the TV, where's the jury? It's all a load of shit, innit ... I'm just stating the facts, d'you know what I mean?" After the threat was made, the defendant sat quietly for the rest of the hearing, just saying "OK, thank you," at the end. In another Crown Court, a defendant was sentenced over video-link to a 16-month custodial term for robbery. As the judge delivered the sentence – using a certain amount of jargon: "commensurate with the nature of the offence", "category range", "position aggravated" and so on – the defendant sat entirely silent and motionless, giving no indication of whether he understood what was being said.

### Underlining the disparities

The references mentioned earlier are to generally courteous and respectful treatment of court users by practitioners. While this was the norm, the researchers also noted some interactions which underlined the social divide between the professionals and laypeople in court. The representative of an appellant in an IAC case chuckled when making his closing comments about his client's case, even while the appellant continued to cry openly about her children who – she had just told the tribunal – were living alone in Ghana. The researchers over-heard occasional disparaging or unsympathetic comments among practitioners after court users had left the courtroom; as when lawyers joked with each other about the unusual name of a baby who was the subject of care proceedings (during the hearing, the judge had asked the mother to confirm the spelling of the name and said, in a kindly way, "lovely name"). In the magistrates' court there was laughter at the end of a pre-trial hearing during which the defendant – a young woman charged with assaulting staff in her care home – had cried, shouted and sworn in the dock. Her lawyer said to the prosecutor and legal advisor: "I told you she was having a bad day!"

Not only were there apparent socio-economic, cultural and educational disparities between most court practitioners and most court users as individuals, but these disparities were embodied in court processes and procedures. It was clear that the language and styles of communication in court, along with the complexity, formality and ritualised nature of proceedings, and even court aesthetics (the grandeur of some courtrooms or court buildings, the formal dress of most practitioners), could all conspire to widen the gulf between the social world inhabited by court users and the social world of the courtroom.

The nature of this gulf between social worlds is illustrated by much of the observational data presented in the earlier discussions about court users' stories of conflict, loss and disadvantage, and the ways in which these stories played out in the courtroom. The observations gave rise to many further examples – among which some of the most telling were from the criminal courts. Here, many defendants immersed in cycles of disadvantage and offending behaviour often appeared to be largely impervious to the interventions (whether punitive or supportive) of the justice system.

A female defendant was observed pleading guilty to having breached her community order because of her failure to carry out unpaid work. A long-term heroin user, her ability to comply with the various requirements of the order was questioned by her defence solicitor, who referred to her chaotic lifestyle: she was living in a hostel, appeared to be continuing to use heroin – having dropped out of drug treatment, and had recently broken her foot. She had three children, of whom the eldest was about to be adopted. In the dock, the defendant admitted to having breached her order and gave a thumbs up to her partner – who was sitting, anxious and restless, in the public gallery – as the magistrates left the courtroom to confer. When the magistrates returned, the chair passed a sentence of 28 days' custody for her "wilful refusal to comply" with the community order. As she was escorted out of the dock, she shouted: "Do I do half?" Her partner replied: "You'll be out in 14," and the two blew kisses to each other. In another magistrates' court, there was discussion about the drug and alcohol use and mental health needs of a female defendant in her late teens said to pose "a high risk to known adults". Reference was made in court to a number of agencies which were involved in her care, and a mental health worker was in attendance at the hearing. The defendant was sentenced to 14 weeks' custody for an assault on her sister, having previously received a community order – with which she was not complying – for a similar offence against her parents. In the dock, she spent most of the hearing with her hood up and hand over her face. When passing sentence, the magistrate told her to stand up and look at him; she got to her feet, but closed her eyes. A male defendant in a plea hearing sat in the dock with his hands over his ears for much of the proceedings. As an interpreter tried in vain to communicate with him, the magistrates decided to remand him in custody pending his next appearance, scheduled for the Crown Court in several months' time. Cases like these raise the question of whether an active choice *not* to engage, or 'expressed rejection of the function of the courts' (Kirby, 2019: 167), might itself be considered a form of participation, and represent the exercise of agency by court users whose scope for action is highly constrained.

Several of the criminal cases observed – including the three just mentioned – made clear the inherent limitations of formal criminal justice responses to the multiple social, psychological and emotional problems with which much offending is associated. The *proportionality* of criminal justice responses to some of the offences observed coming before the courts could likewise be questioned. A defendant – said to have learning disabilities and to be "barely literate" – pleaded not guilty to a charge of breaching a restraining order because he had (possibly accidentally) sent his ex-partner a Skype contact request. The magistrates discussed arrangements for the forthcoming trial, and agreed to stand the case down in time for the defendant to make the coach for his 250-mile journey home. While questions as to the effectiveness and proportionality of judicial proceedings are outside the scope of the current study, the cases just cited point to the pertinence of the issue of court user participation to these much wider considerations.

## Disconnection

In sum, it appeared that the process by which court users' stories were translated in the courtroom was also – by virtue of the complexities of court language and procedures, the silencing of court users, and the manifestations of the disparities between the court users' social worlds and that of the court – a process whereby individuals were gradually disconnected from proceedings and thereby marginalised. To deploy the theatrical analogy that is commonplace in discussion of the courts, court users can thus be said to move from centre stage to the periphery over the course of proceedings. This analogy is used by Smejkalová, who (as noted earlier) writes of real-life problems being translated 'into the language the law recognizes'. She describes 'the split role of the layperson' who is:

at the same time a participant in a trial[16] where a specialized, subjectively incomprehensible language is used, while being an outsider, a spectator of this drama, not fully capable of accessing what is actually happening. She is physically on the stage but not fully participating in the discourse; she has not fully entered the enclosed space, which is capable of producing the result to her dispute. (2017: 72)

A different perspective on the marginalisation of laypeople in court is offered by Owusu-Bempah (2020), who argues with reference to the criminal courts that the existence of 'barriers to meaningful communication between the defendant and the court' result in the situation where '[i]nstead of being viewed as the subject and key stakeholder of the criminal process, the defendant is often treated as an object on which the criminal law is imposed'. McKeever makes a similar point about appellants in tribunals. She notes that although various structural features of the tribunal system, particularly its 'relative informality', are intended to facilitate participation, in practice, 'legal decision makers adopt a legal perspective on what constitutes relevant information ... The result is that the appellant becomes an object in his/her own case rather than a participant in it' (2013: 579).

## Conclusion

For scholars such as those just cited, the '*appearance* of participation' (McKeever, 2013: 578; emphasis added) may thus mask a reality of highly constrained engagement in judicial proceedings. In Chapter One of this volume, it is noted that effective participation in the court process is deemed, in law, to be essential to justice; and the previous chapter demonstrated that court-based practitioners are aware and supportive of this legal principle, even if they have varied understandings of the precise meaning and functions of 'participation'. What this chapter has shown is that, while many practitioners make considerable efforts to help court users participate in court, the forces militating against effective participation – arising from the very nature of the judicial process and the social and power differentials it exposes – are significant. The following, concluding chapter will consider what kinds of policy and practical reforms, at both national and international levels, could help to meet the attendant challenges to the fair and effective delivery of justice.

## Notes

[1]  Either in casual conversation or in the course of formal research interviews that coincided with observation visits.

[2]  Other recent, UK-based studies involving structured observation of court hearings include Gill et al (2018) on asylum hearings; Trinder et al (2014) on litigants-in-person in private family law cases in England and Wales; McKeever et al (2018) on litigants-in-person in the civil and family justice system in Northern Ireland.

[3]  While proceedings are generally adversarial, a semi-inquisitorial approach is sometimes followed; for example, for cases involving litigants-in-person (LIPs), the *Equal Treatment Bench Book* advises judges and magistrates to consider 'adopting to the extent necessary an inquisitorial role to enable the LIP fully to present their case' (Judicial College, 2020: 23).

[4]  www.gov.uk/courts-tribunals/employment-tribunal

[5]  Several of the observed IAC cases were in the aftermath of an investigation into organised fraud at English language test centres, which resulted in the revocation of tens of thousands of visas. A Public Accounts Committee report on the scandal found that 'the Home Office's flawed reaction to a systemic failure by a private company has had a detrimental impact on the lives of over 50,000 overseas students the Home Office accused of cheating' (Public Accounts Committee, 2019).

[6]  The much-criticised IPP sentence was abolished in 2012, but the abolition was not retrospectively applied. As of 31 December 2019, 2,134 IPP prisoners remained in custody, of whom 93 per cent were post-tariff (Ministry of Justice, 2019).

[7]  These are court users who, in Benesh and Howell's terms, have 'a very high personal stake in the outcome, but little control over it' (among whom they include 'criminal defendants, civil litigants, victims, and parties to domestic disputes'): a situation they found to be associated with low levels of confidence in (US) state and local courts (2001: 205).

[8]  The tribunal hearings, like those in the criminal courts, were open to the public; however, tribunal staff – while welcoming – tended to be curious about our presence, tended to confirm with the judge that the observation could proceed. Approval was obtained from HMCTS and

thereafter the judge or magistrates in each individual case (who some-times additionally sought consent from the parties) to conduct the Family Court observations.

9 As discussed in Chapter Two, the Youth Justice and Criminal Evidence Act 1999 provided for a range of 'special measures' intended to assist vulnerable or intimidated witnesses to give evidence, including use of screens in the courtroom and live video-link, and intermediaries to facilitate communication.

10 Which has been noted elsewhere with regard to criminal advocates (Hunter et al, 2018); see also Kirby (2017) and Henderson (2015).

11 The disparities in proportions of LiPs between the different settings largely reflect the scope of legal aid provision. Publicly funded legal representation is available for most criminal defendants, parties in public law and some private law family cases, and appellants in asylum, but not (for the most part) immigration IAC cases. With very few exceptions, legal aid cannot be accessed for representation in ET cases.

12 As discussed in Chapter Three, procedural justice theorists argue that legal authority is most likely to be regarded as legitimate by members of the public if they experience the *processes* of justice as fair – with fairness incorporating respectful treatment, having a voice and neutral decision making (Tyler, 2006, 2007).

13 The guardian is appointed by Cafcass to represent the interests of the child in proceedings.

14 The need for clearer communication in the courtroom, and the provision of information in simple, accessible language, is a particular focus of a recent JUSTICE Working Party report on improving participation by court users (JUSTICE, 2019).

15 Owusu-Bempah has critiqued the general assumption, reflected in case law, that defendants' right to effective participation in their trial 'can be exercised by proxy through one's lawyer' (2018).

16 She uses the term 'trial' to refer to 'any type of legal proceeding before a judge' (2017: 62).

## References

Atkinson, P. (2015) *For Ethnography*, London: Sage.

Benesh, S.C. and Howell, S.E. (2001) 'Confidence in the courts: a comparison of users and non-users', *Behavioral Sciences and the Law*, 19(2): 199–214.

Ewick, P. and Silbey, S.S. (1998) *The Common Place of Law: Stories from Everyday Life*, Chicago: University of Chicago Press.

Gill, N., Rotter, R., Burridge, A. and Allsopp, J. (2018) 'The limits of procedural discretion: unequal treatment and vulnerability in Britain's asylum appeals', *Social and Legal Studies*, 27(1): 49–78.

Henderson, E. (2015) 'Communicative competence? Judges, advocates and intermediaries discuss communication issues in the cross-examination of vulnerable witnesses', Criminal Law Review, 9: 659–678.

Hunter, G., Jacobson, J. and Kirby, A. (2018) *Judicial Perceptions of the Quality of Criminal Advocacy*, London: Solicitors Regulation Authority and Bar Standards Board.

Jacobson, J. (2018) 'Balancing accessibility and authority: towards an integrated approach to vulnerability in the criminal courts', in P. Cooper and L. Hunting (eds) *Access to Justice for Vulnerable People*, London: Wildy & Sons, 219–233.

Jacobson, J., Bhardwa, B., Gyateng, T., Hunter, G. and Hough, M. (2010) *Punishing Disadvantage: A Profile of Children in Custody*, London: Prison Reform Trust.

Jacobson, J., Hunter, G. and Kirby, A. (2015) *Inside Crown Court: Personal Experiences and Questions of Legitimacy*, Bristol: Policy Press.

Judicial College (2020) *Equal Treatment Bench Book: February 2018 edition (March 2020 revision)*, London: Judicial College.

JUSTICE (2019) *Understanding Courts: A Report by JUSTICE*, London: JUSTICE.

Kirby, A. (2017) 'Effectively engaging victims, witnesses and defendants in the criminal courts: a question of "court culture"?' *Criminal Law Review*, 12: 949–68.

Kirby, A. (2019) 'Engaging with legitimacy: an examination of lay participation in the criminal courts', PhD thesis, University of Surrey, available from: http://epubs.surrey.ac.uk/851936/

MacCormick, N. (2005) *Rhetoric and the Rule of Law*, Oxford: Oxford University Press.

McKeever, G. (2013) 'A ladder of legal participation for tribunal users', *Public Law*, 7: 575–98.

McKeever, G., Royal-Dawson, L., Kirk, E. and McCord, J. (2018) *Litigants in Person in Northern Ireland: Barriers to Legal Participation*, Belfast: Ulster University.

Ministry of Justice (2019) *Offender Management Statistics Bulletin, England and Wales Quarterly: Prison Population: 31 December 2019*, London: MoJ.

Owusu-Bempah, A. (2018) 'The interpretation and application of the right to effective participation', *International Journal of Evidence and Proof*, 22(4): 321–31.

Owusu-Bempah, A. (2020) 'Understanding the barriers to defendant participation in criminal proceedings', webinar, 14 May, available from: www.law.ox.ac.uk/events/understanding-barriers-defendant-participation-criminal-proceedings

Peters, J.S. (2008) 'Legal performance good and bad', Law, Culture and the Humanities, 4: 179–200.

Public Accounts Committee (2019) *English Language Tests for Overseas Students*, London: House of Commons.

Smejkalová, T. (2017) 'Legal performance: translating into law and subjectivity in law', *Tilburg Law Review*, 22(1–2): 62–76.

Steele, E.H. (1984) 'Review: morality, legality, and dispute processing: Auerbach's "justice without law?"', *American Bar Foundation Research Journal*, 9(1): 189–205.

Trinder, L., Hunter, R., Hitchings, E., Miles, J., Moorhead, R., Smith, L., Sefton, M., Hinchly, V., Bader, K. and Pearce, J. (2014) *Litigants in Person in Private Family Law Cases*, London: Ministry of Justice.

Tyler, T.R. (2006) 'Psychological perspectives on legitimacy and legitimation', *Annual Review of Psychology*, 57: 375–400.

Tyler, T.R. (2007) 'Procedural Justice and the Courts', *Court Review*, 44: 26–31.

# FIVE

# Looking Ahead: Towards a Principled Approach to Supporting Participation

Penny Cooper

## Introduction

This study began with a review of national policy, and in Chapter Two a picture emerges of fragmented policy development and procedural changes affecting court user participation. The focus of national policy development has been on criminal and family court users who are deemed 'vulnerable', although the definition has become increasingly fuzzy within the legal system of England and Wales and contrasts with usage of the term 'vulnerable' in other professional spheres. A major part of this study was made up of practitioner interviews and court observations through which four key research questions were addressed: in short, what does it mean for a lay person to participate in court, why does it matter, what promotes/inhibits their participation and what are the implications for participation of limited legal aid, court reform and the urgent shift to remote hearings in response to the COVID-19 pandemic?

Chapters Three and Four contain findings from 159 interviews and 316 hours of observations. This uncovered, for the first time, practitioners' concepts of court user participation. The result: *Ten Points of Participation* – six relating to form and four relating to function (see Chapter Three, Box 3.1: Conceptualisations of Participation and at Table 5.2: Ten Points of Participation as a provisional framework for court user guidance). Observational data provided many examples of practitioners' sympathetic and respectful treatment of court users, as well as their efforts to promote and support court user participation. Notwithstanding, there remain significant barriers to participation – for example, lack of legal representation, complex law and procedure, and impenetrable legal language in the courtroom.

This chapter addresses the fifth and final research question: What future developments in policy and practice, across the justice system of England and Wales and beyond, could ensure that participation is better supported? In order to take a broad perspective when addressing this question, an international review of initiatives for young or otherwise vulnerable witnesses was conducted. The aim was to explore what England and Wales might learn about supporting participation from other jurisdictions, as well what other jurisdictions might have learnt from England and Wales. The review revealed multiple examples of international 'export' of practices, including canine support for witnesses in court, witness intermediaries and ground rules hearings, as well as learning opportunities from remote witness assessments being conducted in New South Wales, Australia. This chapter also considers adaptations to hearings as a result of the initial COVID-19-related emergency changes to court proceedings. In conclusion, it is argued that, while it has been easy to pay 'lip service' to *effective participation* in law and practice, it is harder to gain an understanding of what it means in practice. New principles are recommended for future research and policy development so that court user participation may be central to future court reform.

## International review

The international review aspect of this study incorporated a literature review (the methodology for which is detailed later), as well as information gathered on international trips.[1]

### *Methodology for the literature search*

The Westlaw UK database was searched[2] for innovative measures/adjustments for court users. It was apparent that 'vulnerable' is not a universal term used to refer to witnesses for whom adjustments are made; therefore, the search included, but was not limited to, references to 'vulnerable' witnesses or parties.

In order to focus on recent developments and a manageable volume of results, only publications after 1 January 2016 in the English language were included in the Westlaw sweep. The Westlaw search resulted in a return of 308 journal articles. After an initial perusal of the titles of the articles and their abstracts, a total of 11 recent articles were identified as relevant. The Google Scholar research resulted in 113 publications. Article abstracts were reviewed for relevance and, once duplicates as compared to the Westlaw UK results were excluded, two further articles were identified as relevant. In addition to the Westlaw UK search, numerous permutations of the search terms were entered into Google Scholar, Google and Twitter in a quest for other published material, including news stories, reports, educational videos and guidance.

The international review identified six types of initiative aimed at promoting participation of vulnerable court users:

- witness intermediaries;
- ground rules hearings;
- therapy and court facility dogs;
- pre-recording witness testimony in full;
- specialist hearing suites;
- specialist guidance for judges.

All six initiatives seek to alter for the better the interaction or the circumstances of the interaction between the court user and the practitioners in a hearing.

## Witness intermediaries

The term 'witness intermediary' is used in this section to describe someone who helps convey questions to and answers from a witness. However, the intermediary role described here takes a variety of forms: some intermediaries relay questions, others conduct the questioning themselves, others help plan communications and only step in if questioning breaks down. All the roles aim to reduce anxiety and/or promote good quality communication. In England and Wales, eligibility is related solely to age or incapacity, but elsewhere (as for example in New South Wales, Australia) it may also be restricted to witnesses in particular geographical locations and types of cases.

In South Africa, the role was established for child witnesses in 1992, with the aim of reducing the trauma associated with giving evidence. There, the intermediary accompanies the child witness in the video-link room, translating and relaying questions into child-appropriate language, 'buffering aggression and intimidation and informing the court when the witness tires or loses concentration in order for the presiding officer to adjourn the court' (Jonker and Swanzen, 2007: 95).

In Norway, the intermediary is a specialist forensic interviewer who is observed by the judge and counsel from an adjoining room via video-link or one-way glass. After their interview, the intermediary consults with the judge and counsel, who are given the opportunity to suggest topics to be covered or contradictions to be explored. The interviewing intermediary returns to question the child on the agreed topics until all are satisfied (Hanna et al, 2010: 10). In Sweden, evidence can be taken from children in advance of the trial in a procedure controlled by an examining magistrate. Israel also has a system of child examiners or 'youth interrogators' who collect evidence from children for use in court (Spencer and Flin, 1990).

In 2019, Chile implemented new legislation aimed at enabling child witnesses to give their best evidence, which includes a provision for witness intermediaries. This development sits against the backdrop of Chile's transition from an inquisitorial to an adversarial legal system as it has sought to incorporate 'respect of human rights and international standards' (Gómez, 2010). Law 21.057 regulates the treatment of children and adolescents[3] who are complainants in sexual abuse cases. Article 3 of 21.057 sets out the *six principles* of application which can be summarised as follows:

- creating conditions at trial that are in keeping with the child/adolescent witness's best interests;
- supporting their right to be heard;
- supporting their voluntary participation as a witness;
- preventing their secondary victimisation by creating an environment which is appropriate to their individual needs;
- the timely investigation and prioritisation of a case involving a child's/adolescent's complaint;
- safeguarding the dignity of every child/adolescent.

The parties, their lawyers and the presiding judges remain in a traditional courtroom linked by closed-circuit television to the witness. The lawyer states a question, the judge repeats it in a form that they are content with and the intermediary hears the question (as conveyed by the judge) through an earpiece and repeats it to the witness. The witness will neither see nor hear what is happening in the courtroom. However, the court can see and hear the intermediary via the TV link.

Chile's intermediary model is similar to South Africa's; the question is relayed by a neutral person using a calm pace and tone. However, Jonker and Swanzen reported that in South Africa the use of an intermediary relaying questions has shortcomings, which have given rise to a number of problems:

The power of the intermediary is very limited, since the intermediary is perceived to be nothing more than an interpreter (and not an expert witness) and the court can at any time insist that the intermediary repeat the question exactly as it was phrased. A further disadvantage of the present system is that the intermediary does not have the authority to comment on a question and give an opinion as to whether a child understands a question or not. The intermediary is powerless to intervene and argue that questions should not be asked in a particular sequence or not phrased in a certain manner. (2007: 106)

At the time of writing, the Chilean intermediary model has been operational for under a year and a protocol allowing the intermediary to intervene is being trialled.

Witness intermediaries have been available in England and Wales since 2003 (see Chapter Two). Their role, as set out in section 29 of the Youth Justice and Criminal Evidence Act 1999, is to communicate the questions to the witness and the replies given. This version of the intermediary role, 'the English model', consists of the intermediary assessing the communication needs and abilities of the witness and advising practitioners how best to accommodate those needs and abilities. In contrast to the role in the jurisdictions described earlier, the intermediary in England and Wales does not undertake forensic questioning, although they closely advise and support those who do. Research has demonstrated how intermediaries in England and Wales enable a witness to provide and questioners to elicit more accurate and complete information (for example, Wilcock et al, 2018). In court hearings, intermediaries make recommendations for ground rules for questioners to follow and intervene only if communication breaks down. (The international evolution of the ground rules hearing is discussed later.)

The English intermediary model has been successfully adopted in modified form in Northern Ireland and in the states of New South Wales, Victoria (Cooper and Mattison, 2017) and the Australian Capital Territory. Since 2016, in the Australian state of New South Wales, reflecting the geographic dispersal of witnesses and intermediaries, many witness assessments are conducted remotely using video technology. Plans for an intermediary scheme in Tasmania are at an advanced stage, while South Australia is moving from a volunteer communication partner scheme to a 'fee-for-service' model (Parliament South Australia, 2020). New Zealand has also implemented its own version of the English intermediary model, and research has found that professionals are overwhelmingly in support of the new role (Howard et al, 2019).

Professionals in India are said to be exploring the use of the English model of the intermediary (Shukla, 2018), although the applicable guidelines for a vulnerable witness communication facilitator are more akin to the South African model where the intermediary relays the questions:

> the respective counsels for the parties shall pose questions to the vulnerable witness only through the facilitator, either in the words used by counsel or, if the vulnerable witness is not likely to understand the same, in words or by such mode as is comprehensible to the vulnerable witness and which convey the meaning intended by counsel. (Delhi High Court, nd: 9–10)

The Republic of Ireland has legislation which allows for the use of an intermediary, but it is 'seldom used' (O'Leary and Feely, 2018). In at least one criminal trial in the Republic of Ireland in 2016, the services of an English intermediary were used (Gallagher, 2016). Intermediaries operating under the 'English model' have also assisted on an ad-hoc basis in cases in Jersey (Channel Islands), Scotland and British Overseas Territories.[4]

While the use of witness intermediaries appears to be growing in popularity, there is relatively little published research on their effectiveness and no known research comparing the effectiveness of the different models described earlier.

## Ground rules hearings

The English approach of a ground rules hearing prior to the recording session, at which lines of questioning are agreed seems to have merit; for this to work well, the bench must be prepared to take an active role in setting the parameters for the cross-examination and re-examination of the witness. (Scottish Court Service, 2015: 36)

Ground rules hearings (also discussed in Chapter Two) are a judicial case management tool for setting the parameters for the treatment of a witness or party at a hearing so that they may participate effectively. The practice originated in England and Wales when a ground rules meeting/hearing was requested by witness intermediaries (Cooper et al, 2015). Ground rules hearings and subsequent planning of questions in line with the ground rules should be a collaborative exercise.

The ground rules hearing should cover, amongst other matters, the general care of the witness, if, when and where the witness is to be shown their video interview, when, where and how the parties (and the judge if identified) intend to introduce themselves to the witness, the length of questioning and frequency of breaks and the nature of the questions to be asked. (*R* v *Lubemba*; *R* v *JP* [2014] EWCA Crim 2064, para 43)

Ground rules hearings, an established feature of the English legal system in cases where court users are deemed vulnerable, feature in the criminal justice systems in Scotland and three Australian states. They have been incorporated into primary

**Table 5.1: Comparing approaches to ground rules hearings**

| Jurisdiction | Ground rules hearing procedure statute, rule or practice guidance | Year procedure was first written into statute, rule or practice guidance |
|---|---|---|
| Criminal Justice System, England and Wales | Criminal Procedure Rules, Rule 3.9(7) (see also Criminal Practice Direction, paragraph 3E). | 2014 |
| Family Justice System, England and Wales | Practice Direction 3AA Vulnerable Persons: Participation in Proceedings and Giving Evidence, paragraphs 5.2–5.7. | 2017 |
| Criminal Justice System, Victoria, Australia | Criminal Procedure Act 2009, Part 8.2A – Ground rules hearings and intermediaries, page 23, paragraph 13. | 2018 |
| Criminal Justice System, News South Wales, Australia | Criminal Trial Courts Bench Book, District Court Criminal Practice Note 11. | 2019 |
| Criminal Justice System, Australian Capital Territory | Evidence (Miscellaneous Provisions) Amendment Act 2019, Part 2. | 2019 |
| Criminal Justice System, Scotland | Vulnerable Witnesses (Criminal Evidence) (Scotland) Act 2019, section 1ZD. | 2019 |

legislation in Scotland and two Australian states (Victoria and the Australian Capital Territory). Legal provisions for ground rules hearings differ according to the jurisdiction, although all have their origins in the ground rules hearing concept created[5] in England and Wales (Table 5.1).

In a unique piece of legislative drafting, the Australian Capital Territory ground rules hearing provision is applicable to all witnesses in criminal proceedings:

> A court may, at any time, if satisfied that it is in the interests of justice, direct that a ground rules hearing be held for a witness in a criminal proceeding.
>
> ...
>
> (1) At a ground rules hearing for a witness in a criminal proceeding, the court may make any direction the court considers is in the interests of justice, including any of the following:
>
> (a) a direction about how a witness may be questioned;
>
> (b) a direction about how long a witness may be questioned;
>
> (c) a direction about the questions that may or may not be asked of a witness;
>
> (d) if there is more than 1 accused – a direction about the allocation among the accused of the topics about which a witness may be asked;
>
> (e) a direction about the use of models, plans, body maps or other aids to help communicate a question or an answer;
>
> (f) a direction about the use of a support animal by the witness;
>
> (g) a direction that if a party intends to give evidence that contradicts or challenges the evidence of a witness or that otherwise discredits a witness, the party is not obliged to put that evidence in its entirety to the witness in cross-examination. (Chapter 1A Ground rules hearings – criminal proceedings 4AB(1) and 4AF)

Support animals (see (f)) are available to help calm anxious witnesses when they give evidence, but are also available to witnesses waiting outside Canberra criminal courtrooms.

International approaches to the provision of canine support both inside and outside the courtroom are discussed in the following section.

### Court 'facility dogs'

It is important to note the difference between 'therapy dogs' (also known as 'companion dogs') and 'facility dogs' in the justice system. Therapy dogs support a witness before and/ or after an investigative interview or hearing. Facility dogs accompany a witness while the witness gives evidence and are specially trained to do so. The two are closely connected, but it is the facility dog which can have a direct effect on participation in court.

> [Facility] dogs are specially trained to a high standard and are allowed in actual police interviews or courtrooms ... [Therapy] dogs should not go beyond providing comfort in waiting rooms before or after an interview/trial. Due to their lack of training and unpredictability, they are not suitable to be present during a police interview or during court proceedings. (Spruin and Mozava, 2017: 39)

The first recorded instance of a *facility* dog being used to support a witness in court was in the US state of Mississippi in the early 1990s (Spruin, 2016). Their use has spread to most other US states; however, evidence supporting the use of facility dogs remains sparse. Grimm argues that the use of facility dogs for child victims is 'constitutionally suspect' and should be excluded on account of the availability of other support mechanisms, such as videotaping of testimony, video-link, dolls, stuffed animals and child advocates (2013: 292). Conversely, it has been argued that facility dogs 'fill a gap for witnesses when traditional comfort items and support persons fail to ease their anxiety' (Holder, 2013: 1187). Six attorneys interviewed for a small US study supported the provision of witness support by court dogs, although one respondent noted that they should also be available for the defence, not just prosecution witnesses (Donaldson, 2017). A study with mock jurors provides initial evidence to suggest that facility dogs 'may not prejudice jurors against defendants or bias jurors in favour of the witness they accompany' (Burd and Mcquiston, 2019: 11).

A survey of US and Canadian criminal justice system practitioners who had experience interviewing child witnesses with and without the use of a facility dog found that 'respondents believed that utilising facility dogs both enhanced witnesses' credibility and helped [forensic] interviewers to build rapport with witnesses' (Spruin et al, under review).

The presence of a facility dog providing the witness with support in court has been recognised in at least three US states (National Crime Victim Law Institute, 2013). In 2013, in *State of Washington, Respondent* v *Timothy Dye, Petitioner No 87929–0*,[6] the Supreme Court of Washington said:

> Generally, we give trial courts wide discretion to control trial proceedings, including the manner in which testimony will be presented. We recognize that some trial procedures, such as providing a child witness with a toy on the stand or shackling a defendant at trial, may risk coloring the perceptions of the jury. But trial courts are capable of addressing these risks. Here, the trial court acted within its broad discretion when it determined that Ellie, the facility dog provided by the prosecutor's office to the victim Douglas Lare, was needed in light of Lare's severe developmental disabilities in order for Lare to testify adequately. (Para 1)

The Courthouse Facility Dogs Foundation in the US cites 234 facility dogs working in 40 of the 50 states as of 27 November 2019 (Courthouse Dogs Foundation, 2020), a substantial increase on their previously published figure of 148 dogs in 35 states as of 19 September 2017.

In Chile, a facility dogs program has been running since 2009, having started in conjunction with the Courthouse Dogs Foundation which provides professional training to the Chilean Bocalan Trust.[7] The Courthouse Dogs Foundation also reports (2020) that the Australian state of Victoria's Office of Public Prosecutions has a facility dog. Best practice recommendations for wider implementation in Australia have been made (Morrison, 2019). Dogs also support witnesses in court in Canada (Grant, 2014; Warnica, 2015) in eight out of 13 provinces (Courthouse Dogs Foundation, 2020). In *R v Marchand and Marchand*,[8] a 14-year-old complainant in a sex offence case was accompanied by a dog alongside the dog handler in the witness box:

> The testimony of the handler included evidence of the effectiveness of service dogs such as Caber in situations similar to the one before the court. The evidence was compelling that service dogs such as Caber have a calming influence on witnesses who must testify about difficult matters, and that these dogs allow the witness to effect-ively communicate his or her evidence, without creating interference or distraction. (Para 5)

In one small Canadian study, seven court officials perceived the use of a courthouse facility dog to be beneficial for children and young people who are experiencing challenges testifying in court; the study also called for further evidence-based research on the use of dogs in court to support vulnerable witnesses (Glazer, 2018: 52).

Although not part of a formal scheme providing facility dogs, a young witness's autism support dog accompanied them in the video-link room in Northern Ireland in 2018. The dog sat behind the witness's chair while they gave evidence.[9] The intermediary, who had made the recommendation for the dog to be present, reported that the witness coped very well and did not need to stroke the dog. This is the first known instance of a dog in the video-link room in the United Kingdom. It is also known that a dog accompanied a vulnerable witness to give pre-recorded evidence in a criminal matter in Sydney, Australia.[10] These two examples did not involve a dog specially trained for the courtroom; rather, they were instances of ad-hoc applications for canine support which the judge granted. Belgium, France and Italy also have facility dog schemes (Courthouse Dogs Foundation, 2020) and in England, for research purposes, Dr Liz Spruin has 'imported' a specially trained facility dog from the US.[11] These are small steps towards more expansive use of facility dogs to support witnesses in hearings.

### *Pre-recording witness testimony in full*

Pre-recording of witness testimony may be partial or full. Full pre-recording includes not only the witness giving their account (commonly referred to as evidence-in-chief), but also the witness's responses to an opposing party's challenge to that account (commonly referred to as cross-examination). Of all the special measures for vulnerable and intimidated witnesses in criminal courts in England and Wales, this was the last to be introduced. While the pre-recording of interviews in place of evidence-in-chief is a long-standing practice for eligible witnesses, pre-recording of cross-examination only began in 2014 in pilot courts (see Chapter Two). By 2018, technological difficulties were delaying roll-out in England and Wales (Cooper and Mattison, 2018). Contrast Australia, where, although each state has its own particular eligibility criteria and procedures, pre-recording of child witness evidence in its entirety is commonplace in criminal cases and has been for years in most states (Corish, 2015: 187).

Reviewing the practice of pre-recording the testimony of child witnesses in criminal cases in Australia, Norway and England and Wales, the Scottish Court Service's 'Evidence and procedure review' noted that practitioners are 'convinced that there are clear benefits to be had from a systematic and structured approach to the use of audio-visually recorded forensic interviews as a witness' principal evidence, and from the recording of cross-examination' (2015: 25). The review's vision for recording child witness evidence in its entirety was realised in the Vulnerable Witnesses (Criminal Evidence) (Scotland) Act 2019. This requires the court to enable a child's evidence to be given (and recorded) in advance of the hearing in front of a specialist judge unless it is an exceptional case.

### Specialist hearing suites

Some courts have a specialist approach to particular kinds of cases; for example, Family Drug and Alcohol Courts (England and Wales) take a therapeutic, problem-solving approach to cases, which means the focus is not only on finding the best care plan for the child, but also on substance misuse treatment for the parent. Other courts taking specialist approaches are operated by practitioners specifically trained to deal with certain cases – for example, sexual offences courts in India and in Antigua and Barbuda. The international review also revealed examples of innovative, specially designed, calming environments aimed at supporting court user participation where the complainant is a child.

The Goa Children's Court, which has been operating for some 16 years, has pink walks and the judge's table is placed so that the child can 'sit near the judge rather than across from her'. Delhi has gone even further; children can 'wait in a separate room designed like a crèche with toys and colouring material; the courtrooms have one-sided glass booths so the accused can see the proceedings, as is their right, but the child does not have to see the accused' (Sriram, 2017). There are parallels with the new Glasgow Evidence and Hearings Suite. Opened in November 2019, it was designed to enable child witnesses to pre-record their evidence and for vulnerable witnesses to give evidence remotely away from the formality of a traditional courtroom. The suite includes a calming 'sensory room' with special furnishings which can be also be used as a remote video-link room. There is also an evidence room with one-way glass so that a child witness can be observed being questioned. Similar suites are planned elsewhere in Scotland (SCTS, 2019; BBC, 2020a).

### Specialist judicial guidance

There are diverse examples from overseas of publicly available judicial guidance aimed at supporting participation. Guidance may be relatively brief and broad in scope; for example, Colorado's 'Access to the courts: a resource guide to providing reasonable accommodations for people with disabilities for judicial officers, probation and court staff':

> This directive is issued to ensure equal access to and full participation in court and probation services and programs by people with disabilities, including attorneys, litigants, defendants, probationers, witnesses, victims, potential jurors, prospective employees and public observers of court proceedings. (Colorado Judicial Department, 2004: 4).

The 15-page resource highlights a wide range of adaptations, including talking slowly, writing things down, taking periodic breaks, 'scheduling court proceedings at a different time to meet the medical needs of the individual; providing a coach or support person at the proceeding; or allowing videotaped testimony or the use of video conferencing technology in lieu of a personal appearance' (Colorado Judicial Department, 2004: 9).

California Courts' 'Elder abuse pocket reference guide' (Mosqueda and Judicial Council of California, 2012) focuses on the needs of a specific cohort of court users and runs to 106 pages. It contains not only legal but also medical guidance for those dealing with elder abuse cases.

The Judicial Education Institute of Trinidad and Tobago publishes particularly extensive guidance, including a 311-page *Criminal Bench Book* on the JEITT E-book platform (2015) and a 113-page 'Gender equality protocol for judicial officers' (2018). A section titled 'Use of alternative means of giving evidence' states that for complainants in cases of sexual offences and for children:

> video conferencing, video digital recording, depositions taken by the Registrar or a Master using computer-aided transcription or audio-digital recording or both, telephone or other alternate electronic means including telecommunications application software using Voice Over IP. (Judicial Education Institute of Trinidad and Tobago, 2018: 78)

The status of the guidance is described within the document:

> It simply represents suggestions on the best practices to be adopted when faced with inequality as a result of gender or any other source of discrimination. It seeks to provide the Judicial Officer with guidance on how to approach adjudication in a manner that will allow for more than just a strict application of the laws. (2018: IV)

In India, 'Guidelines for recording of evidence of vulnerable witnesses in criminal matters' (nd) is a 19-page document emanating from the High Court: 'The purpose of this protocol is to present guidelines and mandatory recommendations, to improve the response of the justice dispensation system to vulnerable witnesses' (Delhi High Court, nd: 2). The protocol provides an overview of potential adjustments: a person appointed by the court to attend to support the witness, prohibition on the publication of the child witness's identity, comfort items, courthouse familiarisation tour, meeting the judge, communication ('descriptive aids'), video-link, screens, image or voice altering or any other technical device.

## Reflections on innovative support for participation

The cross-fertilisation of ideas from one jurisdiction to another, though widespread, has also tended to be ad hoc and unco-ordinated. International initiatives described earlier, as well as national policy developments described in Chapter Two, share common features. They are as follows:

- Slow to spread: initiatives have frequently taken years, sometimes decades, to be more widely adopted in new jurisdictions.
- Under-researched: their effectiveness is rarely the subject of academic study.
- Niche: they have been applied only to court users deemed vulnerable enough to need special assistance.
- Temporary 'fixes': the traditional mores of court culture which dictate how most court users participate remain unchanged.

While there is a multitude of national and international developments which have a clear goal of enhancing participation, few are explicitly grounded in a theory/principles of participation. Practitioners' contrasting accounts of what participation entails and why it matters, set out in Chapter Three of this volume (see, in particular, Box 3.1), provide a provisional framework – elaborated later as the *Ten Points of Participation*. This framework requires further elaboration through research with court users which could, for example, examine the extent and impact of enduring barriers to participation such as the language, formality and emotional stakes in the courtroom. It is hoped that framing participation according to these ten points will take us on a route to a better understanding of *effective participation*, but there is still some way to go.

National policy developments for vulnerable witnesses were originally justified not because they would enhance participation, but for more practitioner–centric reasons – because it was thought they would improve the quality of a witness's evidence. In the 20 years since special measures were first introduced, the legal narrative on adaptations in court has begun to focus more on *effective participation*, but without concomitant attention to what it means to participate and to do so effectively. This study has explored practitioners' conceptions of participation. What participation means to court users and what makes it *effective* is much talked about, but remains too little explored. Taking an idea from the world of gardening,[12] the best time to address effective participation of court users was 20 years ago, and the second best time to address it is now.

In England and Wales, a report by the law reform organisation JUSTICE called for fundamental change to the way in which hearings operate (Marks, 2016). The report redefined the concept of courts and tribunals as flexible spaces and urged greater use of technology; the authors identified an opportunity to be seized. The HMCTS courts modernisation programme, falling behind and with overrunning costs (National Audit Office, 2018), has not yet seized that opportunity. However, for the first time, there was a pilot of 'video hearings' in the tax tribunal, where appellants and representatives from the tax office attended remotely from their home or office. It was independently evaluated by Rossner and Tait (2020): '[P]articipants were able to access their hearings easily, understood the proceedings and considered the format to be appropriately formal. This was despite the fact they experienced frequent technical disruptions.'

The implications of the modernisation reforms that HMCTS has been pursuing, especially in the criminal courts, have given rise to many concerns about remote attendance (Gibbs, 2017; Padfield and Hawker, 2017) and the need for 'significant investment' to improve court audio–video equipment (Fielding et al, 2020:11). Remote hearings may never be appropriate for some court users, according to the interim findings of an Equality and Human Rights Commission study into vulnerable defendants in the criminal justice system: 'Most of our evidence focused on the barriers that video hearings can present to defendants with a cognitive impairment, mental health condition and/ or neuro-diverse condition. We found that for many people with these impairments, a video hearing would not be suitable' (EHRC, 2020: 10).

However, the concerns raised about the reforms go much wider than this. The House of Commons Justice Committee (2019) sounded alarm bells:

> Courts service modernisation, including use of better IT to be more efficient, is long- overdue. But we have found that poor digital skills, limited access to technology and low levels of literacy and legal knowledge raise barriers against access to new services provided by digital means ... We received powerful evidence of a court system in administrative chaos, with serious staff shortages threatening to compromise the fairness of proceedings. (Para 149)

Then, in the spring of 2020, an already stressed court system was forced to make sudden, radical changes to the way in which hearings are conducted and thus how court users participate.

## Court reform, the COVID-19 pandemic and court user participation

On 23 March 2020, the Prime Minister announced strict curbs on travel and social contact in order to prevent the transmission of COVID-19 (BBC, 2020b). It does not appear that the courts in England and Wales could immediately turn to a pre-set pandemic response plan 'to ensure the continuity of vital court operations' (Task Force on Pandemic Preparedness Planning for the Courts, 2007: 3) with, for example, provisions to facilitate press and public access to remote hearings (Task Force on Pandemic Preparedness Planning for the Courts, 2007). In England and Wales, the decision was taken to keep open some 'priority courts' (MoJ, 2020), while the majority closed to lawyers and the public. Overnight, the centuries-old presumption in favour of face-to-face hearings was replaced with a presumption in favour of hearings facilitated by technology so that participants could join in from separate locations ('remote hearings'). This was a very rapid and unanticipated acceleration of a trend that was already in progress, under the courts modernisation programme.

The approach was, 'where it can be safely done and without risks to the integrity of the legal process, the wheels of justice should keep turning at their pre-crisis rate'.[13] HMCTS, the Ministry of Justice and the judiciary necessarily worked fast and hard to produce extensive guidance for judges and lawyers involved in remote hearings. There were pressing practical issues such as which video platform to use and how to prepare electronic bundles of documents for hearings.

Judges were given the discretion to determine how the remote hearing would replace the traditional face-to-face, oral hearing in court: for example, by telephone (*Anwer* v *Central Bridging Loans Ltd* [2020] EWHC 765 (Ch)), by video (*A Clinical Commissioning Group* v *AF and Others* [2020] EWCOP 16), by a combination of telephone and video (*Kavaarupo* v *Nursing and Midwifery Council* [2020] EWHC 731 (Admin)) or by evidence and submission in writing (*Gil* v *London Borough of Camden* [2020] EWHC 735 (QB)).

It rapidly became clear that practitioners and court users could have very different experiences (Kitzinger, 2020), resulting in 'a gulf between lawyers and lay parties' perspectives' (Jaganmohan, 2020). One barrister and sometime tribunal chair summed up the position as follows:

> The fact that some lawyers or participants would rather engage in conventional, in-person, hearings does not

mean that one held remotely has not been fair. Certainly, there are different dynamics, particularly around the human inter-reaction between witness and questioner and between advocate and tribunal. But whether that materially alters the instinctive assessments that are a feature of the conventional process and, if it does, whether one loses anything that is truly useful and reliable is open to question. (Norris, 2020)

Despite a steady stream of new guidance for lawyers,[14] advice for court users was exceedingly brief and of limited value since it came with no explanation of what it means to 'participate effectively' or what 'adjustments' to a remote hearing might be possible:

Audio and video hearings provide an additional channel for conducting a hearing and should be as accessible as possible. But they may not be suitable for everyone. Please tell the court or tribunal if there are any circumstances about yourself or your case which may affect or impair your ability to participate effectively in an audio or video hearing. This will inform the judiciary's decision. Reasonable adjustments will be made. (HMCTS, 2020)

HMCTS had rightly identified the issue of participation for court users, but without providing practical guidance. It is suggested that placing effective participation at the heart of the design of practical guidance for court users would be a good place to start. Using our empirical findings, and in particular the *Ten Points of Participation* (see Chapter Three generally and Box 3.1 in particular), we have suggested what the guidance might cover in Table 5.2.

Use of the *Ten Points of Participation* to frame guidance for court users is one example of their application. The *Ten Points of Participation* can also help practitioners to reflect on their

**Table 5.2: Ten Points of Participation as a provisional framework for court user guidance**

| | Participation entails: | Guidance might cover: |
|---|---|---|
| 1 | The provision and/ or elicitation of information for the court | The way the court user can provide information (including evidence) and how the court will provide it to the user |
| 2 | Being informed about proceedings | Sources of information about how the hearing works and sources of advice on use of accessible language without reliance on legal jargon |
| 3 | Having legal representation | Sources of legal representation and information about funding so that participants may consider representation and understand that it is intended as a facilitator of, not a substitute for, their participation |
| 4 | Protection of well-being | Adaptations (including but not limited to special measures) and how they may be sought and applied according to the needs of the court user and the case |
| 5 | The 'management' of the court user, such that disruption to proceedings is minimised | The court user's responsibilities and potential consequences (for the individual and the court process) of disruption |
| 6 | Presence at proceedings | Implications of virtual versus physical presence, and the bases on which informed choices might be made (where applicable) about whether, and how, to attend proceedings |
| | **Functions of participation:** | **Guidance might cover:** |
| 7 | The exercise of legal rights | What legal rights are and how they differ depending on the type of court user and court |

(continued)

**Table 5.2: Ten Points of Participation as a provisional framework for court user guidance (continued)**

| 8 | Enabling court decision making | How the court user's participation can facilitate decision making |
|---|---|---|
| 9 | Legitimation of court processes and outcomes | How having a 'voice' in proceedings can contribute to perceptions of the fairness of the process and outcome |
| 10 | Potential therapeutic benefits | Potential benefits to the individual, separate from the legal outcome, that may arise from participation |

own understandings of participation and thus their approach to court users before, during and after a hearing. For example,

- Which aspects of participation, if any, do they regard as most important, and do they regard any as unimportant?
- Do they explicitly discuss with court users the court's expectations of their participation, and how it contributes to the overall process?

Court user participation is also a necessary consideration when guidance for practitioners is produced. Note, for example, that advocates' robes – worn in the courtroom for some hearings – have been dispensed with for COVID-19 remote hearings:

- 'Advocates are not required to wear Robes for any hearing. Smart business wear is, however, appropriate for hearings where the advocate(s) can be seen' (Godsmark, 2020: para 18).
- 'Dress professionally, but not in robes unless specifically asked to do so and appear as if attending the court or tribunal in person' (ICCA, 2020: 6).

Is this decision to dispense with robes because advocates might not have access to their robes? Perhaps it is to prevent advocates feeling awkward joining a remote video hearing in robes from home? It may have been a practitioner-centric decision; however, from the perspective of court user participation, the judge and advocates wearing 'robes' might have particular advantages in remote hearings. It might assist court users to see at a glance who is who. (In a traditional courtroom, the physical location of the judge and advocates usually indicates their role and position in the power hierarchy, but that is lost on a standard video conferencing platform.) Robes, or even just gowns (rather than wigs and gowns), could add legitimacy to a remote hearing. Robes might also add weight to judicial attempts to manage disruptive participants, something that is particularly relevant when judges report a 'growing problem of participants not respecting the reality that although they were not physically present in a court room, they were taking part in court proceedings with all the constraints on behaviour that implies' (Burnett et al, 2020).

Urgent changes to court procedures have given rise to rapid preliminary research, including a consultation at the request of the President of the Family Division (Ryan et al, 2020). In *B (Children) (Remote Hearing: Interim Care Order)* [2020] EWCA Civ 584, the President noted 'a qualitative difference between a remote hearing conducted over the telephone and one undertaken via a video platform'. There is, of course, also a qualitative difference between participating remotely and participating in a court or tribunal room. Emergency measures will give judges and practitioners first-hand experience of some of the challenges of participating remotely and, perhaps, new insights into the challenges already faced by vulnerable witnesses participating remotely under special measures provisions.

## Conclusion

Participation by lay court users in oral hearings is deemed by law to be essential to the delivery of justice. However, what precisely is meant by participation, and its functions, are not clearly or consistently defined. Ongoing policy and practice reforms variously support and undermine participation – for example:

- On the 'support' side are the increasing provision for vulnerable court users; growing efforts to make court proceedings more comprehensible generally; and (arguably) greater efficiency or speed of proceedings.
- Factors on the 'undermine' side may include legal aid cuts; court closures and associated use of remote methods of attending court; and loss of 'local justice'.

Practitioners recognise the importance of participation and of their own role in supporting it, although they vary in how exactly they understand the term. Practitioners also do much to support participation in practice; however, the findings of this study should encourage them to remain vigilant about the barriers to participation and to keep under review the extent to which it is achieved in practice.[15] It is clear that participation can be severely constrained by multiple factors, including the wide disparities between court users' social worlds and the formal world of the courtroom.

There was already an accelerating trend towards replacement of physical attendance at court with remote methods – including online pleas in the criminal courts, online cases in civil courts, attendance by video-link in criminal and other courts, and the potential development of entirely virtual hearings. There were two contrasting rationales supporting this trend: protection of the vulnerable, as well as cost and efficiency savings, under the umbrella of the wider court reform. The past few years have also seen many practitioners, academics and other commentators raise significant concerns about remote court hearings and remote attendance and about the implications for participation by court users, access to justice and open justice. There has been little research or analysis which has addressed these concerns in a thorough or systematic way.

The COVID-19 pandemic has been a major impetus for rapidly expanded use of alternatives to face-to-face court attendance and hearings, at least temporarily and potentially over the medium to longer term. At a minimum, it compels us to reflect on the implications for remote participation at court hearings, and to challenge some assumptions about these developments. Questions that are raised include:

- Does wider use of remote court hearings provide opportunities to overcome barriers to participation – for example, excessive formality and complexity?
- Are there circumstances, or parts of the justice system, in which remote attendance must always be avoided and, if so, why and how?
- How can learning about good and poor practice and procedures be compiled and shared – both nationally and internationally?

There is no doubt that COVID-19 has acted as an accelerant to the HMCTS court reform programme. Which reforms introduced under the emergency measures stand the test of time when the immediate health crisis has past remains to be seen. It is possible that the challenges of participating in virtual hearings will fuel support for a return to face-to-face hearings, at least until there is further research, better technology and more detailed planning of virtual hearings.

## Aspirations for research, policy and practice

For hundreds of years, the traditional approach to hearings in England and Wales has been one in which participants are co-located and communicating face-to-face. Exceptions to the traditional means of participation in court have been made for those who are distressed, young, incapacitated or unable to attend court because they are physically unwell or overseas. Internationally, innovative ideas to promote participation have been shared, imported and adapted. These initiatives have been relatively slow to take root in new jurisdictions and remain under-researched, niche, temporary 'fixes'. For the vast majority of court users, the 'usual way' of participating has meant face-to-face in court. Barriers to participation exist for the majority of court users: these arise, for example, from the complexity of the law and the language of the courtroom; the emotional price of being in a hearing about conflict, loss and disadvantage; and the often wide social, cultural and educational disparities between most court practitioners and most court users as individuals.

When the emergency measures were introduced to tackle the spread of the COVID-19 virus, the new experimental way of participating in a court hearing was remotely. The advice for practitioners soon became legion, but the advice for court users was minimal; it promised 'reasonable adjustments' for 'effective participation' in remote hearings without saying what these meant.

Case law[16] and policy, while referring to effective participation, are largely silent on the form that participation should take or its functions. This study now offers a framework – albeit a preliminary one because further research is required with court users. It is intended that this framework, based on the *Ten Points of Participation*, should guide policy- and practice-oriented engagement with witnesses and parties so that they might better understand what to expect in court and what is expected of them. It should also form the basis of much-needed future research involving court users.

Looking ahead, justice researchers and policy makers around the world have a key role to play in placing court user participation at the heart of court reform through:

- engagement with court users to better understand from their perspective what it means to *participate effectively*;
- coordinated, international, cross-jurisdictional information sharing about issues affecting court user participation;
- research into new, creative approaches that extend beyond remote hearings which simply emulate a traditional hearing.

The mid- to long-term implications of COVID-19 are unknown, although inevitably public funding, including for justice, will be severely tested. Some practitioners may favour a return to 'traditional' hearings (if that is even possible), while others may hope that remote hearings become the 'new normal'. Research shows that 'traditional' hearings can be marginalising and disempowering for court users; however, remote hearings, if poorly configured, might retain the old barriers to participation and add new ones. Whatever direction court reform takes, it requires a new approach based on a better understanding of 'effective participation'. For this to happen, it is the responsibility of researchers and policy makers, as well as those who work in the courts and tribunals, to place the participation of *all* court users at the heart of permanent court reform.

## Notes

[1] Fortuitously, for other professional reasons not funded by this project, the author of this chapter visited Australia, Belize, Chile, Northern Ireland, Scotland and the US as an invited conference speaker during the course of this project, where practitioners and judges readily shared examples of adaptations in courtrooms in their jurisdictions. Thanks are due to the following organisations which facilitated the author's visits/research in the field in jurisdictions outside England and Wales: ACT Human Rights Commission, Caribbean Association of Judicial Officers, Department of Justice, Northern Ireland, Foreign and Commonwealth Office, Fundación Amparo y Justicia (Chile), Judicial Institute for Scotland, Law Society of Scotland, New South Wales Department of Communities and Justice, New South Wales Police Department and NSW Ombudsman.

[2] Initial search term in September 2017: '(witness or victim or defendant or party) AND (vulnerab★ or intimidated or young or child or disab★) AND (special measure★ or adjust★ or adapt★) AND (in court or trial) AND (innovat★ or reform★)'.

[3] Adolescents are defined as those who are between 14 and 18 years of age.

[4] Source: private correspondence between the author and intermediaries and judges.

[5] The concept of the ground rules hearings was devised and developed by the author in the course of intermediary training from 2003 onwards and subsequent research about intermediary practice in England and Wales.

[6] Decided: 26 September 2013. Full judgment available from: http://caselaw.findlaw.com/wa-supreme-court/1645704.html

[7] Email correspondence between the author and the Director of the Bocalan Trust, Chile.

[8] 2016 BCSC 1680.

[9] Information provided by email to the author from the intermediary in the case.

[10] Information provided to the author in a meeting with the judge in the case.

[11] Email correspondence (27 September 2017 and 3 October 2017) and meeting with Dr Spruin.

[12] 'The best time to plant a tree was 20 years ago. The second best time is now.'

[13] Judge Daniel Alexander QC in *Heineken Supply Chain BV v Anheuser-Busch Inbev SA (Rev 1)* [2020] EWHC 892 (Pat), para 28.

[14] At the time of writing, in total 84 new COVID-19 remote hearing guidance documents were on the HMCTS website. They had been gradually uploaded between 23 March and 17 April 2020, with some general in nature and others applicable to specific courts or tribunals. See www.judiciary.uk/coronavirus-covid-19-advice-and-guidance/

[15] This accords with the recommendation in the JUSTICE report on *Understanding Courts* that 'There should be an expressly stated overriding objective – across all jurisdictions – that professionals should have as a primary consideration the effective participation of lay users. In other words, that the professionals adapt proceedings to ensure lay users comprehend the process' (JUSTICE, 2019: 108).

[16] For example, see *R* v *Thomas* [2020] EWCA Crim 117.

## References

BBC (2020a) Law in Action, 'Supporting evidence', 5 March, available from: www.bbc.co.uk/programmes/m000fvvp

BBC (2020b) 'Coronavirus: strict new curbs on life in UK announced by PM', 24 March, available from: www.bbc.co.uk/news/uk-52012432

Burd, K.A. and Mcquiston, D.E. (2019) 'Facility dogs in the courtroom: comfort without prejudice?', *Criminal Justice Review*, 44(4), 1–22.

Burnett, I., Etherton, T. and McFarlane, A. (2020) 'Message for Circuit and District Judges sitting in Civil and Family from the Lord Chief Justice, Master of the Rolls and President of the Family Division', 9 April, available from: www.judiciary.uk/wp-content/uploads/2020/04/Message-to-CJJ-and-DJJ-9-April-2020.pdf

Colorado Judicial Department (2004) 'Access to the courts: a resource guide to providing reasonable accommodations for people with disabilities for judicial officers, probation and court staff', available from: www.thearc.org/file/ADAresourceguide.pdf

Cooper, P., Backen, P. and Marchant, R. (2015) 'Getting to grips with ground rules hearings – a checklist for judges, advocates and intermediaries', *Criminal Law Review*, 6: 420–35.

Cooper, P. and Mattison, M. (2017) 'Intermediaries, vulnerable people and the quality of evidence: an international comparison of three versions of the English intermediary model', *International Journal of Evidence and Proof*, 21(4): 351–70.

Cooper, P. and Mattison, M. (2018) 'Section 28 pre-recorded cross-examination: what is in store for advocates in 2018', *Criminal Law and Justice Weekly*, 182: 7–9.

Corish, S. (2015) 'Issues for the defence in trials with pre-recording of the evidence of vulnerable witnesses', *Criminal Law Journal*, 39: 187–97.

Courthouse Dogs Foundation (2020) 'Where dogs are working', available from: https://courthousedogs.org/dogs/where/where-united-states/

Delhi High Court (nd) 'Guidelines for recording of evidence of vulnerable witnesses in criminal matters', available from: http://delhihighcourt.nic.in/writereaddata/upload/Notification/NotificationFile_LCWCD2X4.PDF

Donaldson, K.M. (2017) 'Defense and prosecuting attorney perceptions of facility dogs in the courtroom', Walden University, doctoral dissertation, available from: http://scholarworks.waldenu.edu/cgi/viewcontent.cgi?article=5042&context=dissertations

The Equalities and Human Rights Commission (2020) 'Inclusive justice: a system designed for all – interim evidence report – video hearings and their impact on effective participation', available from: www.equalityhumanrights.com/sites/default/files/inclusive_justice_a_system_designed_for_all_interim_report_0.pdf

Fielding, N., Braun, S., Hieke, G. and Mainwaring, C. (2020) 'Video enabled justice evaluation', Sussex Police and Crime Commissioner and University of Surrey, available from: http://spccweb.thco.co.uk/media/4851/vej-final-report-ver-11b.pdf

Gallagher, C. (2016) ' "At the moment, court is a very frightening place for a child" – young victims in Ireland's legal system', *The Journal*, 24 May, available from: www.thejournal.ie/child-court-protection-2784424-May2016/

Gibbs, P. (2017) *Defendants on Video: Conveyor Belt Justice or a Revolution in Access?*, London: Transform Justice.

Glazer, M. (2018) 'Assessing the perceptions of the use of a courthouse facility dog program with child and youth witnesses', Electronic Thesis and Dissertation Repository, 5265, available from: https://ir.lib.uwo.ca/etd/5265

Godsmark, N. (2020) 'COVID-19 Nottinghamshire, Derbyshire, Lincolnshire Protocol', 10 April, available from: www.civillitigationbrief.com/2020/04/14/covid-19-nottinghamshire-derbyshire-lincolnshire-protocol-hhj-godsmark-qc-designated-civil-judge/

Gómez, S.E., updated by Fernández-Acevedo, F.J. and Depolo, R. (2010) 'Update: essential issues of the Chilean legal system', Hauser Global Law School Program, available from: www.nyulawglobal.org/globalex/Chile1.html#_Regarding_the_Criminal_Procedure%20Re

Grant, M. (2014) 'Hawk, Calgary police dog, to help child witnesses in sex abuse case', 29 October, available from: www.cbc.ca/news/canada/calgary/hawk-calgary-police-dog-to-help-child-witnesses-in-sex-abuse-case-1.2817476

Grimm, A.L. (2013) 'An examination of why permitting therapy dogs to assist child-victims when testifying during criminal trials should not be permitted', *Journal of Gender, Race and Justice*, 16(1): 263–92.

Hanna, K., Davies, E., Henderson, E., Crothers, C. and Rotherham, C. (2010) *Child Witnesses in the New Zealand Criminal Courts: A Review of Practice and Implications for Policy*, New Zealand: New Zealand Law Foundation.

Her Majesty's Courts and Tribunals Service (2020) 'HMCTS telephone and video hearings during coronavirus outbreak', 18 March, available from: www.gov.uk/guidance/hmcts-telephone-and-video-hearings-during-coronavirus-outbreak#court-and-tribunal-users

Holder, C. (2013) 'All dogs go to court: the impact of court facility dogs as comfort for child witnesses on a defendant's right to a fair trial', *Houston Law Review*, 50: 1155–88.

House of Commons Justice Committee (2019) 'Court and tribunal reforms', HC 190, 31 October, p 3, available from: https://publications.parliament.uk/pa/cm201919/cmselect/cmjust/190/190.pdf

Howard, K., McCann, C. and Dudley, M. (2019) ' "It's really good … why hasn't it happened earlier?" Professionals' perspectives on the benefits of communication assistance in the New Zealand youth justice system', *Australian and New Zealand Journal of Criminology*, 1–20.

Inns of Court College of Advocacy (2020) 'Principles for remote advocacy', Version 2, 16 April, available from: www.icca.ac.uk/wp-content/uploads/2020/04/Principles-for-Remote-Advocacy-version-2.pdf

Jaganmohan, M. (2020) 'Remote hearings: a gulf between lawyers and lay parties?', The Transparency Project, 29 March, available from: www.transparencyproject.org.uk/remote-hearings-a-gulf-between-lawyers-and-lay-parties/

Jonker, G. and Swanzen, R. (2007) 'Intermediary services for child witnesses testifying in South African criminal courts', *SUR International Journal of Human Rights*, 6(4), 91–113.

Judicial Education Institute of Trinidad and Tobago (2015) *Criminal Bench Book*, available from: www.ttlawcourts.org/jeibooks/books/ttcriminalbenchbook.pdf

Judicial Education Institute of Trinidad and Tobago (2018) 'Justice through a gender lens: gender equality protocol for judicial officers', available from: www.ttlawcourts.org/jeibooks/books/geptt.pdf

JUSTICE (2019) *Understanding Courts: A Report by JUSTICE*, London: JUSTICE.

Kitzinger, C. (2020) 'Remote justice: a family perspective', The Transparency Project, 29 March, available from: www.transparencyproject.org.uk/remote-justice-a-family-perspective/

Marks, A. (2016) 'What is a court? A report by JUSTICE', available from: https://justice.org.uk/wp-content/uploads/2016/05/JUSTICE-What-is-a-Court-Report-2016.pdf

Ministry of Justice (2020) 'COVID-19 stakeholder update', email to stakeholders, 31 March.

Morrison, J. (2019) 'The dog helped them find their words', Churchill Fellow Report, available from: www.churchilltrust.com.au/fellows/detail/4336/Julie+Morrison

Mosqueda, L. (2012) 'Elder abuse pocket reference: a medical/legal resource for California judicial officers', San Francisco: Judicial Council of California, available from: www.courts.ca.gov/documents/ElderAbusePDoc.pdf

National Audit Office (2018) *HM Courts and Tribunals Service: Early Progress in Transforming Courts and Tribunals*, London: NAO.

National Crime Victim Law Institute (2013) 'Facility dogs: Helping victims access justice and exercise their rights', NCVLI Victim Law Bulletin, available from: https://law.lclark.edu/live/files/21750-facility-dogshelping-victims-access-justice-and

Norris, W. (2020) 'Remote hearings; here to stay or just while needs must?', 16 April, 39 Essex Chambers, available from: www.39essex.com/remote-hearings-here-to-stay-or-just-while-needs-must/

O'Leary, C. and Feely, M. (2018) 'Alignment of the Irish legal system and Article 13.1 of the CRPD for witnesses with communication difficulties', Disability Studies Quarterly, available from: https://dsq-sds.org/article/view/5587/4887

Padfield, N. and Hawker, T. (2017) 'Editorial: sentencing via video link', Criminal Law Review, 8: 585–6.

Parliament South Australia (2020) Hansard, Grievance Debate: Communication Partner Service, 5 February, House of Assembly, available from: http://hansardpublic.parliament.sa.gov.au/Pages/HansardResult.aspx#/docid/HANSARD-11-37075

Rossner, M. and Tait, D. (2020) 'Courts are moving to video during coronavirus, but research shows it's hard to get a fair trial remotely', The Conversation, available from: https://theconversation.com/courts-are-moving-to-video-during-coronavirus-but-research-shows-its-hard-to-get-a-fair-trial-remotely-134386

Ryan, M., Harker, L. and Rothera, S. (2020) 'Resource: remote hearings in the family justice system: a rapid consultation', Nuffield Family Justice Observatory, May, available from: www.nuffieldfjo.org.uk/resource/remote-hearings-rapid-consultation

Scottish Court Service (2015) 'Evidence and procedure review report', March, Edinburgh: Scottish Court Service, available from: www.scotcourts.gov.uk/docs/default-source/aboutscs/reports-and-data/reports-data/evidence-and-procedure-full-report---publication-version-pdf.pdf?sfvrsn=2

Scottish Courts and Tribunal Service (2019) 'New evidence and hearings suite for children and vulnerable witnesses opens', 18 November, Scottish Courts and Tribunal Service, available from: www.scotcourts.gov.uk/about-the-scottish-court-service/scs-news/2019/11/18/new-evidence-and-hearings-suite-for-children-and-vulnerable-witnesses-opens

Shukla, R. (2018) 'Vulnerable witnesses and criminal justice system: role of intermediaries', 30 June, available from: www.livelaw.in/vulnerable-witnesses-and-criminal-justice-system-role-of-intermediaries/

Spencer, J.R. and Flin, R.H. (1990) The Evidence of Children: The Law and Psychology, London: Blackstone Press.

Spruin, E., Dempster, T. and Mozova, K. (2020) 'Facility dogs as a tool for building rapport and credibility with child witnesses', International Journal of Law Crime and Justice.

Spruin, E. and Mozova, K. (2017) 'Using specially trained dogs in the Criminal Justice System', British Psychological Society, Special Edition: Reviews of Presentations, and Symposia at the DFP Annual Conference 2017, ISSN: 2050–7348, Forensic Update 125, September, pp 30–41.

Sriram, J. (2017) 'The teddy bear courts: Goa's pioneering children's courtroom', 30 July, available from: www.vikalpsangam.org/article/the-teddy-bear-courts-goas-pioneering-childrens-courtroom/#.Xm5a3i2cY1I

Task Force on Pandemic Preparedness Planning for the Courts (2007) 'Guidelines for pandemic emergency preparedness planning: a road map for courts', March, American University Washington, DC and Bureau of Justice Assistance, available from: www.txcourts.gov/media/1353181/PandemicRoadMapFINAL-031407.pdf

Warnica, M. (2015) 'Zebra Centre support dog helps child witness testify', 6 March, available from: www.cbc.ca/news/canada/edmonton/zebra-centre-support-dog-helps-child-witness-testify-1.2984754

Wilcock, R., Crane, L., Hobson, Z., Nash, G., Kirke-Smith, M. and Henry, L.A. (2018) 'Supporting child witnesses during identification lineups: exploring the effectiveness of registered intermediaries', Applied Cognitive Psychology, 32(3): 367–75.

# Index

References to figures, tables and boxes are in *italics*. Page numbers followed by 'n' refer to notes.

## A

*A Clinical Commissioning Group* v
   *AF and Others* [2020]  161
Advocate's Gateway (TAG)  39
*Anwer* v *Central Bridging Loans Ltd*
   [2020]  161
Arnold, J.  34
Asperger's Syndrome  35, 36
asylum seekers
   and conflict  113–14
   participation in
      practice  110, 113–14
   special measures  38–9
   vulnerability  24, 38–9, 122–3
   *see also* Immigration and Asylum
      Chamber (IAC)
Atkinson, P.  106
Australia
   court facility dogs  153, 154
   ground rules hearings  *149*, 150
   pre-recorded witness
      testimony  154
   witness intermediaries  147
autism  92, 153

## B

*B (Children) (Remote Hearing:
   Interim Care Order)* [2020]  165
Bach Commission (2017)  49
barriers to participation
   Bach Commission (2017)  49
complexity of legal process/
   language  25, 127–9
and court reform programme  90
disconnection  135–6
disparities (practitioner/user)  132–5
legal aid  49, 90
litigants in person
   (LiPs)  46, 48, 90
post-LASPO  49, 90
practitioners' views  89–90
silencing court users  129–32
structural and cultural  89–90
translation and
   disconnection  127–36
video-enabled
   participation  30–1, 160
and vulnerability  21–5, 89
Benesh, S.C. and Howell,
   S.E.  137n7
Brown, K.  21
Burd, K.A.  152
Burnett, I.  165
Burton, M.  27
Busby, N.  48

## C

Canada, court facility dogs  153
care proceedings  96–7, 109–10,
   116–17, 126, 133
child witnesses  29, 31–2, 144–6,
   152, 153, 154–5, 155–6

children
  in the Family Court 31–2, 76
  protection of wellbeing 76
  specialist hearing suites 155
Children and Family Court
  Advisory and Support Service
  (Cafcass) 31, 74, 76, 125
Chile
  court facility dogs 153
  witness intermediaries 145, 146
Citizens Advice Bureau (CAB) 48
Civil Justice Council 21–2
closure of courts 53–4, 90
Cobb, Mr Justice 23
communication
  importance of 11
  and vulnerability 26, 28, 39
complexity of legal process/
  language 25, 45–6, 72–3,
  127–30
conflict, nature of in the
  courts 112–15
coroners courts 16n18
  practitioner accounts 68, 71,
  72, 78, 95
Coroners and Justice Act
  2009 22, 26
court closures 53–4, 90
court facility dogs 151–4
court fees 44–5
court reform
  programme 49–54, 159
  closure of courts 53–4, 90
  concerns about 159–60
  court users at heart of 168–9
  COVID-19 pandemic 167
  impact of reforms 120, 166
  online forms and processes 52–3
  remote court attendance 51–2
court staff 67, 68
  conceptualisation of
  participation 73, 75, 78, 79
  facilitation of participation 94–5
  functions of participation 81,
  83, 88, 89
  personal well-being 96–7

courts/tribunals, structure
  of 5–7, 6
COVID-19 pandemic 2, 51,
  160–2, 164–5, 167, 168, 169
criminal courts
  court fees 44
  defendants, special
  measures 29–31
  evaluation of special
  measures 26–31
  ground rules hearings 28, 29,
  149, 150
  guidance for practitioners and
  judges 39, 40–1
  legal aid 42–3
  remote court attendance 50–1
  special measures 25–31, 122–3
  vulnerability 24, 29–31,
  40–1, 122–3
  witnesses 25–30, 40
criminal courts, practitioners and
  users 68
  complexity of legal process/
  language 128–9
  conceptualisation of
  participation 73–4, 75, 77,
  78, 79–80
  disparities (practitioner/
  user) 132, 133–5
  facilitation of participation 94,
  95, 124
  functions of participation 81,
  82–3, 85, 87, 88–9
  intermediaries 122
  litigants in person (LiPs) 124
  loss and
  disadvantage 115–16, 118
  participation in practice 108–9,
  115–16, 118, 124, 128–9, 131,
  132, 133–5
  pre-recorded witness
  testimony 154–5
  remote court attendance 50–1,
  90, 91, 92, 132
  responsiveness to vulnerabilities
  and need 122–3
  silencing court users 131

well-being of practitioners 96
Criminal Practice Directions 9,
    28, 30, 40–1
Criminal Procedure Rules 9, 28
cross-examination
    by abusers 32–3
    pre-recorded witness
        testimony 154–5
    and vulnerability 28, 29,
        32–3, 40
Crown Court, practitioners and
    users *6*
    complexity of legal process/
        language 128–9
    litigants in person (LiPs) 48, 124
    observing court proceedings *104*
    participation in practice 108,
        124, 128–9, 132
    remote court attendance 132
    special measures 122
    vulnerability 24, 122–3


**D**

decision-making, as function of
    participation 82–4, *163*
defendants
    and complexity of the law 128–9
    court fees 44
    disparities (practitioner/
        user) 133–5
    facilitation of participation 122,
        123, 124, 128–9
    and intermediaries 30, 92
    with learning disabilities 92
    legal aid for 42–3, 47
    loss and
        disadvantage 115–16, 118
    marginalisation of 136
    participation in practice *108–9*,
        115–16, 118, 122–3, 124,
        128–9, 131–2, 133–5
    remote court attendance 26, 50,
        55*n*6, 160
    right to a fair trial 8–9, 11
    self-representation 47–8,
        124, 128

silencing of 131–2
special measures 29–31, 40
therapeutic benefits of
    participation 88–9
vulnerability of 22, 26, 29–31,
    40, 47–8, 160
    *see also* criminal courts; criminal
        courts, practitioners and users
digital literacy 52–3
disabilities, people with 11, 156
disconnection 135–6
discretion, judicial 27, 34, 35, 37,
    41–2, 152, 161
disparities (practitioner/
    user) 132–5
dogs, facility 151–4
domestic abuse 33, 50, 121
Domestic Offences Bill 33
*Duffy* v *George* [2013] 35


**E**

elder abuse cases 156
Employment Tribunal (Constitution
    and Rules Procedure) Regulations
    2004 34–5
Employment Tribunal (ET) *6*
    barriers to participation 48
    fees 44–5
    litigants in person (LiPs) 48
    Procedure Rules 10
    special measures 34–7
    vulnerability of users 24,
        34–7, 48
Employment Tribunal (ET)
    practitioners and users *68*
    conceptualisation of
        participation 71
    and conflict 112–13
    facilitation of participation 93,
        94, 95, 110, 124
    functions of participation 83, 86
    litigants in person (LiPs) 48, 110,
        113, 124, 131
    observing court proceedings *105*
    participation in practice 110,
        112–13, 124, 131

and personal well-being 97
remote court attendance 90, 92
*Equal Treatment Bench Book*
  (ETBB) 10–11, 36, 40, 41
equality of arms 42–9, 81–2
Equality and Human Rights
  Commission 160
European Convention on Human
  Rights (ECHR) 8
Ewick, P. and Silbey, S.S. 111

**F**

facilitation of participation
  complexity of legal process/
    language 127–30
  court reform programme 166
  participation in practice 120–6
  practitioner accounts 89–98, 166
  remote court attendance 131–2
  silencing court users 129–32
facility dogs 151–4
fair trial, right to 8–9, 22, 30,
  36, 80–2
Family Court *6*
  ground rules hearings *149*
  and legal aid reforms 45, 46–7
  remote court attendance 50, 165
  special measures 31–5, *149*
  vulnerability of users 9–10, 23,
    31–4, 121
Family Court, practitioners and
  users *68*
  conceptualisation of
    participation 71, 74, 76, 78, 79
  conflict 114–15
  disparities (practitioner/user) 133
  facilitation of participation 94–5,
    121, 123–4, 124–5
  functions of participation 81, 82,
    83, 84, 85–6, 88
  humanising quality of
    participation 125–6
  litigants in person (LiPs) 46–7,
    123–4, 124–5, 131
  loss and
    disadvantage 116–17, 118

observing court proceedings *105*
  participation in practice 109–11,
    114–15, 116–17, 118, 121, 123–
    4, 124–5, 125–6, 130, 131, 133
  personal well-being 96–7
  remote hearings 165
  silencing court users 130
Family Drug and Alcohol
  Courts 155
Family Justice Review (2011) 31
Family Practice Direction
  3AA 10, 33
Family Procedure Rules 9–10, 33
fees 44–5
fitness to plead 8–9, 54*n*1
formality of court proceedings 10,
  25, 35, 127–30
functions of participation
  practitioner accounts *70*, 80–9
  *Ten Points of
    Participation* 162–5, *163–4*
future research 168–9

**G**

*Galo* v *Bombardier Aerospace UK*
  [2016] 36
gender quality protocol 157
Gibbs, P. 51
*Gil* v *London Borough of Camden*
  [2020] 161
Gill, N. 42
Godsmark, N. 164
Gómez, S.E. 145
gowns/robes 26, 164–5
Grimm, A.L. 151
ground rules hearings 28, 29,
  36–7, 148–51, *149*
guidance for practitioners and
  judges 39–42

**H**

*Hak* v *St Christopher's Fellowship*
  [2015] 36
Henderson, S. 40
HM Courts and Tribunals Service
  (HMCTS) 10, 53, 159, 162

Holder, C. 151
House of Commons Justice
    Committee 51, 160
humanising participation 83–4,
    90–1, 125–6

I

Immigration and Asylum Chamber
    (IAC) 6
    Procedure Rules 10
    special measures 37–9
    and vulnerability 24,
        37–9, 122–3
Immigration and Asylum Chamber
    (IAC), practitioners and users 68
    conceptualisation of
        participation 71, 73, 74, 77, 78
    conflict 113–14
    disparities (practitioner/
        user) 132–3
    facilitation of participation 93
    functions of
        participation 81–2, 86, 87
    judicial discretion 42
    loss and disadvantage 118–19
    observing court
        proceedings 105, 121
    participation in practice 110,
        113–14, 118–19, 121, 122–3,
        130–1, 132–3
    and personal well-being 96
    remote court attendance 91
    responsiveness to vulnerabilities
        and need 123
    silencing of court users 130–1
India
    specialist hearing suites 155
    specialist judicial guidance 157–8
    witness intermediaries 147
information-provider/elicitation
    role 70–1, 163
informed participation 72–3, 163
innovative support measures
    international review 143–58
    nature of 158–60
intermediaries
    for defendants 30

in the Family Court 32, 34
    practitioners' views 72, 78,
        92, 122
    witness
        intermediaries 28–9, 144–8
international review 143–58
    court facility dogs 151–4
    ground rules
        hearings 148–51, 149
    methodology for literature
        search 143–4
    pre-recorded witness
        testimony 154–5
    specialist hearing suites 155–6
    specialist judicial guidance 156–8
    witness intermediaries 144–8
intimidation 22, 27, 33, 35, 75
Ireland, witness intermediaries 147
Israel, witness
    intermediaries 144–5

J

Jaganmohan, M. 161
Jonker, G. 144, 145–6
judicial guidance 10–11,
    36, 40, 41
    international review 156–8
Judicial Working Group (2013) 40
judiciary (views/actions of) 67, 68
    complexity of legal process/
        language 128–9
    conceptualisation of
        participation 71, 74, 76, 77
    facilitation of participation 93,
        94, 95, 122–5
    functions of participation 81–3,
        84, 86, 87, 88
    guidance for effective
        participation 10–11
    humanising quality of
        participation 125–6
    intermediaries 122
    litigants in person (LiPs) 123–5
    personal well-being 96
    remote court attendance 90, 91,
        92, 132

responsiveness to vulnerabilities
and need 122–3, 125–6
silencing court users 130–1
JUSTICE 52, 53–4, 159
*JW Rackham* v *NHS Professionals
Ltd* [2015] 35

**K**

*Kavaarupo* v *Nursing and Midwifery
Council* [2020] 161
Kirby, A. 134
Kirk, E. 48

**L**

language, legal 25, 45–6,
72–3, 127–30
Law Commission 8–9
Law for Life Advice Project 45–6
Law Society 45
lawyers (views/actions of) 67, *68*
conceptualisation of
participation 71, 72, 73, 78, 79
facilitation of
participation 93, 95
functions of
participation 82, 85–6
humanising participation 126
personal well-being 96, 97
remote court attendance 91
responsiveness to vulnerabilities
and need 123
learning disabilities, people
with 30, 35, 36, 92
Lee, R. 47
legal aid
eligibility for 32, 42–3,
49, 138*n*11
impact of reforms 41, 45–9
*see also* litigants in person (LiPs)
Legal Aid Agency 43
Legal Aid, Sentencing and
Punishment of Offenders Act
2012 (LASPO) 42
Leggatt, Sir Andrew 34
legitimacy of judicial
process 84–7, *163*

litigants in person (LiPs)
and Asperger's Syndrome 36
court users' experiences 36, 46–9
difficulties of 45–8, 131
domestic abuse cases 33
Employment Tribunal (ET) 113
facilitation of participation 94–5,
123–5, 137*n*3
Family Court 32, 33, 45
guidance for practitioners and
judges 40–1
increasing numbers of 32,
45, 120
and legal aid reforms 43, 120
participation in practice 110,
113, 123–5, 131
practitioners' views of 77,
90, 94–5
silencing of 131
vulnerability 25, 43–8
live video-links *see* video-enabled
participation
loss and disadvantage, nature of in
the courts 115–19

**M**

MacCormick, N. 127
magistrates' courts, practitioners
and users *6*
conceptualisation of
participation 75, 77
disparities (practitioner/
user) 133–4
facilitation of participation 95
functions of participation 85, 87
litigants in person (LiPs) 47
observing court
proceedings *104–5*
participation in practice 108–9,
115, 116, 128–9, 131, 133–4
remote court attendance 90, 91
management of participation
process 76–8, *163*
marginalisation of laypeople 135–6
McDermott, M. 48
McFarlane, Sir Andrew 45

McKeever, G. 10, 11, 46, 136
Mcquiston, D.E. 152
Mozova, K. 151
Munby, Sir James 32

## N

National Audit Office 49
New Zealand, witness
intermediaries 147
Norris, W. 161–2
Northern Ireland, court facility
dogs 153
Norway, witness intermediaries 144

## O

observed realities of
participation *see* participation in
practice
online forms and processes 52–3
over-participation 77
Owusu-Bempah, A. 8,
136, 138*n*15

## P

participation (general)
concept of 3
functions of 70, 80–9,
162–5, *163–4*
impact of reforms 166
practitioners' conceptualisation
of 69–80, 162–6, *163–4*
as a right 8–11, 80–2, *163*
*Ten Points of Participation* 70, 142,
158, 162–5, *163–4*, 168
*see also* barriers to participation
participation in practice
(observed) 103–38
commonalities 111–19
complexity of legal
process 127–30
conflict 112–15
disparities (practitioner/
user) 132–5
humanising and sympathetic
responses 125–6

institutional parameters
of 107–11
litigants in person (LiPs) 123–5
loss and disadvantage 115–19
observing court
proceedings 104–7
remote court attendance 131–2
responsiveness to vulnerabilities
and need 121–3
silencing court users 129–32
supporting and facilitating
participation 120–1
telling the stories 119–26
translation and
disconnection 127–36
Peters, J.S. 112
Police and Justice Act 2006 22, 26
policy and practice 19–56
court reform programme 49–54,
120, 159–60, 166
in criminal courts 25–31
in the Employment Tribunal
(ET) 34–7
equality of arms 42–9
evolution of special
measures 25–39
in the Family Court 31–4
guidance for practitioners and
judges 39–42
in the Immigration and Asylum
Chamber (IAC) 37–9
international review 143–58
legal aid 42–3, 45–9
nature of developments 158–60
special measures, observed use
of 121–3
and vulnerability 21–5
Pollert, A. 48
practitioner accounts 65–99
barriers to and facilitators of
participation 89–98, 166
conceptualisation of
participation 69–80, 70
decision-making 82–4
effective participation 158–9
functions of
participation 70, 80–9

informed participation 72–3
intermediaries 122
legitimacy of judicial
  process 84–7
management of participation
  process 76–8
participation as a right 80–2
and personal well-being 96–7
practitioners as facilitators 92–7
presence of the
  participant 78–80
protection of users'
  wellbeing 75–6
provision/elicitation of
  information 70–1
rationale and methodological
  approach 66–9, *68*
remote court attendance 90–2
representation 73–4
*Ten Points of
  Participation* 162–5, *163–4*
therapeutic benefits of
  participation 87–9
pre-recorded witness
  testimony 29, 154–5
presence of the
  participant 78–80, *163*
probation officers 74, 129
procedural justice theory 85–6,
  88, 138*n*12

**R**

*R (on the application of Unison)
  (Appellant)* v *Lord Chancellor*
  [2017] 45
R. v *G* [2017] 27
*R* v *Lubemba*; *R* v *JP* [2014] 148
*R* v *Marchand and Marchand* 153
*R* v *Rashid* [2017] 30
*R* v *Zafer Dinc* [2017] 28
race discrimination 113
*Re W (Children) (Abuse: Oral
  Evidence)* [2010] 32
remote court attendance/
  hearings *see* telephone hearings;
  video-enabled participation
representation (general)

practitioners' views 73–4
suggested guidance for *163*
tribunals 10, 34
*see also* litigants in person (LiPs)
research methodology 3–6, 12–14
right to a fair trial 8–9, 22, 30,
  36, 80–2
robes/gowns 26, 164–5
Rossner, M. 159

**S**

Safeguarding and Vulnerable
  Groups Act 2006 37
*SC* v *UK* ([2005] 8
Scotland
  ground rules hearings 148, *149*
  pre-recorded witness
    testimony 154–5
  specialist hearing suites 155–6
self-representation *see* litigants in
  person (LiPs)
sexual offences
  child witnesses 145, 153, 157
  observed hearings 108
  special measures 29, 155, 157
silencing court users 129–32
Single Justice Procedure 53
Smejkalová, T. 127, 135–6
social divide (professionals/
  laypeople) 132–5
South Africa, witness
  intermediaries 144, 145–6
special measures
  criminal courts 25–31, 122
  Employment Tribunal (ET) 34–7
  Family Court 31–4, 121
  Immigration and Asylum
    Chamber (IAC) 37–9
  observed use of 121–3
specialist hearing suites 155–6
specialist judicial guidance 156–8
Spruin, E. 151, 152, 154
Sriram, J. 155
*State of Washington, Respondent*
  v *Timothy Dye, Petitioner No
  87929–0* 152

statutory sector practitioners'
   accounts 67, *68*, 74, 76, 94
study parameters 4–7
Susskind, R. 52
Swanzen, R. 144, 145–6
Sweden, witness
   intermediaries 144

## T

Tait, D. 159
Talbot, J. 30
tax tribunals 159
telephone hearings 37, 42, 90, 92,
   157, 161, 165
*Ten Points of Participation* 70, 142,
   158, 162–5, *163–4*, 168
therapeutic benefits of
   participation 87–9, *163*
therapeutic jurisprudence 88
therapy dogs 151
Thomas, R. 41
Tkacukova, T. 47
Trinder, L. 46
Trinidad and Tobago, specialist
   judicial guidance 157
Tyler, T.R. 85

## U

*UK – AM (Afghanistan)* v *Secretary
   of State for the Home Department*
   [2017] 38–9
UN Convention on the Rights of
   the Child 31
UN Convention on the Rights of
   Persons with Disabilities 11
unfair dismissal 110, 112
unfit to plead 8–9, 54*n*1
United States
   court facility dogs 151–2
   specialist judicial guidance 156

## V

Victim Personal Statement 88
victims
   children 151

cross-examination by
   abusers 32–3
rebalancing of system 25
remote court attendance 50
therapeutic benefits of
   participation 88
video-enabled participation
   barriers to 30–1, 160
   benefits of 91–2
   court facility dogs 153–4
   court reform
      programme 50–1, 161–2
   and COVID-19 pandemic 51,
      160–2, 164–5, 167, 168, 169
   disadvantages of 28, 51, 84, 90–
      1, 159–60, 165
   and intermediaries 144
   legal provision for 26, 55*n*6
   observations of 107, 131–2
   practitioners and users'
      views 27–8, 30–1, 90–2, 161–2,
      165, 166–7
   pre-recorded witness
      testimony 29, 154–5
   rationales for 166–7
   silencing court users 132
   specialist judicial guidance 156–7
   tax tribunals 159
virtual court attendance *see*
   video-enabled participation
voluntary sector
   practitioners 67, *68*
   conceptualisation of
      participation 71, 72, 78, 79–80
   facilitation of participation 95
   functions of participation 82
   remote court attendance 92
vulnerability 7–8
   asylum seekers 24, 38–9, 122–3
   as barrier to
      participation 21–5, 89
   characteristics/factors 23–5
   and communication 26, 28, 39
   criminal courts 9, 24–7, 29–31,
      40–1, 122–3
   Criminal Practice Directions 9

cross-examination 28, 29,
  32–3, 40
current policy and practice 21–5
defendants 22, 26, 29–31, 40,
  47–8, 160
and digital literacy 52
Employment Tribunal (ET) 24,
  34–7, 48
Family Court 9–10, 23,
  31–4, 121
Family Procedure Rules 9–10
guidance for practitioners and
  judges 39–42
Immigration and Asylum
  Chamber (IAC) 24,
  37–9, 122–3
and judicial discretion 41–2
in law 22–3
litigants in person
  (LiPs) 25, 43–8
as observed in
  court 115–19, 121–3
remote court
  attendance 51, 91–2
witnesses 9–10, 21–9, 31–7, 39,
  40, 122, 143, 142–59
Vulnerable Witnesses and
  Children's Working Group
  (VWCWG) 32
Vulnerable Witnesses (Criminal
  Evidence) (Scotland) Act
  2019. 154–5

**W**

well-being
  of practitioners 96–7
  of users 75–6, *163*

Westlaw UK database 143
Williams, K. 44
witness
  intermediaries 28–9, 144–8
Witness Service 67, 71, 93
witnesses
  child witnesses 29, 31–2, 144–6,
    152, 153, 154–5, 155–6
  civil courts 21–2
  court facility dogs 151–4
  criminal courts 25–30, 40
  cross-examination 28, 29, 32–3,
    40, 154–5
  Employment Tribunal
    (ET) 34, 35, 36
  Family Court 31–3
  ground rules hearings 148–51
  Immigration and Asylum
    Chamber (IAC) 37
  intermediaries 28–9, 144–8
  participation in practice
    (observed) 109, 110, 112,
    122–3, 124
  practitioners' views 70–1, 75,
    82–3, 93
  pre-recorded
    testimony 29, 154–5
  special measures 25–39
  specialist judicial guidance 156–8
  vulnerability 9–10, 21–9, 31–7,
    39, 40, 122–3, 142–59

**Y**

Youth Justice and Criminal
  Evidence Act 1999 (YJCEA) 9,
  22, 23, 25–6, 29, 146

## OH, THANKS

To Dr. Adrian Frazier and Mike McCormack for heralding
and guiding.

# Table of Contents

Awake  *Jimi McDonnell* ................................................ 1

Adam's Fib  *Jennifer McCarrick* ..................................... 5

Night Jasmine  *Colm Byrne* ......................................... 9

The Animal  *Brid Buckley* ............................................ 25

Poetry  *Davnet Heery* ................................................. 27

Amusements  *Ciara O'Dowd* ........................................ 37

Iran – Axis of Power  *Anna O'Leary* ............................. 43

My Big Brother  *Elizabeth Cox* .................................... 57

The Date  *Joe Jennings* ............................................... 65

Care Assistant  *Brid Buckley* ....................................... 71

Poetry  *Trevor Conway* ............................................... 77

Roulette  *Caron Mc Carthy* ......................................... 85

Winter Wonderland  *David O' Doherty* ......................... 89

The School Bag  *Caron Mc Carthy* ............................... 105

The Perfect Cup of Tea  *Trevor Conway* ....................... 115

Statue  *Brid Buckley* .................................................. 119

Poetry  *Jimi McDonnell* .............................................. 123

Boats Passing  *Ciara O'Dowd* ..................................... 131

Poetry  *Brid Buckley* .................................................. 141

Nativity  *Jennifer McCarrick* ....................................... 145

The End  *Joe Jennings* ................................................ 151

About the Authors ....................................................... 152

## Introduction

It is a pleasure to welcome a new anthology of writing which covers fiction, memoir and poetry. While this collection trips through the various genres it carries the reader through different times, moods and geographies; here the past and the future interweave while fantasy and realism blur the contours of the here-and-now. Here are seasoned voices and here too are those we are hearing for the first time. In each one there is much craft and imagination — not to mention a welcome touch of recklessness — and each separate voice is lit from within by an imaginative spark. Best of all, the anthology succeeds admirably in the first task of any collection — it brings to our attention these separate voices in full song as it whets the appetite for more.

Enjoy.

Mike McCormack

# Awake
## Jimi McDonnell

The smell of the McDonalds, familiar, perfected in laboratories to tempt the masses, drifts out onto the street. But Galway isn't hungry this morning. Outside a chemist's clinically-cold white edifice, a queue of orange twenty-somethings queue, yawning, checking their make-up in mirrors or texting. 'Triple-points on all tanning products today!' declares a poster in the window.

Down a bit there's a café, a place of no consequence that manages to stay open. The chairs sit around the tables, whispering fondly to the sugar bowl.

'And then this fat Yank sat down on me, I thought he'd never leave.'

The demerara chuckled. The chair was plain, simple, sturdy, but had a sense of humour that those stuffy Laura Ashley 'feature pieces' could only dream of.

The smell of shit rises out from under the paving stones on Shop Street. The rats are down there, singing: 'Welcome to Galway, did ye enjoy the boat race?'

A bunch of kegs line up outside Taaffe's.

'This country will never progress,' says one, 'until it deals maturely with its dependence on alcohol. Our culture runs deeper, surely, than a few pints, having the craic.'

Then, there is silence amongst the other kegs until one of them clears his throat, farts, then says: 'Now for ye.'

The other kegs roar in approval and collectively launch into Willie McBride.

Galway is waking up; you can see it in the bleary eyes of the drunks. Where Shop Street forks into High Street on one side and Mainguard Street on the other, a scrawny, bearded man channels into this waking madness. He beats his hand hard against his chest, letting out incoherent roars mixed with snatches of Pink Floyd lyrics.

'You are only coming through in waves!' he tells a bewildered pair of American tourists.

Behind him stands the placidly-yellow health-food shop, benevolently bearing witness to the unhinged ravings before it. There is an ad in the window for vitamin supplements, featuring a smiling couple. It hoped to suggest wellness, equilibrium, serenity — the man who stood in front was having none of it. His fingers click incessantly as if trying to light a spark from short-circuiting wires.

The three-storey pub across the way is imposing and quiet, recovering from the bout of indigestion that had caused it to spew its charges on to last night's street. The building knows it is tied to these young bucks, and anticipates neither their coming or going. It faces winning goals, spilt pints, sloppy kisses, assembly-line cover bands and vomit with the same stony silence.

Further down, on High Street, the red and white fishmongers seems to be beaming today. Red peppers, cauliflower and courgettes are on display, but they are mere trailers to the main feature of monkfish, salmon, squid and bream. In spitting distance of chain stores, it is resolutely upbeat, open and smelly.

The street gives way here to confusion. A barber's; a pub with fishing tackle and Zippos in the window; two shops selling overpriced jumpers to obliging tourists; an Internet café nearing extinction; a boutique clothes shop; a charity store. They stand together, unwilling teammates in an unconvincing scrum.

At the end of this street a road emerges uncertainly, an unwelcome strip of tarmac between two pedestrianised streets. Cars seem to soak up this trepidation, stalling as people pass blithely in front of it. At the corner was one of the town's most popular pubs, adopting a casual lean.

'Coming in for a coffee later, are ya?' it asks. 'Fine. But there's pints here too; just so you know, no hassle.'

This is Quay Street slowly coming to life. The toy shop opens its small door, welcoming curiosity but not robust enjoyment — these are handcrafted toys, and the place feels like a museum. Next door the vintage clothes shop haughtily sniffs, and dresses and blouses wait, weary from being tried on but never bought. A few doors down, passing three snoozing restaurants, is another bar. It hosts numerous stag and hen parties and seems to inhale people but right now it is dormant, sure of its place and happy to enjoy this respite.

A tiny newsagents is anxiously open for business, sending cigarettes, newspapers and chocolate bars on their way to anonymous offices and cluttered apartments. Nearby, at the end of the street, the fish and chip shop sprawls like an overfed cat, happy and satisfied with itself.

Meanwhile, the river moves on, under the bridge, past the Spanish Arch. The Claddagh is quiet, eight hours before high tide.

## Adam's Fib
## Jennifer McCarrick

It seems like I've gotten a bit of a name for myself — through no fault of my own, naturally, but there it is. It's typical, isn't it? No matter what happens the woman always gets the blame, and being the first woman I get the blame for everything. It's so unfair.

I mean — 'the curse of Eve' — what the hell is that all about? You'd think I'd invented menstruation, the way they go on. I suffered it too, just like all the rest of you, and do you know why? Not because God was angry with me, but because I could handle it, unlike *him*. You know who I mean — Adam. Really, what a pussy. He'd cry for hours if he as much as got a thorn in his foot. Even after I'd pulled it out, he wouldn't be able to walk for the rest of the day. There was no way he could bleed for days on end without dying. So it was left up to me; simple as that. And as for childbirth — don't talk to me! Three children I bore that ungrateful whelp and what do I get in return? Sons! You'd think God would've granted me the comfort of a little girl after all that toil, but no; that would be going too easy on me altogether. Instead I end up with three wreckers. Then Cain slays Abel over some foolishness and is banished (only God knows to where) and I'm left with Seth, who, just between you and me, is a little too much like his father, what with the whinging and the finger-pointing. I love them all, of course, but it's a trial at the best of times.

What galls me the most is this nonsense about my being made from Adam's rib. Pure fabrication, that's what that is — like so much else. The Garden of Eden, the snake, the apple — all lies!

Here's what really happened: Adam was made first, but like all prototypes he was... shall we say, somewhat flawed? Not that he wasn't lovely looking and everything;

5

he was quite dashing, for all that. It's just that there were some issues which needed ironing out, if you know what I mean. For one thing, he was terribly vulnerable — I mean, his bits dangling on the outside like that — that was an accident just waiting to happen. And then his survival instinct wasn't quite as honed as it should have been. A few nights in the garden without a proper meal and a fire and he was practically at death's door. So God decided that for all his magnificence Adam needed a mate — someone with the practicality and work ethic needed for survival in the world, because — and this is the funniest part — all that stuff about there being no pain or death in the garden is hogwash. After all, we were mortal, weren't we? The earth was a harsh place for a mortal; even then, without all the wars and whatnot that they have today.

So, that's where I came in, and in making me God used all the same tricks he used in making Adam, but this time he tidied things up a bit, you know — tweaked the fine tuning that bit more. I was given stronger instincts, sounder logic, and the ability to win almost any argument. I was the earth in which Adam's seeds would grow and flower. Then — maybe so that Adam wouldn't feel inferior, or maybe so neither one of us could dominate the other — God left me lacking in brute force. This was a mistake, in my opinion — but there was no point in kicking up a fuss about it. The thing to do then was just to get on with it as best I could.

Adam was quite pleased to see me — at first anyway. He liked the animals and everything but I think secretly he was a bit lonely for human company in the garden. The garden, by the way, was really more of an unkempt wilderness, overrun by wild creatures hunting and eating each other, and it was cold at night. We couldn't survive as we were in such a place; that much was obvious. We needed shelter, and food, and water, and clothes to keep our bodies warm. So we set to work, digging a hole in the ground for refuge, making traps to catch animals for meat and fur, making fire to cook with and keep us warm — and tools to work the land so we could grow things. And all the time I had to keep nagging him to get the smallest thing done.

'Adam', I'd say, 'Did you gather wood for the fire? Have you sharpened the spears today? Can you help me plough the ground for the planting?'

And he'd do as I asked mostly — though often with bad grace — because he had been busy sunning himself in a tree or playing with a mouse or something. And because I kept at him, eventually the work got done and we thrived in the garden. Then God made others in our image, since we had worked out so well, and they spread half-truths about us, which turned into malignant lies and ruined my image forever.

It was Adam's fault, really. He told them stories of how there was no work to do before Eve, how he had slept out underneath the stars without worries or knowledge, in peace among the wild animals. How the apple and snake got worked into that I'll never know. We grew apples, and ate them of course. Why would God give us fruit if we weren't meant to eat it? And the poor snake that was just going about the business of its survival like the rest of us got an awful bad rap of it too. Well, I can empathize. Men can be such cruel, ungrateful things. You toil away, giving them the best years of your life, then suddenly they turn on you and accuse you of stifling them, of weighing them down with cares and woes and wailing infants. They forget that if it wasn't for you they'd probably have been eaten by a woolly mammoth long ago. They forget because it suits them to forget that they need you to help them bear their burdens, and their children.

As I've said, they are magnificent creatures — but fatally flawed. That is the real curse of Eve. Bear it with good humour, my daughters, unless you want to be remembered like me — as a temptress and a shrew. Know that God the creator feels your pain, and she sympathises with you.

# Night Jasmine
## Colm Byrne

This much I can tell you; her name was Iseult. She had long brown hair, no... long hair that drifted into curls and sort of lifted up into bright bits at the end. I met her once, perhaps twice. This is the point. I'm not entirely sure.

Let's see, green eyes, she was thin, no bra needed kind of girl and touched by sun but not in a way that made her more attractive. Her complexion was... I don't even know why I am bothering to describe her because there are people — and she was one, whose inviolate presence submerges features that cannot be fixed on, whose very encounter with is remembered through sensation not memory, whose words sweep your thoughts, crumbling them. That you enter this void voluntarily, it's true. That you know it doesn't matter what they appear as anyway, is also true, because once you enter their reality the problem becomes what you are *not*, anymore.

It was years ago. I'm writing about it now because the distance of time, maybe memory, perhaps other factors... I think writing it down will help me make sense of it. This is pretty much how I remember it.

Where we met; it was Ranelagh, in a supermarket. It was a high-end supermarket. I had been working through the night trying to devise a motif for a black-oak chair for my first real client. Impossible with my simple Quaker style. A friend phoned, time-wasting on about a sale of French wine. The kind I like, she insisted, full-bodied, smooth, and cheap. I was not in the mood for this, but then she said the grape was from an unusual vine from Languedoc.

I needed the break, she had me at cheap, so I drove down; only six bottles left. I started to put them in a case when I felt the prickly presence of someone extremely close. I shot a, what are you looking at? glance.

'That's Languedoc Carignan, isn't it?' a bright voice asks.

'Yeah. Carignan,' I reply, not turning.

'It's really, really good. Last six?' the woman asks.

Then this guy appears, I assume her boyfriend, his arms cradled, holding goats cheese, tostinis, emmental, olives, that kind of thing.

'Everything but the Gruyere,' he says to her and precisely then, they both look down beside the wine because there also, is the last piece of Gruyere.

I've a confession. I was trying to be funny with the 'had me at cheap' cliché. The reason I was here at this moment, getting this particular wine was on account of my first girlfriend. Sylvie, on holidays, in a piscine, in a campsite in Languedoc. I loved her. I was 10. Every day I would wait for her in the piscine, shivering in my little red togs, but she would always come. I really did love her and think of her often. Similarly with the Gruyere; a Swiss girl called Miriam with a foul tongue who smelled of sheets and made cheese for a living. The manner of compulsively connecting with women from my past through quixotic associations, while completely transparent to me, baffling to others makes it simple to understand, in a long-winded way, that this beautiful woman standing behind me in the local supermarket in Ranelagh was neither getting my cheese nor my wine. Ever.

'I tell you what-' she begins.

'No,' I finish.

'Why don't we make a deal? I'll promise-'

'You'll promise?' I laugh, almost barking.

'I always keep them you know,' she says forcefully.

Her boyfriend looks blankly at her, then me, then wanders off. She bends down to her knees slowly, turns to me, her warm breath on my ear, 'We're having a party.'

I stand and head to the checkout with my Languedoc and Gruyere. She follows, a little dented, but still in pursuit. This must be a really good vintage, I thought.

'I don't know much about wine,' I tell her over my shoulder a little loudly, 'but any of those behind me are good.'

'You can come to our party if you bring *that* wine.'

'Great. See you there,' I lie, pay, and walk out the door.

After I load up the back of my estate, I look up the street to see the two of them, arms full of groceries. No bags of course. She walks unevenly in worn out shoes. Does she have a limp? I'm trying to figure out if one leg is shorter than the other when she turns. A harsh glare back. My head sort of snaps back and to the right with the intensity of it. She stops, touches her boyfriend's arm and he looks back.

Somehow that head movement thing was interpreted as a complex gesture; first as an invitation for a lift, then polite refusal (by her look), insistence (by my continuing to stare), humble acceptance (his), followed by lavish praise for my generosity to strangers and responded in turn with a general feeling of good will towards mankind. All with nothing said.

Next thing, they are in the back of my car. My carpentry tools and bits of wood get tossed to the back except for a piece of freshly cut redwood. She examines it, holds it to her nose, inhales deeply. Then she pulls out a bottle of the wine. I drive off immersed in a backward rationalising brain-frap as to why I'm giving these people a lift at all. Her leg, I conclude. She circles the foil of the bottle with her finger, slowly.

'Nah-ah,' I say.

'Why do you want them *all*?' she asks, putting it down.

I look back at her boyfriend with a raised, direction-seeking eyebrow.

'Milltown,' he says.

'I thought we lived in Ranelagh?' she asks.

'It's more Milltown.'

'Which is it?'

'Milltown.'

For the next five minutes down Sandyford road there's not a word said. It's a comfortable silence, like three close friends at the end of a road trip from Donegal, for example, looking forward to getting home. She runs her fingers across the side window. He reads a scrap from the Quaker carpentry book I'd been writing and abandoning forever.

'Stop!' she shouts.

I brake suddenly. Jesus! A child, what?

Out she jumps and races down a lane. I look out, then at him. He shrugs.

'I'm Robert, by the way, and that's-'.

'Where did she go?'

'Don't know.'

He has nothing to add to this, so doesn't. We wait. The sun is out and shining right on my face. I'm trying to hold on to my irritation but the unusual warmth feels good. I close my eyes, drifting with the Dublin spring thrum.

The door slams. I jolt up and turn to see her with a baby's bottle and God help us, a kitten. A black, skinny, mud-slicked thing barely keeping it together. It mewed and coughed and sneezed continuously. One eyelid would stick on the down-blink and then it would pop open quickly as if it just saw something amazing. It was dying.

'You know what? I think that kitten is-' I say.

'Well, we have to take care of it,' she cuts in, nulling any argument. I shift into gear and drive off. She tries to coax it into taking the milk but it tries to get away from her.

'What's your name?' she asks.

'Aodh.'

'I meant the cat. Are you really Aodh? Is that like A-ud, A-ya? Is that really your name? What kind of name is that?'

'It's the kind of name of the guy driving you home.'

Disinterested or even disappointed perhaps.

'It means thunder, fire,' I add too quickly.

'What do you do with your thunder, Aodh?'

'Nothing yet. You?'

'Iseult.'

I laugh so hard, I belch.

'What's so funny?' she asks.

'Gaeilgeoir parents.'

'Inis Mor.'

'Right. Iseult is just slightly more thundering and magnificent than Aodh.'

'It's true,' she laughs.

By now the kitten has escaped. Robert tries to locate it to no avail. The mewing turns to a plaintive wailing which we listen to in silence until we turn down a cul-de-sac. Robert points to a place to park.

'Oh no, Prostitute-face!' says Iseult. I look up a gravel driveway of a sprawling red-brick Victorian to see a busty red-head dominate the flight of granite steps to the house.

'She looks mad. I'll go-' says Robert.

'No, I will. And I'll find a box for Amud,' she says hopping out.

My offence must have registered because Robert shook his head laughing, as if the misappropriation of my name was a by-the-by with Iseult.

We try to locate the kitten while Iseult gets a lecture from their landlady pointing at a dirty VW camper in the driveway. Iseult throws up her hands and goes inside. The landlady peers into the van, then disappears into the house next door.

'Don't worry about it,' he says.

'Worry about what?'

We were both at the back of the car now, all doors open, looking in plastic bags, under mats.

'I was with friends a couple of years ago in Sardinia,' he begins, 'We had all chipped in to charter a boat but were two hands short. In Cagliari, two expert sailors, as they billed themselves, approached us to crew in exchange for a lift to Corsica. It wasn't our plan to sail there but somehow our plans got changed. One of these sailors was Iseult, the other a bit of a mystery, a Russian guy. We were 100 metres out and I could tell they knew nothing about the sea, sailing and as I found out quite quickly, could barely swim.

On the first day, there is Iseult, sunning herself out on deck. It's all quiet and open sea when this gust comes through and just lifts her hat; one of these huge, wide brimmed affairs. It lifts right up, up and then down to the sea. Now, you can't stop a boat — not for this. Turning it around, searching, it would take... I don't know, an hour. She got really upset. She insisted we turn the boat around. I said no. Absolutely no way. It was late and I wanted to make land. It just wasn't safe. She began sobbing. I couldn't believe it. Then she begins this moaning. It's a hat! The Russian looks over at me, then disappears below deck.

That's when things fell apart. I turn my head to see her jump in after the hat. Immediately we snap into man-overboard. I signal the skipper, throw the dinghy over and dive in. Short story; it was an hour before Iseult, myself and the hat were back on board

Anyway, that night, out on deck alone with her, after I felt I was no longer going to smack her, asked why she took such a risk. Why, for such a small thing? She looked at me as if I should know. As if it was obvious. And then she said, "Robert, it's not the hat, it's the thing behind the hat."'

He paused for a moment. I lifted a piece of balsa wood and underneath was the little kitten.

'She said "It's not the hat, it's the thing behind the hat." And that was when I fell in love with her,' he said.

I scooped up the dead kitten with a round wood panel. Something odd about the way he said it, something sad and prescient.

Iseult appeared with the box. We all went quiet for a moment considering the life of the little animal.

'Can you bring him out to the back for me?'

Well, I did and we buried the cat and then we went in to their kitchen and drank tea and talked about South America.

And then... the detail gets lost. I remember the bookends. I remember meeting them, going there, I remember the end and afterwards but inside the house, most everything that happened there just fades. The strange thing is, the second weekend is crystal clear. Crystal.

That first weekend: bookends. Going backwards, I remember it like this: It's two days later — after I had met them at the supermarket and had driven them home. I've spent the entire weekend there. Now I'm leaving their house. I am looking up the driveway from my car. It's about 5:30am. I see Iseult standing on the steps. There is blood on her dress and on the ground in front of her. There is blood on my hands. I'm fumbling with the gears. The wheels spin on the gravel as I leave. My one compelling thought is, despite the obvious urgency, will I ever see her again? With one last look back, my thought is, what will it be like if I *never* see her again?

Earlier, Iseult and I were in the conservatory, relishing the dark and deep in conversation. Everyone else had gone to bed. She got up to show me a plant she was nurturing; a jasmine that blooms only at night. She fingered the white flowers which were strange and milky bright in her hands. She handed me scissors to cut a bunch for her. When I finished I turned to see her standing there watching me, naked. She seemed very calm and matter-of-fact. She lit up a cigarette.

'Can you give me the flowers?' she asked

She carefully examined them, discarding all but one. She took the flower and traced it down across her neck, to the side of her breasts and to her hips, laughing when it tickled her. She repeated this on the other side.

I went right up to her keeping just a hair away from her skin as I smelled her in one go from her neck down to her breasts, on to her belly and down past her hips. Behind the powerful scent of the jasmine was another smell. The smell of the islands, of Inis Mor, the smell of sea, of ash, of French perfume. I could taste it as I went over her hips. I wanted to bite into her. I was slipping into warm darkness. My mouth closed over her skin. I felt a drifting sensation. Then I stood up with a jolt, a panic. I retreated back into the dark of an overhanging beech, panting. It was like I brushed against an electric fence I failed to see.

She laughed knowingly and put her shirt back on. We sat and smoked a cigarette in silence.

'I want to swim,' she then said, 'Let's go for a swim in the sea. In my van — to Howth.'

'No, I don't think so. It's a little dangerous.'

'You're a little boring, A-mud.'

'Yet you're still here.'

'Predictable hand cleaver, stick-in-the-A-mud with his boring Quaker furniture. Can't take a risk?'

Was she being childish and mean because I had just rejected her or because she was tapping into some truth about my work? I thought about the motif.

'Iseult, people like you claim to take risks but you've nothing to lose, which makes you particularly uninteresting to people like me, who do.'

'OK, come with me. We'll drive to Belfast, take the ferry to Scotland, then to Holland, over to Sweden, to Iceland then cargo boat to the Canada-'

'What's the risk for you?'

'I give up Robert. He stays.'

I pulled her toward me, kissed her. She leaned in and bit hard on my lip. I swept her up with my right arm and put my weight on her. And then I felt it again, like being tugged under surf. It was that feeling of a void, like before, only now it was very powerful. I barely managed to break off. She looked straight through me, reading me instantly. There was a vicious look in her. I held her stare. She leaned back very slowly, imperceptibly. Then she kept leaning back, falling as if in a faint. She fell straight back to the top of a glass table. I immediately threw my hands behind to stop her fall and my left hand went straight through the glass, neatly slicing a gash four inches across my wrist. Blood pumped.

We wrapped it tightly and I held it above my chest. I had to get to hospital, but I didn't want to leave. If I did, it would be the end. She followed me out to the steps as if she knew it too. I stopped to say something to reassure her, but we kiss. It was probably the best skin to skin contact I have ever felt. Not just the sensation of lips and tongues, a connection or even a feeling. As the life blood seeped from my wrists, I understood. It wasn't a void I entered, it was the emptying out of everything that hadn't worked in my life up to that moment. In that kiss, that contact, it was the same with her.

Then, it ended. She whispered into my ear, something. What did she say? *Something*. I walked away. Why could I not remember?

Later, I began to revisit the moment in my mind, obsess about it over and over, and soon lost the way of myself. I retreated to my work, but now of course I had my motif.

Then came my first success, then another, and quite soon my furniture became other people's obsession. I couldn't care less. I had mine; it was Iseult.

I knew this much, I had to meet her again. But I didn't. Not for a long, long time. Not until I had everything ready

The second time, the second weekend was their going away. Iseult made lunch after I drove over. Robert fired up the barbeque, put some olive oil on prawns and gave them a quick sear. The original visit was never referred to. They chatted animatedly about their plans. The sun shone hazily through the glass veranda as I watched Iseult toss the prawns into a salad of tomatoes, feta and crunchy lettuce. I still remember the taste of her sweet balsamic. The six month trip to South America was going to happen at last, they told me. On Monday they were to drive to South American in Iseult's VW.

From lunch to evening was pleasant and soporific. Iseult took a nap at one stage. People began to arrive and look after themselves. I looked at the brake lines in the VW with Robert and a buddy of his. There was a drip underneath which he sealed. When we returned, the party was in full swing. I had a nagging concern, but Iseult wouldn't hear about it. They would have to take care of these things themselves on the road anyway, she said dismissively. About fifty turned up, it could have been a hundred, for the enormous house absorbed them like a plant taking water. My Carignan wine was quickly consumed. Robert went out for more. When he returned he tore up a parking ticket in front of everyone. I thought it oddly grandiose, something I couldn't put my finger on.

I had a long chat with him about travelling and the aid organisations he was going to hook up with en-route. There were several encounters with Iseult but I became wary of her early on. I was uncomfortable talking to her for any extended period. It was as if things were unfolding in a way of her choosing and it was all amusing in a flighty way. I moved past her once in a hallway and my hand brushed her hip. She grabbed it, then threw it away.

'Meat cleaver,' she laughed.

My hands: rough, scarred and oversized coming at the end of knotted forearms from years of working with wood were like cleavers. I felt an odd surge, unusually so, despising her.

Sometime about 3am there were six or seven of us dancing in Iseult's bedroom; an enormous space dominated by elaborate plasterwork and walls of ruby red with dark tones. It had corners to disappear into and luxurious couches for legs to intertwine. The air was still moist and warm. She danced erotically with a glistening black girl, their bodies grinding against each other to a hypnotic drum beat. I didn't like it. The two of them then sat beside me on the couch, whispering, giggling and kissing. The other girl put her arm around me, fanning my face. She was high.

'Do you want a taste?' asked Iseult, holding my face to the girl's brown-red lips.

This was all bullshit as far as I was concerned. So I asked about Prostitute-face.

'So much blue eye shadow!' shouted Iseult over to me.

'I wonder what she calls you,' I replied.

Why I was taking the side of the hard-faced landlady I have no idea.

'What do you think she would call me?'

'I think she would call you The Cripple.'

There was a stunned silence in the room. She turned the music down.

'Why do you think,' she asked slowly and deliberately, 'she would call me that?'

Everyone looked back at me.

'Because,' I said, just as slow, 'you walk *funny*.'

'I think you should leave,' she said quietly and I was suddenly outcast.

And of course I got up and left. But the next thing I remember is her and I laughing our heads off over bad knock-knock jokes out in the garden.

I slept that night on a couch in the large conservatory. It was warm amongst the plants. I woke up once to find Iseult sitting beside me in the dark smoking a cigarette, lost in thought. I looked up at her, put my head back down and fell asleep.

The following day we took a drive out to Howth to road-test the van. It was blustery but seemed to be getting hotter and more humid. Their plan to leave the next day seemed to be a needless rush.

'How about that brake line?' I asked on the beach.

'It's grand,' said Iseult and added something else but her words were whipped away by the wind.

Robert announced he would go to bed early that night. Before he retired, he went over their route with me. He talked about Iseult quite a bit. Despite her independent spirit she needed a lot of looking after, he told me. I asked about her limp.

'Sometimes she goes too far.'

'What do you mean?'

'Don't you remember what I told you?' like I wasn't getting it. 'Too far,' he repeated distractedly.

The story of the hat? I wondered, looking out to the blooming jungled garden. It was at this point that I began to understand why I came back to the house. Why I had to come back, no matter what would happen. It was simple. I was in love with Iseult. And I realized too, that Robert was addressing this point exactly. He smiled and bid me goodnight.

I went from room to room exploring. It was dark and quiet; that 2am quiet. The air hung warm and super-saturated. Everything was packed away in boxes, labelled and ready to be taken by movers to storage. I browsed a few books that were left on shelves; art, Celtic myth and religious ethnography. The only room I didn't go to was the conservatory. I kept that for last, because I knew for certain that Iseult would be there, waiting.

When I felt ready, I found her wandering amongst the plants, touching one, whispering low to another, spraying water on others. Then she stopped at one in particular, stared at it, yanked it from its roots and tossed it on the ground. She then stood on it, crushing the juice out of it.

'Saying goodbye?'

She looked up, irritated.

'Are you spying, A-mud?'

'A-mud is dead. We buried him in the garden remember?'

'Poor, poor A-mud.'

'I don't know, I think he had a good last few minutes.'

There was quiet for a while as she wandered deep into an overgrown area.

'Do you have anything to smoke?' she asked suddenly, standing up.

I shrugged.

'What are we going to do until dawn?' she asked.

I walked over to her, stood away for a moment, then undid her blouse. Taking a good long look at her, I put my hand under her pretty, odd shaped breast and brought her close. I went over her skin just like last time, smelling the jasmine on her. It was deep in every pore. Smelling the islands off her, just like before. My mouth closed over her taut, moist skin. The kiss was as I remembered it on the steps. Everything was exactly as I remembered it, except we made love this time. The animal instinct for fucking underlining the messy, hungry, deep-seated ravaging — this messiness between two reasonable and educated adults who bore the pseudo-sophisticated mark of success and status — made the consuming, this animal fucking, all the more intense and fast and blazing. We went from room to room, from kitchen to bathroom. We stopped to eat. We found a bottle of wine, fucked again, then smoked tobacco someone had left using newspaper as rollies. We walked into the garden naked, exploring and floating on things imagined above in the inky-blue. She disappeared into an old ivy-licked shed where the owner stored costumes. I heard a low whistle and saw her running out wearing a deer mask. There was a chase. I grabbed her by the wrist and fucked her roughly under the magna carpa. We came back into the house, our skin goose-bumped, feeling raw. We ate again. We started over with kissing in the warm conservatory. It didn't end. Not seem to. We lay down naked on the cool white tiles, her hair spreading out star-like and she told me ancient stories. She slept. The jasmine slowly began to close as the light came up. I talked about the future, I drifted, I turned, and she was gone.

I was in the shower when Robert came down stairs next morning. I heard them both in the kitchen, noisily chatting about ordinary things. Listening to them gave me a pang. Their van started up with a backfire. I dressed quickly and went outside just as they were throwing the last few things in the back.

'It's time,' said Robert.

'Already?' I asked, 'You're going right now? Breakfast?'

'10,000km to go. I want to get at least one in this morning.'

Iseult was beaming brightly. The two of them were. She threw her arms around me and I squeezed tightly. Robert shook my hand firmly and got in. Iseult came close, removing a blade of grass from my jumper.

'You remember what I said to you on the steps?' she asked coyly.

'The steps. From last-' but no, not at all. She did say *something*...why can't I...

She smiled playfully waiting for things to slide over and under and over and fit neatly into place. But they didn't.

'You have to stay,' she said flatly. I didn't understand.

She detached from me, stood back.

'Well. I do keep my promises Aodh. I did.'

And then this is how it ends.

She gets in the van. They begin driving down the road, waving back, beeping. Before they turn the corner, the red-haired woman comes out of her house approaching crab-like, her blue eye shadow blotches of dark sea. She stands, peering so close I see a bead of sweat roll down her bleached moustache to the swell of her lip.

'Poor craturs! Poor, poor craturs,' she says.

I watch the van go to the end of the road. Beeps, *see-you*, echo.

'Sorry?' looking at her, then at the van as it nears the corner.

'Such a lovely couple they were. Despite an' all.'

'Oh, Iseult and Robert. Yeah, they're off!'

'Such a tragedy. Awful. Awful.'

'Pardon?' as the van winks in the morning sun and turns out of sight.

'Horrible way to go. I told them that camper wasn't safe.'

'What are you talking about?'

'Terrible.'

Talking about? I stand away, my mouth suddenly very dry, my breath short, trying to comprehend. She is talking about...?

*See you*, echo.

'Coming back? I do myself,' she says

'What!?' I'm nearly shouting now as if talking over an incredibly loud engine.

'What are you saying?' my heart rocketing.

The noise is now like a screeching jet but I hear through it. The words of Iseult. I hear what she said on the steps. I hear them.

'What?!' I shout at the woman again. Her mouth moving to Iseult's words but not saying them.

'Just started on their journey. Horrible accident.'

'What the FUCK are you saying?' and I nearly add Prostitute-face.

Iseult's words in the roar. What she said. Words uttered that were able to wipe clean the memory of everything that happened the first weekend. Now all was sliding, under and over and neatly locking into place. I remembered. Words so uttered that could let her keep her promise to meet again, for a second time, this time.

'Just around the corner. Well you were there. The funeral. Dead now a year-'

I didn't hear the end of it. I race down the road. I could hear the blap-blap of their Volkswagen. I can hear it. I shout with all my previous and sudden thunder, 'Iseult! Iseult!' I can hear the van close, then far, then close. I can smell jasmine! I run and run and run and run. It begins to rain. I can smell jasmine.

# The Animal
## Brid Buckley

I get down on my haunches to approach the animal carefully. Its neck is long and held low. I creep a little closer. I have never seen this kind of animal before. The animal pretends not to notice me. I put out my hand slowly. It starts but allows me to pick it up. Its fur is warm and soft against my bare arms. I can't get the animal to fit my shape exactly. I try to bundle its legs into a comfortable position for both of us but have no choice but to let them hang awkwardly as I turn the door handle and leave. Outside it is daylight. A winter sun sits high in the sky. Once my eyes have adjusted to the glare, I walk until we find a narrow path through the field. It's not a real path, more a line where the grass has been trodden. We walk for a long time and the animal grows heavier in my arms. It is dusk and all the puddles are dusty pink and rippled like the inside of a mouth. I sing little songs. I sing all the songs I can remember. The arc of the animal's spine rounds as it slumps against my body. It sleeps a while.

We walk and walk until the land grows cold and dark. The animal wakes and turns in my arms, kicking a little. I cannot tell if it is trying to get away or just to get more comfortable. My arms are heavy and aching with the weight of it, but I am afraid it cannot walk. We climb a hill. I cannot catch my breath. Branches slap against my arms. Thistles graze my ankles. I keep walking. My arms are so numb now that I can barely feel the animal's fur against them. I cling to the sensation of its bulk and warmth. I focus my attention on the circle on my left arm on which I can feel the steady heat of the animal's breath. I have run out of songs to sing. It kicks again in my arms but I hold it firm. The animal relaxes and nuzzles deeper into my body.

Its snout fits the crook of my elbow so well that a lump forms in my throat.

We reach the brow of the hill. I stop. There are more fields to walk. In the distance, black mountains arch. A patch of sea where the moonlight has caught it glistens like a silver fish. I am more tired than I have ever been in my life but I don't want to let go of the animal. I look out at the horizon and wonder if I am hurting the animal more than I am helping it. I squint out into the night's blackness and try to decide whether I should put the animal down. But where will it go? What will it eat? Because although we have walked a long way together I still can't be sure of its nature.

## CAMELLIA

Marvelling at the camellia's survival, that it endured salt,
the thrashing westerlies and plain neglect,

I move it to more sheltered ground
a single bud clinging still to a stripped branch
rust-burn on its crimson heart.

My mother's birthday gift,
in the early days of her widowhood,
*Because I know you like them*, she'd said,

having driven alone across the Burren,
her gesture reining-in memories of harsh words,
our silence salve to the wounds.

I see my daughter beaming from that sunny photo,
the grey tabby trapped mid-leap in her firm arms
her plastered fingers testimony to earlier frays

and the original camellia that flourished on her placenta
displaying the blooms that frame her blond head.

# THE MOTHER SPEAKS

Afterbirth

The sort of thing
you might expect
from savages—
imagine asking for it
then taking it home
and burying it
in the garden
to nourish
the flowering shrub
she'll plant on it
by the kitchen door
out of direct sunlight
a camellia, fancy!

In my day
we incinerated them.

## THE FATHER SPEAKS

Labour

At your request
I passed the photos
on to your sister
who wouldn't dream
of showing them
to her husband
– suitable
for medical personnel only
we're all agreed –
so they're here enclosed
we can't keep them.
How you've coarsened
since you left …
must be the company
you keep.

# THE PARTNER SPEAKS

When her waters broke
she threw up the lentil soup
we'd had at dinner.

I chucked the rest of it
into the garden
and in the same spot
dug the hole for the camellia.

In the night
she buried the placenta
planted the shrub

and patting the raw earth
beseeched the unformed spirits
not to prick her child's hand.

That summer lentils wound like wild peas
through the camellia's branches
dotting them with tiny indigo flowers.

# THE BROTHER-IN-LAW SPEAKS

It was there in the fridge
when I left the champagne to chill.
I thought it was steak
until the mother carried in the plate
and lifted up the membrane
to show us the see-through sac
her baby had grown in.
The window was high over the street
And where the mother stood blocked the kitchen exit
so I dived for the front door, landing in the garden.
I almost puked.
As we were leaving
she offered us newly-laid eggs
gift-wrapped, dressed with parsley.
*I can't take them*, I said.
*They remind me of grandfather's farm*
*and the smell of warm milk.*

Davnet Heery

# THE BIRTH MOTHER SPEAKS

They're cut now these cruel canines and me too—
freed. I've served my time, been chewed and bitten.
Over and back, that gum gnawing grinding
has my nipples zinging electric,
verging on combustion, take-off.

This is the day for weaning!
I make a bran poultice with sage and parsley,
add vinegar to disguise the scent,
wrap my breasts in cabbage leaves,
and hike into the wilderness, the child on my back.

All day I parry requests for titty—
walk the tracks, rest, walk, sleep.
The child puzzles where the milk has gone,
*Up to the sky,* I say,
pointing to the jet plane's trailing drip.

## CAMELLIA (2)


Fortnightly she feeds the camellia
15mg of sequestered iron diluted in a gallon can.
She pours liberally over the roots
and from a fine rose sprays the leaves.

The plant has begun talking to her
turning lemon-yellow from tip to mid-leaf
when hungry. And its appetite is voracious!
But it has not flowered.

Has she mistaken a young shoot for mature stock
expecting it to bloom while still fragile or
launched a currach that is yet a chrysalis
to wrestle winds before its hide has hardened?

# CAMELLIA (3)

Aboriginals tell their stories
when retouching 'the living caves' at Oenpelli,
fingers trace marks other generations made,
fresh pigments animate the spirits.

Regularly, I check the camellia's leaves, feed and mulch its roots,
bring my mother's spirit back;
as the granite boulder stands guardian against the elements
nurturing the plant, I mother myself.

Four strong buds hold firm on the new growth
and seven embryos wait and wonder.
The green sheens avocado...so all is set now
for a burst of life on my birthday and I know

this is how it will go, setbacks and recovery,
moving on nevertheless, each new spring a bonus.

# THE PARAKEET

She flew in
colours squawking,
parakeet in blue, indigo and red;

torched a trail palette blazing,
spurned monochrome
painted bold;

squirreled away
whatever glistened
velvet or satin, sequins or pearls;

hatched and moulded
herself a vision,
diamond 'n bevel, shimmer 'n shine;

feathers cavorting
wall to ceiling.

# CLOSE CALL

On an ordinary day
death crept in
turned the taps on full
let my life-blood run.

On an ordinary day
fortune smiled
measured out more string
my child birthed me.

## Amusements
## Ciara O'Dowd

Five teenagers with shoes full of sand are trailing up the hill, weary from a long day of flirting and posturing. They will not go back to the caravan park yet. Although they crave comfort and food, there are too many unspoken moments hovering in the air to face their parents. Five pink noses, breath that smells of forbidden cigarettes, and a girl has grass in her hair. The village boasts nothing more than this hill — one wide, sweeping road careering from the country road up to the coast. Uneven buildings cluster either side; some appear at risk of toppling right over. At the brow of the hill, the teenagers will stop; the plump one needs to catch her breath. The dappled light of the June evening picks out the faded sparkle in the red letters over the *Amusements* arcade.

There are few caravans in the park now; it's all modern mobile homes. Almost all have the doors thrown open. If you squint through the sun you may see people moving around inside. There was a barbeque last night on the deck to the right and charred meat still flavours the air. Someone is humming and there's the low rumble of a TV with a bad reception. In the shower block, one shower is rushing and another dripping. The day is unravelling into the dusk. All of the inhabitants are unwinding, waiting for their children to come home, and hoping they'll stay out a little longer.

In the mobile home with the varnished decking, Adam and Lisa are using up the dregs of the bottle of Shiraz they shared with the Bonners. Lisa thinks it is bitter, past drinkable, but she hates waste. She also dislikes the idea of Adam enjoying it all. She watches him sip as he idly turns the pages of a golf magazine. He isn't reading; they both know he isn't, but it makes clear that he doesn't want to talk. Once, she used to wonder what he was thinking about.

Now, she looks out the window and across the park to the tiny swatch of blue he insists on calling 'the view'.

Without a word, Lisa takes her glass and crosses to the door. Her husband's gaze lifts momentarily. He opens his mouth and then decides against braving the ravine of conversation. Lisa balances her glass on a ledge outside, looks out across the park and lets her face find the sun. All day, she has been avoiding it: a sun hat, Ray Bans. Now, she craves the last lingering warmth.

In a mobile home in the shadow of the sand banks, two women are hunting for cigarettes. Neither knows that the other is looking, or the search might be easier and more successful. Ellie eventually spies the box under the sink when her mother is in the bedroom, pretending to fluff pillows and fold towels. There are only two inside and one is squashed at the tip.

Her mother won't take her sleeping tablet for hours yet, so there is time to fill. There'll be achingly painful conversation, tepid tea and soap operas. She fills a glass with water from the tap. The intact cigarette is now up her sleeve. Her mother comes out of the bedroom with a pile of clothes that needs sorting. She puts them on the table and begins to fold. Ellie sees her eyes are full of tears again, her shoulders rounded with grief. She slips out the door. At the foot of the dunes, she collapses on a heap of rushes and puts the cigarette in her mouth. Only then does she realise she has left the lighter behind, no doubt hidden somewhere else. Ellie sucks on the unlit cigarette and tries to exhale all of her frustration.

Bernie is flicking through the TV channels and thinking about swimming. She has come this week on the spur of the moment. A car loaded with kids stopped in the traffic outside the window of her office. Like a great gust of sea air, the sight shook something out of her. By the time Brendan had rung, she was on the road out of the city.

'Like one of those chick-lit novels,' she told him. 'Where the heroine takes off on an adventure.'

She heard him smiling at the other end of the phone. Now she picks up a paperback and thumbs through it to find her page. In the mornings, she stays in bed reading, listening to the kids gathering outside. Then she potters around in her pyjamas, attempting to tidy. Sometimes it is then the nightmares find her; half-remembered visions creeping up on her, and she gets back into bed. The nightmares where everything she owns has been sold around her — her car, her house, her wedding ring. There are worse nightmares, when Brendan is in prison and she is curled up at the base of the prison wall, crying and pleading.

The inherited caravan had once been a joke, a source of amusement. Now, it's a refuge. The curtains are dusty and she fingers the fabric. Perhaps she should replace them. She hasn't found a way to suggest it yet, but if needed, they could live here. They could commute to the city, stock up on provisions once a week. Shivering at the thought of the place in winter, she banishes the vision, and decides to swim.

Unclipping her togs from the makeshift clothesline, Bernie sees Lisa on her deck, lost in thought. She catches her eye. They smile and wave. They have never been friends; they beep playfully at each other when their BMWs are caught in traffic. It strikes her for the first time that as everyone knows Lisa's husband is having an affair, so everyone knows Brendan is bankrupt. A laugh escapes her, completely involuntarily, the noise knocking her sideways. There is no reason to fear everyone finding out, for surely everyone already knows. She rolls up a towel, then pulls the front door shut and heads for the sand dunes.

Bernie pauses on the edge of the path, squinting through the sun to see Lisa put down her wine glass and scramble in a corner of the deck. She holds up a towel triumphantly. Lisa's flip-flops smack against the path as she runs towards her, waving. She's breathless when she arrives, and trembling, coming face to face with this woman who she barely knows. As some kind of greeting spills out, her bikini slips out of her towel. She reaches over to pick it up off the ground, and shakes the dust out of the scarlet material.

'You don't mind?'

'It may be tepid,' Bernie says. 'If we're lucky.'

Ellie sees the two women approach, and remembers to take the cigarette out of her mouth. For a moment, Lisa thinks Bernie is going to ignore her, but they both pause as Ellie struggles to her feet.

'You don't have a lighter?' Ellie asks, shielding her eyes from the sun. 'I'm worse than a teenager, hiding from my mother.'

They shake their heads.

'Swimming?' Ellie asks.

As she says it, the prospect unexpectedly catches her and spins her around. Just as her father had spun her, when she was light enough to stand on his feet without injury.

'Can I come?' Ellie says.

The wind sends the cigarette fluttering away. It is the first breath of wind Ellie has felt all weekend and Bernie notices it too, the breeze playing with her skirt. Lisa can't think of any excuse to back out now, or of anywhere that she can go without having to return and explain herself to her husband.

Despite her protests, they wait for Ellie to fetch her things. Silently they follow the wooden pathway through the dunes, until they reach the sand. They speed up as they start to speculate about the temperature of the water. Lisa kicks off her shoes and sand tickles her feet. Half way to the water's edge, they realise they need to change and so, giggling, they huddle, wrap towels around themselves, and shimmy out of their clothes. Lisa doesn't pause to fold her shorts, afraid she'll lose her nerve. She stuffs her bra and knickers into a pocket and covers the heap with her towel. Ellie stumbles down the sand after her, her body uncoordinated after months of tension and pain. Bernie is the fastest and the most elegant. She lengthens her stride, intent on reaching the water first, then launches herself into the waves, and is stunned into silence by the cold burst.

Shrieks from the women explode in the sky and all three are blinded by the day's last beams of sunlight. Another wave and Lisa is sent flying, losing her grip on the stony bottom and flailing as she falls. Her fingers find only spray and seaweed and with a final kick, a shriek and a splutter, she surrenders to the sea. Ellie's knees are stinging, where they had been scorched earlier by the sun. As she throws back her head and goes under, also spluttering, she sees her father's outline through the water's surface. Refusing to hold her, as he'd always done, simply letting her know he was there. He is there. When she comes up again, gasping, and realises he is gone, the pain is too much and she plunges downwards again.

In the dunes, the girl with grass in her hair is droning on about song lyrics and picking at a mole on her ankle. Her companion gives up trying to force the last flame out of the lighter and stands up to see who is shrieking. The sand shifts under his feet as he shades his eyes. Only in outline he sees the familiar shape of his mother, in the triangle of women throwing words at each other over the tossing of the waves. The ground shifts again; he slides down the dune but catches himself. He wrenches his arm on the grass as he recovers and tears spring to his eyes. The girl whimpers, sensing his pain. If he could slap her without retribution, he would. He pushes her away. The day has been too long. He is hungry and tired; fury consumes him. He wants his adolescence to pass, and quickly, because everyone else is having much more fun.

## Iran – Axis of Power
*Anna O'Leary*

### I

Wake! For the Sun, who scatter'd into flight
  The Stars before him from the Field of Night,
  Drives Night along with them from Heav'n, and strikes
  The Sultan's Turret with a Shaft of Light.
                        *----Omar Khayyam*

His restless pacing comes to an abrupt halt as he unbuttons his crisp white shirt.

'I'll show you,' and I detect urgency in his voice as he holds his shirt open.

'Look!'

I'm unprepared for the horror of his mutilated flesh just inches from me. I'm in the home I share with his son. Our main reception room overlooks a secluded walled garden, and the scent of jasmine drifts through open French windows.

'Shah?'

'Them.'

His unsteady gait has little to do with age or neat vodka, but is a consequence of inhuman punishment when he was a political prisoner.

His torture has been barely spoken of because his son wishes to avoid all political discussion. Ridges, lumps and bumps are crossed by tracks of taut flesh, and every inch of his torso is a patchwork of layered skin. No part was spared. I imagine it would feel like a rough-hewn pebble path if one were to run ones fingers over it.

'They did that!'

'That and more.'

The pain that has punctuated his life is sculpted around his eyes.

'How?'

'They tied me on and heated it up,' and the memory is obviously raw. He buttons up his shirt, but I want to know more; see more.

'Is your back the same?'

'Everywhere is the same.'

'Terrible. Can I see your back?'

He unbuttons his shirt, turns, hoists his arms over his head and pulls it up around his shoulders.

His mutilated back is not the same. The taut burnt skin has disjointed diagrams all over it, but with none of the fleshy lumps that protrude from his chest and stomach. Quivering only a trifle he pulls his shirt down and buttons it. He pours chilled vodka and drains the glass in one swig.

'They burnt you.'

'They heated it up.'

These are third degree burns. The secret police have the ability to strike terror into everyone's heart, innocent or guilty, breaking bones, pulling out fingernails and drilling into skulls. Expatriates whisper about the torture-rack and the frying pan. To witness the result of such debauchery at close quarters has a sobering effect, as if the cold barrel of a gun was thrust against my temple. I brace myself.

I suspect his torturers destroyed his manhood, as my fiancé has no sisters or brothers. I am eager to shower him with questions, but out of respect I refrain.

'Your feet; them too?' I ask, referring to his unsteady gait, but too shy to ask the really big question.

'Yes. Them too.'

'How?'

He points to his feet and flicks his hand, and I wonder if they were burnt or if he is indicating a lashing. Savak[1], the Shah's secret police, are known to beat the soles of the feet with bamboo. I try to imagine the pain. I suspect he was strapped to an electrified metal table that was heated like a toaster before he was lowered on to it to cook. This electrified table is the frying pan Iranians are afraid to speak of. I have heard expatriates discuss it. Savak is everywhere, creating an atmosphere of terror. Even he does not mention the frying pan.

'Torture,' he says, pouring neat vodka and downing it in one gulp. He has welcomed me into the bosom of his family, and we have established bonds of trust. This is dangerous territory. I rest my elbow on the corner of the table, stung by reality, and realize that nothing is as it seems.

'They would have killed me.'

'You think so.'

'I know so! Because I am an engineer I was saved.'

'How come?'

'Iran had only forty engineers then. They needed me to build the roads and railways.'

'So how did they let you go?'

'They rehabilitated me. Rehabilitate,' he says with bitter scorn in his voice, 'to make me think like them. Only I don't think like them.'

He worked for the government, but now in retirement he runs his consulting engineering practice.

Baba[2], as I call him, was close to Dr. Mossadeq, the democratic Prime Minister who nationalized Iran's oil in 1951 and threw out the British. He too was educated in Germany and Switzerland and shared Dr. Mossadeq's vision to return ownership of the country's greatest asset to the nation.

'Dr. Mossadeq was against the Anglo Iranian Oil Company's economic usurpation.'

He pauses, and drags deeply on his cigarette, while I wait for him to continue.

'Dr. Mossadeq said the land we walk on belongs to us and everything we find in the land is ours.'

His argument appeals to my Irish rebel heart.

'The British operated the world's largest oil refinery here, but the amounts paid by AIOC[3] to the British Treasury exceeded many times over the total paid to Iran.'

In 1950 AIOC earned a profit approaching £200 million from its oil enterprises here, but Iran received only £16 million in royalties, share profits and taxes. They refused to allow Iranian officials to examine their accounts. Mossadeq worked ceaselessly to promote the cause of nationalization, nudging the Shah to rid the country of economic exploitation by signing the act of nationalization.

'It triggered Mossadeq's downfall.'

'How?'

'The British were in a rage. They accused us of stealing their oil! Their oil. The crowds chanted Oil is our blood! Oil is our freedom!'

'So what happened?'

'The British planned a coup d'état, but Dr. Mossadeq was popular, and was tipped off.'

'What did he do?'

'He closed the British Embassy. That's where their agents were. When they were thrown out they had nobody here. They retaliated by blockading and boycotting our oil. They leaned on governments and banks to deny Iran a much needed loan. They asked the Americans for help.'

He paces up and down.

'The Shah ran away and left the army in charge. The CIA teamed up with MI6. Together they hatched a plot.'
I've already heard whispered mention of this plot.

'Shah flew to Rome with Queen Soraya.'
Now is not the time to mention that I stayed as a guest with Queen Soraya's family. Instead I say,

'Old man Aryieh says he gave him a blank cheque as he left, and Shah cashed it.'

'He ran away. That August there were tank battles in the streets between the loyalists to Shah and Mossadeq's supporters.'

'What year was that?'

'1953. Three days after Shah fled Dr. Mossadeq was overthrown. Once the army took control Shah flew back from Rome.'

'How did Shah come back?'

'They emptied the prisons and brought illiterate people in from the countryside to line the streets, and paid them American dollars to shout long live the Shah.'

He explains that with its American experts, the army reinstated the monarchy, and commercial oil rights fell largely to British and American companies. After Prime Minister Mossadeq's government was toppled the army put about five thousand people up against the wall, or killed them on the streets. The army, led by General Zahedi, brutalized the people and both Dr.Mossadeq and Baba were imprisoned.

'What happened to the Prime Minister?'

'After three years in prison Mossadeq was placed under house arrest until he died in 1967.'

Baba stands and gulps down another glass of neat vodka. He places the empty glass beside the bottle, and reminds me that his wife is waiting at home. He pulls on his jacket, and laboriously trudges along the street on feet that are unsteady because of torture. One of Mossadeq's inner circles, Baba is lucky to be alive to tell the tale.

I'd arrived in Iran, young and naive and against my family's better judgment, to be a stewardess for Iran Air in February 1976. In 1977 Baba told me his story. That same year, Shah was persuaded to allow the International Red Cross into his prisons, where three thousand 'security detainees'[4] were held in eighteen of them. They recorded the inmates were beaten, burnt with cigarettes and chemicals, tortured with electrodes, women were raped and men sodomised. The Red Cross report named 124 prisoners who died of torture.

## II

Before the phantom of False morning died,
Methought a Voice within the Tavern cried,
"When all the Temple is prepared within,
    Why nods the drowsy Worshipper outside?"

*---Omar Khayyam.*

### December 1975

They had made it sound like a place of ancient barbarity where I would be kidnapped and raped. I made myself deaf to everyone and vowed that no amount of scare stories would deter me from stretching my wings to follow my dream of world travel.

My father lowered himself into the upholstered chair opposite me, and leaned forward.

'There's trouble over there,' he said.

### February 1976

I am on my way to Iran because I chose to ignore all warnings. To be honest I would be afraid to venture out of my cocoon to embark on this journey alone, but we are a group of sixteen with an abundance of adventurous spirit and a great camaraderie. Like spiders, we are spinning our webs as wide as we can.

After gathering speed along the runway the take-off is smooth. We feel the sensation of upward thrust as the jet climbs through mist and cloud. My young traveling companions, all recent graduates of in-flight training school, are seated around the cabin in groups of two or three. They are impeccably dressed and manicured, and most have an air of carefully reined excitement.

Charlotte, who sits next to me, clings to both arms of her seat, her aquamarine eyes are popping out of her pretty head, and I can almost smell her fear. This is her first-ever flight. Newly armed, as she is, with the knowledge that more than two thirds of airline accidents happen during the take-off or landing phase, she is panic stricken. En route to Tehran via Moscow, she is trying to control it. I talk to her in a soothing voice, in the way one tries to calm a fractious filly, while holding a sick bag for her.

We leave London behind, where the economy is beset by an economic crisis driven by oil prices. The oil-boom has changed the axis of power. The Middle East, always a hotbed of great power rivalry, has pivoted center stage. America is importing more oil than it produces for the first time in history. Over the public-address our captain announces,

'We are cruising at 29,000 feet, with a ground speed of 510 miles per hour.'

An hour out Charlotte paints her nails and relaxes somewhat.

I check the map in the in-flight magazine to see exactly where Iran is. The Soviet Union lies to the north of Iran, with Turkey and Iraq to the west; Afghanistan and Pakistan are to the east, and across the body of water known as the Persian Gulf, are Kuwait, Saudi Arabia, Bahrain, Qatar, United Arab Emirates and Oman. Geography is not my strong subject, and this is one place I never expected to travel to. An English stewardess, sporting a golden winter suntan, slides a tray in front of me. I cut into a Persian dish of chicken and rice with plastic cutlery.

On schedule, the Iran Air Boeing 707 touches down in Moscow. I find being behind the Iron Curtain intimidating, and to avoid causing stress for Charlotte I hide my fear of being snowbound in this tightly regimented communist state. Russia in February is arctic cold with snow ploughs busy clearing the runway. I hum the Beatle's hit song, Back in the U.S.S.R.

My dream, since I was old enough to parade around in my mother's high-heels, was to be an air stewardess. As a child I watched my cousin, a glamorous British Airways stewardess, sip tea from a bone-china cup in our farmhouse kitchen. Everything about her impressed me. Her black silk grosgrain skirt, her long legs in black nylons and black patent high heels, her ruby red ribbed sweater and her awesome ruby-red lipstick and nail-varnish. She casually mentioned both Paris and New York in the same breath and the world danced and shone before me. I shared my dream with my beautiful mother before she died, and she assured me that I too could be a stewardess when I grew up.

The primary function of an air stewardess on board a jet is passenger safety, and not handing out boiled sweets and pouring champagne as I had imagined. Passengers are unaware that air stewardesses are really safety-officers in disguise, and can cut the umbilical cord of a newborn at thirty-something-thousand feet. Fire and smoke are the main killers in the aftermath of a crash, and the crew is there to evacuate the aircraft and lead the passengers away from the wreckage. A disturbingly high proportion of accidents occur at night or in low visibility.

I stare into the clouds and say a silent prayer asking my mother to keep me safe. Iran is a long way from my home at the foot of Stacks Mountain in southern Ireland, and for all my outward bravado I am scared to have flown so far from the nest, but am not prepared to admit it. The Holy Sisters of Mercy who run Colaiste Ide, the ultra-strict all girl boarding school I attended, are not at all impressed with my career choice. The college has a splendid academic reputation and prides itself on turning out teachers and the odd nun. With no mother, a healthy interest in boys and little interest in study, the nuns despaired of my antics. Obedience did not come easily to me. If they could see me now they would start a novena to Saint Jude, patron saint of hopeless cases. I imagine the nuns in their long rustling robes, giant size rosary beads clanking, scurrying to the college church to kneel and pray for the salvation of my rebellious soul. I can almost smell their Benediction incense.

It was T.S. Eliot who wrote the journey, not the arrival matters, but this journey is long and tedious because of my profound yearning to get to Iran. We fly over the Caucasus Mountains, over Georgia and Azerbaijan. When the fasten-seat-belt sign comes on the pilot announces we are flying over the Alborz Mountains and tells us to adjust our watches by three hours, making it terribly late in Iran.

The operating crew dim the cabin lights, which will enable the eye to make a rapid adjustment to the dark in the event of a crash landing. The undercarriage of the Boeing 707 locks in the landing position, spurring Charlotte to dig her nails into my arm in a renewed bout of terror as she steps closer to the hysteria she has been fighting ever since we boarded at Heathrow. The twinkling lights of Tehran are barely visible.

The jet touches down and the Pratt & Whitney engine noise intensifies as the captain opens the wing flaps to slow the forward thrust. At Mehrabad Airport, on a cold February 1976, I catch my first glimpse of Iran in the soft light of the half-moon dipping over the horizon as we are escorted across the tarmac to the crew briefing-room. We are officially welcomed and served Iranian chaii from a traditional samovar. The little glasses of black tea are a Persian ritual of hospitality I embrace enthusiastically, and I try to drink it as they do, sipping the tea through a sugar lump held between my front teeth. The traditional tea-ceremony is a perfect start to our exotic new life, and despite exhaustion we are all determinedly smiling.

Crew transport whisks us away. It is almost midnight and I am weary and disappointed by how dull and charmless the place looks, except for the illuminated Shayad monument. The King of Kings, Shah Mohammed Reza Pahlavi, commissioned this impressive edifice in homage to two thousand years of Persian dynasty. Somewhere behind me on the coach one of the girls refers to it in a naughty whisper as 'the Shah's erection.'

### III

And, as the Cock crew, those who stood before
  The Tavern shouted— "Open then the Door!
You know how little while we have to stay,
And, once departed, may return no more."

*----Omar Khayyam.*

I wake as dawn sneaks over the city and the first glimmer of sunlight streaks into my hotel room. The quiet of the morning is shattered by the constant roar and clatter in the traffic-choked street below. Nothing has prepared me for the din of the relentless activity.

I breakfast on delicious hot barbari bread spread with fetta cheese and strawberry jam. To my delight the day reveals a strange and very exciting country full of new sights sounds and smells. Travelling by car or crossing the street is fraught with danger. The congested roads lack pedestrian crossings, so I learn to copy the locals and step on to the road, forcing the intimidating traffic to halt while I cross. Everybody toots his or her horn, all the time, sometimes for no apparent reason. Once the drivers slow enough to notice my blonde hair braided in a French plait the cheeky ones try to attract attention.

Its geographical location makes Iran one of the most strategic areas of the world with its long Gulf coast and its trade through the Straits of Hormuz. At the apex of its power, Iran has unlimited oil reserves and is undergoing a social and economic transformation. The Shah is steering his nation into the twentieth century and the country's enormous oil revenue is visibly changing the landscape. The most up to date Boeing jet fleet, crewed by multi-lingual air stewardesses, is only part of the investment program.

At the chaii khane — teahouse — amid the whirr of ceiling fans and the constant hum of Persian chatter, women and children eat rose-petal ice cream and men suck vigorously on cigarettes. I sprinkle chocolate on my cappuccino and spoon the froth slowly and sensuously, and discover baklava crammed with pistachio nuts and drenched in fragrant syrup and shredded kataifi pastry with thick clotted cream.

I am fascinated by the chador in the same way a small child is held spellbound by a nun's habit. Some ladies wear the long black robe wrapped around them, covering their hair, with a corner of it clamped between their teeth to hold it in place or held tightly under the chin.

Iranians are a very good looking race. Some pretty ladies are heavily made-up, their fashionable denim jeans peeping beneath their chadors, as they sashay along in high heels. The more adventurous, when passing a handsome man will briefly unfurl their chador and make a flirtatious play of readjusting it.

Not everyone covers up, and many fashionably-dressed ladies strike an elegant pose. I observe these exotic women as if they are another species. Our fair skin marks us out in a crowd, and Iranians seem to find us almost as fascinating as we find them. Coming from an Irish Catholic background I find Iran a culture shock, though it is generally considered a stepping-stone between east and west.

Iran Air has European stewardesses based in London, and Japanese stewardesses based in Tokyo, but so far only fifty of us are based in Tehran. I am curious why Charlotte, with her fear of flying, wants to be a stewardess.

'Why did you join Iran Air?'

'To find a husband.'

'Seriously Charlotte?'

'I'm serious!' She giggles, as her pale luminous skin turns pink. Personally I want to discover new places and experience different cultures. Charlotte has a different agenda.

'I want to get married' she says.

Iran Air is the fastest growing airline in the world. Our elegant Mila Schon-designer uniform, with navy matching hand tooled leather luggage, is fashioned from silk and the finest wool. It is exquisitely tailored and completely reversible. For my first flight I wear my hair in a French plait and don my navy hat with the emblem of the Homa bird on the side. I am nervous, but my Iranian colleagues encourage me. They teach me some Persian words, which I write phonetically on a paper napkin. I resolve to learn three new Persian words per flight and I delight the passengers by practicing my newly acquired vocabulary.

My companions are eleven British girls, another Irish girl, one French, one Dutch, and an Australian. We are young and dependent on each other for friendship and companionship in this foreign environment. Jeni and Jill, two fun loving friends, were simply honing their interview skills when Iran Air hired them both. A former schoolteacher in our group assured us we could get jobs as bunny girls at London's Playboy Club when we worried about failing our crew exam.

'All you need are good legs!' Liz said mischievously.

The youngest in our group has come straight from Art College and has a body men dream of. Another elegant girl was a ground stewardess for South African Airways at Heathrow airport, while yet another was a stewardess with Dan Air. The sophisticated Chris worked for the Hermes family in Paris. Our only Australian was backpacking her way around Europe when she was hired.

Twelve of us move to live in three apartments on Andesheih Shish, off Farah Jonubi. There is excessive activity on our street, which resembles a building site, and our shoes sink into the mud. Tehran is under construction with cranes, scaffolding and unfinished buildings as far as the eye can see. Every surface in our apartment is covered in a thick layer of bulldozer dust and as we clean it away more settles. The air here is heavy with putrid fumes created by unyielding traffic jams.

In Tehran an Iran Air stewardess is a creature of great interest and it spurs us into dressing up and making up. Charlotte and I plan a quiet dinner at an Italian restaurant. It feels glamorous to dine out. We order a selection of focaccias, bruschettas, and proscuitto-wrapped asparagus. We sprinkle grated Parmesan cheese liberally on our tagliatelle carbonara al dente. The portly Italian chef appears as we finish each course.

'Everything all right, Signorina?'

With our coffee he offers us drinks.

'Si Signorina! Compliments of the owner.'

We accept the complimentary drinks unaware the owner is one of the handsome young men at a nearby table.

The chef introduces our benefactor, Aleksander, the lean young man with the curly hair and the trendy John Lennon glasses. Aleksander's skin is a smooth golden olive, his black hair thick and curly, high cheekbones, and bright dancing eyes. He invites us to join his table.

'Have you been to Key Club?'

'Key Club,' I say, 'I have never heard of it.'

'Majid, they don't know Key Club.'

Aleksander, his dark brown eyes teasing, takes great delight in this and compares Key Club to a Californian nightclub, and then to a famous London nightclub I have been to only once. He pauses to draw breath.

'Is it the best nightclub in Tehran?'

'Sure! It's one of the best in the world' he announces triumphantly. I am dubious such a place exists here, but as Aleksander is gorgeous I want to check it out. I must have agreement from Charlotte, as we are in a strange city, in an even stranger country, and I find myself contemplating a trip to a club I have never heard of.

[1] SAVAK — *Sazeman-e Ettelaat va Amniyat-e Keshvar*, National Information and Security Organization, was the domestic security and intelligence agency of Iran from 1957 to 1979.

[2] Baba is the Persian word for Dad.

[3] AIOC (Anglo Iranian Oil Company).

[4] 'Security detainees' were political prisoners.

## My Big Brother
## Elizabeth Cox

It's kind of a secret, but my big brother was born with magic on his fingertips. Nobody speaks of it (perhaps because some things are too obviously true to doubt) so there's no proper account of that morning. It seems that as they brought him from Mother to cot he dipped his tiny pink hands into the vat of magic that accompanies every birth. Magic is the most marvellous of substances, a delicate mixture of elements that contains worlds of possibilities. Every midwife needs just a spoonful of the silvery stuff to soothe the pains of the parent and ease the breathing of the infant. How a newborn with barely the sense to cry could have misappropriated the carefully guarded brew is a mystery. The few conversations that touch on that day protest that the lid was to be sealed the whole time. Something must have gone awry though, there is no other possible way he could have contracted the fine dust that flecked off like sugar whenever he touched something important. It would catch your eye when he picked up his sword or put down a favourite book. Of course, a whisper is sometimes heard that the lid was airtight. That something caught the light before he was passed across the room, the very instant he stretched out of the womb.

Those murmurs only started up in the days before he left home to grow up as a man. Not sly asides against his character, just friends and neighbours reminiscing and marvelling how quickly he had grown. He had been a smart active boy, mischievous but not hurtful. Too busy to sit down for a meal, he would run to play with his friends, food half-consumed in his wake. As a young man he was agreeable and witty, destined to succeed. Learning was never a problem. He took interest in all that crossed his path and read voraciously, trying to discover more, another ploy always up his sleeve.

It was like that when he got his sword. He wasn't a violent boy by any stretch of the imagination, but after reading so many swashbuckling tales, he felt the need for a sword. Swordplay wasn't discouraged where we grew up, per se, but other less brutal defensive techniques were felt to be easier for a young person to pick up. The elders were much more willing to show off their boxing skills or explain their prowess with the sheep's crook than to lumber a child with a hunk of metal and tell them to swing. In fact, each of them blankly refused his request, fearing the easily distracted boy would make off with a sword and come back with a missing appendage. My big brother was not so easily put off. One elder, a retired general, was pestered so much he declared that he would train the boy, but he would not provide the equipment. That settled the case for the elders. All of the village were warned to secure their swords, feeling superior in the knowledge that a boy thwarted was a boy bored. Surely after three failed misappropriations (or outright robberies as Mother called them, before making him scrub the skirting boards) he would move on to something else. But no, he endeavoured and endured.

One morning, two months after starting his quest, he turned to me and muttered something about not having "looked for one yet". My big brother then turned on his heel and ran off in the direction of the forest. There was a temptation to follow him, but all that week I had been dazed and mildly blinded by the shining skirting boards. No one was ever told what exactly happened that day. My big brother returned at dusk, a shadow traipsing out of the forest. From the distance he seemed a mobile sapling separated from the woods. When he entered the house, cheeks ruddy and smudged with dirt, he brought in a blast of outside. Pine sap and earth and the scent of a cold fresh wind checked the room as he came indoors. In an addition to his usual garb of naturally distressed denim and cotton t-shirt was a worn brown leather belt. Attached to it was a sheath filled with a beauty. The sword he refused to take off, even after he had scrubbed his face and fingernails. Mother didn't mind, as long as nothing was knocked over and it wasn't used to cut steak.

It didn't fit him exactly. In time it would, but back then it was a few inches too long and would knock his knees when he wasn't paying attention and the belt drooped. It was thin though, light as air in comparison to the others lugged about by men. A wooden leather-bound hilt and steel blade, it had no jewels, but there was a small series of grooves on the broad side just blow the hilt. Sitting out on the stump one day sharpening it, he showed me how if you got a certain type of pebble, smooth but easy to grip, you could rub along the grooves and create hollow sounds, notes that turned to haunting melodies. So obscure, and yet my brother always had this knack for utilizing the useless, finding talent and spark in the plainest of things, or people.

Not long after that, he decided it was time to move on out. The whole village turned out to toast his farewell. That night was full of cheer and banter, more full of feasting than fear. Still so young, they whispered, and yet capable as one twice his age, others would rejoin. Each person that asked where he was off to got a different reply. His bag held little, but stories contradicted whether he would climb mountains and trek cross-country or land in a city full of airs and graces, peddling his charm and marrying royalty. Some proposed he would do it all, they were not far wrong. The sun in the east threw his figure out as a shadow as he started out. Waving goodbye, there was no air of sadness that he would be gone, but a tinge of hope that he would return brighter than ever.

And return he did. The most reassuring sound of my childhood happened during his stays. In the depths of the dark night, a dim pulse would wake me. Confused at first, I would always lie awake and try to puzzle out the sound. Then I'd smile and be lulled back to sleep. It was my big brother, strumming his sword in the night, repeating the beats, playing only for himself. I strained to hear that simple sound that soothed me so. Those simple rhythms meant he was home. Maybe not for a day or a week or not for a month at a time, but he would come back, arriving home laden with gifts of fine coffees, dancing toys and an air of excitement. He would trickle about the house fixing the broken locks Father hadn't gotten around to or painting the ceiling a pale lemon. At one point during his stay he would sit with me of an evening. Mother would bring him a mug of cocoa and, taking a sip, he would launch into a thousand tales.

Never the same adventure twice, he told me how he fought off vicious warthogs (the trick is to take a great bellyful of their scent and blow it back at them). In his quest for maturity he climbed slippery peaks and fought Yetis using snowballs. Once, he had learned from a gossiping eagle that there was a troll-sized cave filled with emeralds in a not-too distant land. He snuck into the nearest library to read all he could about trolls and smuggling emeralds. Three weeks he spent there, camping out in the archives and teasing apples off the desks of lecturers (who have a great fear of doctors). Finding out his fill, he prepared for his trail.

Crawling through bog to reach the ocean-side rocks, he washed that day in the saltwater until night landed and the moon shone orange. Sodium absorbed through the epidermis repels any creature over eight foot tall. As he soaked he chewed carrots and his eyes grew accustomed to the murk of the dark.

He slid over slimy pebbles and crept through the cold sand, a faint sparkle following the movement of his hands on the harder-to-reach rocks. The trace shone brightest on his sword handle. Practised in warthog-baiting, his nose picked up fifteen different scents, one of which was starlight, another emeralds, a third was animalistic deposits. None of the fifteen was troll.

As dawn broke, twelve deer were seen traipsing out of their sea cave dwelling. Slowly they climbed the rocks ill-suited to their hooves, burdened with the green jewels of a dozen royals. These deer were a rare strain of desert stag that had gotten quite a bit lost and then distracted by the presence of sand. They had been fairing poorly in the endless twilight of their new cliff home.

It is said magic led them out.

My big brother was comprehensive in seventeen tongues and could order a hazelnut latté in Juavaland using only the blink of his left eye and a snort of the nostril. He told me his own experiences almost in passing, though those are the ones I pressed for. More important it was for me to hear about the great heroes of men; the eternal fables of kindness and strength. The most ancient of tales was about Gilgamesh — half man, half god and a whole load of brawn. Gilgamesh and his best friend Enkidu went on an unmitigated host of adventures, saving the world from beasts and flames. When Enkidu died Gilgamesh cried for days and days, until maggots crawled out of his best friend's nose.

When my big brother died I didn't cry at all at first. The first thing that happened was a thought: 'No-one else is getting his sword. That is mine.' After that my whole body collapsed. When you cry that much, really cry, your lungs won't hold enough oxygen to let you do anything else, like stand. We all collapsed. Then we all got up together, holding on, clasping hand on elbow, and said goodbye. But he wasn't gone.

He told me once about black holes. About how they suck up everything that comes in their path and how you can't see them, but you can see everything that stands around them. You recognise one because it's not anything, but it's not anything else. It was the same with my big brother. There was a him-shaped hole and we all stood around it. It sucked out stories and thoughts from our breast-pockets, unfinished as they were.

When the time came for me to go off and grow up, I didn't much care to give a toast. I could barely remember telling people what I was going to do, or even choosing it. I just did the only thing I knew anything about. I adventured. I don't know if I wanted to do it or if I just wanted my big brother back.

As time went on I discovered that I didn't like doing anything as much as I liked battling mermen and tripping the light fantastic. At first I followed my brother's fingerprints, but then I changed lightly what I did and how I did it. I shaved the priceless hair off the chin of the warthog with my big brother's sword instead of sticking it in the belly of the pig. In place of the climbing the highest mountains, I dove the deepest seas.

Coming home to visit one time, I bumped into an old friend. I asked her to visit, so we could catch up. After my big brother had died I stopped talking to people as much. I wanted to be alone. This wasn't fair on my friends, but I had only just been able to be happy again. The evening came and she asked me about my big brother, about how he died, something that had been a mystery to those outside our family.

'Did he die fighting trolls?'

No.

'Was he drowned trying to catch the Great Trout of Juavaland?'

No.

'Fell from a branch climbing the Tree to Nowhere?'

'No,' I said.

I told her that he tripped and hit his head and was no more. Simple. It was a great reunion of his pals and much fun was had. His legs were weak and wobbling from dancing, reflexes slow from drinking.

'So he didn't die a hero's death?'

Mother handed us hearty mugs of cocoa. I told my friend not to be disappointed. My big brother was laughing when he died, had been happily enjoying the company of friends.

It was straightforward, not epic. Not as a hero, but as himself.

I took a great gulp of cocoa and launched into the story of my big brother. As I put down the mug, something caught on the corner of my eye. Barely there, on the edge of my messy fingerprint, was a speck of a sparkle that looked like sugar, but wasn't.

# The Date
## Joe Jennings

She was having a glass of wine in the shower when I
arrived. Her housemate let me in. He seemed odd. A
strange one, with deep dark eyes. His angular jaw stretched
into his neck with ease and stubble smothered his cheeks
but not his chin. We walked in single file through the house
into the sitting room. It looked like he was wearing ladies
underwear as a frilly pink line stood above his jeans; either
that or he was wearing extremely feminine jocks.

The room was dimly lit with lamps in opposite
corners. Red scarves had been laid out over the shades
which made the lights glow in a low pink colour. It was a
feeble attempt at making a small room in an old house seem
cosy and pretty. In fact it looked more like a cheap hooker's
bedroom complete with a fold out couch. I took up position
on said couch and the squared jaw housemate tucked
himself up in a blanket on a rug in front of the fire. I didn't
know his name. He didn't say anything at the door apart
from that fact that *she* was in the shower, having a glass of
wine.

I crossed my legs and we sat in silence. The jaw
person stared intently at the crackling flames. I watched
him for a minute or two. He didn't move, except when the
fire spit. Then he looked at me and smiled. I nodded
awkwardly and checked the time. The room was cold. It
was no wonder the odd knickers-wearer sat by the fire.

After five awkward minutes of no conversation, I
decided to break and talk to him.

'So have you been living here long?'

His dark eyes never looked away from the fire and he
scratched his head roughly. I waited. No answer. I sighed. I
was dying for a fucking beer. Seeing that there was no luck
with a dialogue with baldy chin, my eyes searched around

the seedy room. On the coffee table in front of me, there were the makings for a joint, a lighter and a book called *Our Cosmic World*. A bookshelf stood to the left of the fireplace packed to breaking point with all sorts of books which all seemed pink because of the stupid light next to it. There wasn't a television in the room but there were three laptops stacked on each other on a small study desk just beside the door. I checked the time. I waited. The fire spit again. Fuckface turned to me and smiled again. I gave him my typical reply, a nod. He reciprocated and returned to the thrill of a blazing fire.

That weed on the table looked more and more appealing. I was desperate. I tried to converse with the sedated flame addict once more.

'Do you think she's nearly ready?'

No answer. No movement. I grunted in pain. Absolute boredom crossed with my stupid manners. Why didn't I have it in me to just grab the papers and skin up a joint and take the edge off the awkwardness? But no, I sat there smiling at a twenty-something-year-old male wrapped in a fluffy blue blanket staring at a naked flame. I sighed once more. The reflection of the flames bounced in his eyes. I decided to speak again. There was nothing else to do.

'Are you ok buddy?'

'I'm fine. Sorry man.' The fucker spoke. He tossed the blanket off and pulled himself up onto the only other chair in the room. 'I'm so fucking stoned.'

'That's grand man, don't worry.'

He rubbed his face and shot his arms out for a stretch. I couldn't believe that he was facing me now. It was surreal. He was actually looking at me and I thought: Fuck no, I hope he says something. He did.

'You don't mind if I roll a joint do you?'

'No, not at all. Fire ahead, buddy.'

'Sound man.'

He pulled an A4-sized book off the bookshelf and placed it on his lap. Then he grabbed the papers, weed and tobacco pouch off the coffee table. I watched him roll and the silence grew again. I checked the time. She was twenty minutes late already but I suppose that's just women.

The fire spit again. I waited for his dumb smile. There was none. So he was actually sober now, not bad. I thought, now's the time to talk. Perhaps now he'll chat. He licked the joint and sealed it. I cleared my throat and started.

'So have you been living here long?'

'Huh?'

'Have you been living here long?'

'Oh. Well … about … well … probably …t— …thr— … five months. Yeah … five months.'

'Oh really, oh right.'

He grabbed the lighter and sparked the joint. He sucked it hard and released smoke slowly from his mouth. It smelt fucking great. He leaned back in his chair and took another drag. I watched the smoke fill the room and then he shocked me. He spoke of his own accord. I nearly fell out of my seat.

'Sorry man, who are you?'

'What?' My eyebrows arched in a confused fashion. They almost danced on my forehead. 'Are you serious?'

'Yeah well, who are you man?'

'*You* let me in the door. I'm here to see …'

'Oh yeah.' He inhaled again. 'She's having a glass of wine in the shower, man.'

'Yeah, you told me that. Do you think she's ready now?'

'Nearly. Do you want a drag?'

He held out the joint.

'Please, if you don't mind.'

He passed it across the coffee table and I sucked on the thing like it was going to be my last taste of weed. The smoke exited from my mouth and I fell back into the comfort of the couch. Instant satisfaction. Instant relaxation. I inhaled again and felt my head become dramatically lighter. It was strong shit. I returned the joint to its owner. He smiled and I nodded.

The room seemed cosier now. It took on a warm and vibrant feel. I guess you had to be stoned to truly appreciate the mood lighting. I heard movement upstairs and I calmed myself. She was thirty minutes late but I was slightly stoned. It balanced out. The night wasn't so bad and it got better. Jawman rose from his seat.

'Do you want a beer while you wait?'

'Sure, yeah, sound."

He nodded and walked out. I clapped my hands and rubbed them together with delight. Fuck going out at all; the craic was here. Weed, beer, a fire. The fire. The fire bobbed and weaved around the timber and coal. The colours were intense and it spit hard. I nodded and smiled back at the fire. Fuck, I shook my head. I was turning into that freak. And what kind of mutant line of super weed had he given me? No more. That was it.

He returned and handed me a large brown bottle of beer. I looked at the gold label. Cheap Belgian crap, but strong. I twisted the cap off and took a mouthful. Not bad. Ice cold, that was good; not bad at all. I checked the time. Still no sign of her. Knowing my luck, she would probably walk in now and I'd never even get to finish my beer. Typical. But she didn't. I drank it. I swallowed it. I knocked it back. Fuck, it was good. I refused another joint and the lingerie-wearer in the corner kept feeding me with beers. Two. Three. Four beers later and still no sign of her. Rock jaw comforted me though.

'I think I heard her there, man. She's probably coming down the stairs now.'

I nodded. She was well over an hour late. I wasn't that angry. Perhaps it would be a story that we would tell our grandchildren when we were old and grey. That on our first date, she kept me waiting for hours but it was worth it. Who knew? I didn't and certainly Fuckface in the corner, who was completely baked out of his mind, didn't know either.

Another twenty minutes skipped by. Then he lifted his leg and farted. I smirked and he apologised. That is what we were reduced to, him half soiling his ladies underwear and me sitting there getting drunk, smiling awkwardly. I had had enough. It had gone too far. Never mind grandchildren, there wasn't even going to be a date. That's it. She had her chance and she blew it. She fucked it up. I finished my beer and put it on the coffee table with the others. Jawface stood up when I did. He looked confused. His red eyes drooped.

'Are you going man?'

'Ah yeah, just tell her to call me tomorrow. Thanks for the beers and the weed man. Much appreciated. I never got your …'

'No man. We'll go up and get her. Come on. Come on.'

He brushed past me and latched onto my arm. I went with him reluctantly. We went single file in the hall and swung round up the carpeted stairs. He marched on ahead of me. I stood in the landing and did what I did best, waited while he burst into what I suspected was her room. There wasn't a light on. Complete darkness. I turned and saw the bathroom door was slightly ajar. The light was on and droplets of water had been splashed on the white tiles.

I knocked quietly. No answer. I knocked again. Then Stonerboy with his pink frilly underwear shoved me out of the way and barged in the door. There she was, in a heap in the shower, with red stains on the tiled wall, which I believed to be wine, as I raced down the stairs and out the front door, although I wasn't quite sure.

## Care Assistant
### Brid Buckley

She thinks that I am ugly. I take these words from out of her mouth silently but I can see them, lying latent there on the curl of her lip.

'Your trousers are too long for you,' she says and what she means is that my legs are not of a respectable length.

'Your fringe is in your eyes,' she says and what she means is: what is wrong with you that you would not get your hair cut, that you could not be tidy?

It is cramped in this small bathroom; there really is not room for both our bodies. She stands before me completely naked and decides that I am ugly. I wash her wrinkled body in the technically-correct manner. How different all these bodies are to each other; how unaffected I am by them. I am a care assistant, that is the correct professional term. I wear a blue smock and sometimes people mistake me for a nurse. The white towel I hand her is stiff with starch. Kathleen tells me I am holding it at the incorrect angle. What she is really saying is that I am so wearingly ugly that it pains her to look me in the face. There is a moment of awkward silence. I decide to be professional. Perhaps she is lonely. Seventy eight years spent accumulating life experience and nobody to talk to about what she heard on the radio. She has a family. They visit. They talk about what they need to buy for that night's dinner. They talk about putting out the refuse. I choose a topic from our regular rotation of three and wade in tentatively.

'You speak too fast,' she says.

I push her slight into the pile of others to be sifted through at a later stage. I laugh. The corners of my eyes don't wrinkle. When I laugh she sees with disgust that my bottom front teeth are slightly twisted.

'Ah, they all talk very fast in Cork,' I say.

She does not think that I am funny.

'But it isn't the right way to speak. You should get elocution lessons,' she says and I have to look away.

She thinks that I should wear a pencil skirt and have my hair combed and tied together at the nape of my neck. I could do with a trimmer waist, she thinks, and smaller breasts. I should take longer steps when I walk and keep my shoulders straight. She does not tell me any of this but I know she thinks that this is what I should expect from myself. When I mention that my friends Kate and Daniel came to visit over the weekend, she asks did they stay in the same bed and I do not think fast enough to lie.

'They are going out a long time,' I say.

Then I think: why should I have to explain myself or my friends to this woman? What business is it to her what they do or do not do, these friends of mine who do not even know that she exists and is now judging them? She scowls and turns away for a moment with an exaggerated sigh. She thinks that it makes perfect sense that I would be friends with moral degenerates such as Kate and Daniel. When she is dressed and settled I make the tea and toast and think about how she thinks I'm ugly. I am careful to get the honey right to the edges of the lightly toasted bread. I will the clock's hand to move. I am anxious to get out of this kitchen and away from the sickly smell of something sour, something that is going off.

Later that evening I shower a father and a daughter. Tommy first; Aideen is still at mass. We chat while we foam and clean. He is unabashed by his nakedness. He is embarrassed by the fact that it takes two attempts and my extended arm to get up from the shower chair. We are friendly and slightly formal. I wash his body top to tail, and then dry each part of him in the same order that I have washed them in. The towels are soft and fluffy. I douse him in a cloud of powder. After he is dressed, Tommy insists I make us both a pot of tea while we wait for his daughter to return from mass. I have to ask him if he takes milk. I dig around presses to find where it is he keeps the sugar. We sip our tea and talk about the World Cup match.

'Yes,' I say, 'It was awful rough, awful dirty.'

His daughter is taller than me. She does not think about the shape of her body. She has a thirty-three-year-old body but the mind of a girl of eight. She talks a lot, whatever it is that comes into her head. Last night she told me that her mother is dead.

'Oh, that is hard. Do you miss her?'

'Yes,' she said, 'Yes.'

Her voice does not change with what she is saying. I have to listen carefully to discern between what is statement and what is inquiry.

'Are Jerusalem and Galway close together?'

'No, very far.'

'Was David a good king?'

'Yes,' I say. I have heard he was.

'I dressed up as Saint Mary in a play once.'

'Wow, really?'

I ask her to tell me more about this. I dry her body on the bed and help her into a pink nightgown. Her face and body are round. They do not fit a girl of eight. They do not fit a woman of thirty-three either. I ask Aideen to sit on the bed and I plug in the hairdryer. Her long, dark hair grows softer in my hands. It goes all the way down her back.

'I wish my hair was long and dark,' I say. 'I had mine long but it would never grow this long.'

'Yes,' she says. 'Yes,' unaffected.

She does not understand what a compliment is; she does not know what it is to want to be different to how one is. She talks all the while I dry her hair. I flick the dryer on and off and try to keep up with the many destination changes that occur along her train of thought. I would like to speak like this, I think, out of sequence. I wonder who I am to Aideen: a mother or a sister figure? Or perhaps I am more a friend, but of eight or thirty-three?

When her hair is dry, I turn down the covers and tuck her in. We sit and watch Mary Poppins for a while.

'What's the difference between a babysitter and a nanny?' Aideen asks.

'A nanny lives in the house. A babysitter doesn't,' I say, as if it was all as simple as that. Soon it is time for me to go.

'Nurse,' she calls, and I find myself surprised.

I have sat with her and dried her hair; she has told me about her mother. I should correct her. Technically I am a care assistant. When it is time to leave I say: 'Goodbye. It was nice to meet you. Best of luck on your trip to Lourdes.'

She says, 'Goodbye nurse,' in a flat voice, her eyes still on the flat-screen television.

My final call is to Jack's house.

'Oh, it's you,' he says with a smile. I give him his medication and a spoonful of Gaviscon. I call it his Sambuca as always, because I think that that's what it smells like, and he laughs.

'What do you call it?'

He knows but he wants me to say it again. Then the other care assistant Rosemary arrives and there is a lot of laughter. Her laugh is loud and I like it. She's from Kenya but Jack always tells her about a man he worked with from Columbia because he thinks that's where she's from. She does not correct him.

'You look pretty tonight,' he says to me. 'No lipstick though. You're not on a promise tonight?'

We laugh. He will never let me live that one down.

'No Galway man yet then?' he asks.

Plenty of time yet, he thinks. I asked him once how old he thought I was and nineteen was what he said. Rosemary guessed twenty-eight so she thinks I should be getting a move on. She had had three of her four children by that age. I am twenty-five I told them but I remain nineteen and twenty-eight.

'Do you like having green eyes?' Jack asks me.

I give it some thought before answering.

'Yes,' I say, 'The same colour as my father's.'

Jack notices these things, the parts of us that aren't our uniforms. He thinks that Rosemary is beautiful too. I know this because he asks us to move him from chair to bed using the 'Rosemary style' and he says it again and again so that we can all laugh about it. He notices, I decide, as I do, the brown silk that are Rosemary's arms showing between the white of the gloves and the blue of her smock. She is more beautiful than yesterday I think, although she must have looked the same.

'Now Jack, we will have to do some scooching,' she says and we all laugh. 'Scooch' is the word we use for when Jack holds onto the bar above him and shuffles his bottom to get central in the bed.

'Scooch, scooch, scooch,' we say in our own language, 'Scooch, scooch, scooch.'

Their faces switch on like lamps. When it is time to go, I say goodnight to Jack and rest a hand on his shoulder. I make sure he is 'snug as a bug'.

'That I am,' he says. 'Goodnight. Safe home.'

The street is quiet when I step outside. I look into the faces of the people that I pass. I think about all the different faces they must have worn that day and the other faces I cannot see, to whom they may be ugly or to whom they are so beautiful. It is much more than symmetry I decide. It is an array of languages and maths is only one of them.

## On the Wing

I love the ball at my feet,
Running smooth over grass,
Each blade bending, springing back.

He stands before me, keen to lunge,
But I have many tricks to use
As a ruse, and I'm fast.

I'll step over, twist, launch myself
Past his shoulder. He'll resist,
But I'll find a gap.

*I follow the ball; his legs deceive,*
*Weaving a secret tapestry.*
*I want to know his design.*

*If he takes the line, I'll pull him back*
*By the sleeve, where the ref won't see.*
*He's tricky, but he's mine.*

*I can beat him in the race,*
*And there's cover behind.*
*When I turn, I'll do it in his line.*

Who's in the box?
I could play it short inside,
Maybe get the return,

Or drop the shoulder,
Shift from right to left and back.
All he'll see is a blur.

*He likes to feign, but I'm no fool,*
*And though my legs burn,*
*Their eyes will roll if I lose.*

*Slide in hard or stay on my feet?*
*It's all a battle of pretence.*
*What will he do?*

## Connected

She sees many things:
Windows in a whirl of colour.
She sees the multitude,
Knows their status,
The business of their lives,
Her place apart
Among them.

Still she searches.
A picture, some quality it has
– Maybe the humour of the light –
Takes her to a sunny weekend
Lying on a Turkish beach.

*I wonder what he's doing now.*
*Likely looking in the mirror.*

She considers her next trip:
Stockholm? Singapore? Syracuse?

*He was reading that novel,*
*'1984',*
*Telling me about it:*
*People were leaping up and down*
*In their places*
*And shouting at the tops of their voices,*
*The Two Minutes Hate.*

*I really should read that.*

Tapping, constant tapping
Like an endless echo applauding

Through the captured fragments of conversations.
Music slips through an open window.
A sound comes, like a crying child:
A ring-tone wailing.
The name appears.

'Hey Mum, how are things?'

They talk in banalities,
Like a train stopping
On the way to a bigger town.
They talk of other lives:
Her sister's child,
A neighbour's ill health,
Students killed in a car crash.

As the words tumble out, her thoughts creep away:
*This could be the last time I talk to you.*
*I haven't even said sorry.*

'I bought a new thing for the computer,'
Her mother says,
'But I can't get it to work.'

*Why can't I just say it?*

*I'm sorry.*

Like water trickling over her toes,
Rising foam above her knees,
A sense of pride swells inside her,
Modern life a better life
Than all the lives lived before.
But, for all the interactions,

All the easy words thrown and borrowed,
All the voices sounding separate notes,
Life seems, at times, a soliloquy.


Her mother says goodbye.
She looks at the people around her and wonders:
*Is there anything else to search for?*


Moving away from what she sought,
Coming closer to what she needs,
She feels she's always searching,
Her world expanding silently,
Hidden scaffolds and cranes,
Hidden workers, even,
Across the globe.
She sees pages
Sliding out of every window,
Drifting through the fumes,
Between the wires and road signs,
Over cliffs, above the sea,
Pushed along like wandering birds.
Dipping under a bridge, they rise
Above the jagged teeth of Sydney Opera House,
Floating through open windows
Ten floors up.


Her path is blocked.
She pushes and prods,
Afraid to stop.
She sees another window,
Full of books with alluring titles
And covers designed for intrigue.
She looks inside, opens one,
Finds comfort in lines and curves,
Dots, spaces, all their sounds,

The things they represent
And all the feelings they produce
As she moves down the page:

*'I will wake one day and walk away*
*Through fields beyond the touch of hands.*
*Concrete huddled at a distance,*
*My city lights will shine above.*
*I will tread on snapping twigs,*
*On yielding moss.*
*The world will speak in steps and calls.*
*Time measured in shades of blue,*
*Hair will scale down my back.*
*I'll wipe myself with grass.*
*My jaw will disappear like the undergrowth.*
*Food will run, jump*
*Or seek the sun,*
*No traffic light to clip my flight.*
*I will read no book, play no guitar.*
*I will not be online, not be aware*
*Of the latest trends.*
*I will see no pretty face.*
*I'll see poetry everywhere.'*

She closes it,
Looks around,
And all she's known is a shadow
Thrown against a wall,
Flickering by firelight,
But she's been chained,
Unable to see the flames.

Now the path is clear,
She returns to her search.
But in a moment reflects:

*What's missing from my life?*
*I'm interesting, attractive.*
*I have lots of friends.*
*There's nothing wrong*
*With living this way.*
*Who lives without symbols?*
*We all have a stage, a bedroom press*
*To publish our thoughts.*
*We are the age of the individual*
*Attached.*

*Two minutes hate.*

*Two minutes love.*

*I'm happy.*

One message received
Offers bigger breasts.
But she's found what she wants.
She enters sixteen digits,
Her personal details,
And clicks to pay.

Another window offers discussion.
All the familiar, faceless names,
The same design,
So many things,
Seem, to her, like a café.
She closes the window,
Slams down the screen
And unfurls the bed clothes.

She is offline.

## Out of Fashion

*The bobbish burdalane shalt gowl*
*To see the coddleshell a cumberground.*

Every word with its season, its
Own peculiar taste,
Changes shape
As it washes through a generation.
Meaning can't be fastened, it
Hangs like a scarf
Ready to unravel.

We wear our words like colours,
Choose our favourites, change
According to company,
Advertise identity
In phrase and tone.

They're thoughts let loose, unwrapped,
Frayed to threads until they pass.
The dodo drew its last breath
At the hands of men,
Revived by a child's mouth.

Will 'cool' be cold in fifty years?

Centuries from now,
No-one will understand my words,
Which might be best.
I'll be the enigmatic genius
Who said:

*It's been some time*
*Since I've heard the phrase*
*'Having it off'.*

# Roulette
## Caron Mc Carthy

Paul checked the odds. One more horse and he was home free. 7/2 favourite. Not great, a safe bet. Just what he needed to collect on the rest. He pressed the button. Twist of Fate, 7/2, grand down.

'Go for it,' he thought. 'You never know your luck.'

He pressed OK.

Chris saw Paul pressing the button in the racing computer section of the casino.

'He's on a roll, that fucker. He's loaded.' Chris eyed his own chips. Five hundred dollars left. 'That won't get me far.'

'Lucky 32 again, sir?'

The croupier hauled in the chips from the last play.

'Is it on the house?'

'Afraid not, sir. Place your bets, ladies and gentlemen.'

Chris split his chips and put two hundred and fifty dollars on number 32.

'Roll it there, Collette.'

'Sorry, sir.'

'Never mind. Irish joke. Just spin the bloody thing, will you?'

The young girl at the other end of the table had won twice in the last three plays on number 14. Chris felt that his luck had run out.

Spin. Little white ball. Clickity click, clack.

'Black 17.'

The croupier raked in the proceeds for the 'house'.

'Shit.'

The horses lined up at the post. They're off.

'Come on. Come on, ya bastard.'

'Twist of Fate leads by a length. Jason's Creek is closing the gap. As they round the bend, it's Twist of Fate, still the leader. Can he hold it? Jason's Creek is closing in fast, but as they pass the post, it's Twist of Fate that wins this year's Kentucky Derby.'

'Yes!'

'Are we going again, sir?'

'Just a minute. I'll be back.'

Chris took the rest of his chips from the table and headed towards the racing section. Paul stood up from his computer.

'Chris, are you ready to go? Let's have a drink before we head up to the room. It's on me. I'd a bit of luck there in the last race.'

'Paul, I need a grand. I'm out.'

'Tough luck. Didn't do so well on that wheel, did you? I told you the horses were a better bet.'

'Come on, I need it. Just a few more spins. I know I'll get it soon.'

'You're crazy. You'll never get it. Let's just cut our losses and split. We have enough for the next few days.'

'Wanker, come on. You made some tonight. Give me a grand.'

'You know the deal. We said five thousand dollars each, and to leave it at that. Hard luck if you spun yours into the sewer.'

Chris took a piece of paper from his jacket pocket.

'See this?'

Paul looked down at the paper.

'Room 1673.'

'That's not our room.'

'I know. It's his.'

Chris pointed across the casino. A fat balding man, in a grey suit had taken a seat at the roulette wheel.

'Who the fuck is he?'

'You wait and see. Are you going to give me that grand or not?'

'Chris, we made a deal.'

'No. You made a deal. Fuck you.'

Paul watched as Chris turned away from him.

'No, Chris. Don't. Please.'

Chris was already gone. He had given the signal and was heading towards the elevator. The fat man called his chips and followed him. Paul sat in the bar area. Double vodka in front of him. He twisted the gold band on his finger until it pinched his skin.

'Another one, sir?'

The blonde behind the bar stood smiling at him.

'Yeah, give me all that you have.'

The blonde winked at Paul.

'Would you like anything else with the vodka, sir?'

'More ice.'


The elevator door opened half an hour later. Chris looked satisfied.

'Five hundred dollars on number 32.'

'Yes, sir.'

The ball popped along the numbers and settled in a black slot.

'Number 25 has it.'

A woman who looked Hispanic started jumping up and down at the other end of the table.

'I won! Gano! Carlos, gano!'

Carlos stood beside her with a smug look on his face.

'Bueno. Bueno chica.'

Paul looked over at Chris. He'd his back turned to him. Another five hundred dollars went on number 32.

'How could he? This was meant to be our wedding night. All the way to Vegas from Dublin. Just to make it legal. How could he?'

'Another one, sir?'

The blonde was back, still smiling. Paul wondered if cosmetic surgery had advanced to the point of creating the permanent smile.

'Not this time, darling. I'm well chilled.'

She looked at him as if he had said, 'Mickey Mouse had just died in an asylum like a raging lunatic.' A momentary glitch. She recharged the smile for the next suit that sat in Paul's seat.

'Room 1014, please.'

Paul took his key from the reception desk. He looked over at the roulette table one last time as the elevator door shut. Chris was talking to the Mexican couple. He was gesticulating flamboyantly as he spoke. His gold ring shone on his finger under the casino lights.

The room had been cleaned since they had left it that morning. The coffee tray was replenished. Extra sugar. The bed was made. Fresh towels. Paul took a small packet from the pocket of his jeans. Cut a line and scooped it up in Vegas style with a hundred dollar bill. Stripped to his underpants, he rolled back the crisp white sheets on the bed. He was careful not to loosen the part that the maid had carefully tucked in at the side as he climbed into the bed. He put the knife under his pillow and waited.

## Winter Wonderland
### David O' Doherty

*Sleigh bells ring, are you listening?*

Carol singers in Santa hats huddled together in the cold outside The People's Park. The youngest caroller, sporting reindeer antlers, shook a collection bucket as passers-by scurried past the rusting black gates.

*In the lane, snow is glistening.*

Beyond the gates, for one week only, the city centre green space had been transformed into a Winter Wonderland designed to delight children and grown-ups alike. Rickety old benches, with wobbly planks and obscene graffiti, had been draped with green and red throws. Leafless trees that surrounded the perimeter now sparkled under a thousand red and white fairy lights.

*A beautiful sight, we're happy tonight.*

Special-brew-soaked winos — the park's usual clientele — had been chased off. In their place a magnificent old-fashioned golden carousel, with gold lamé lettering and ceramic horses lit up by flashing white lights, took pride of place. Further left, a large snow machine stood draped in silver tinsel as it spewed chalky flakes over revellers.

*Walking in a winter wonderland.*

Impressed by the transformation, Billy Murphy stopped by the carol singers to take it all in.

'What do you think Adam?'

'It's brilliant.'

Billy tossed a euro to the carollers and smiled down at his six-year-old son. At the entrance a jolly man in a snowman costume took their tickets and stamped their hands. Stepping through the gates, they splashed past the sludgy mixture of stagnant water and mulched leaves to the next checkpoint, where a friendly elf frisked them and searched Adam's backpack before waving them through to Winter Wonderland with a smile.

'Wow!'

Adam's attention was immediately caught by the brightly coloured candyfloss stall.

'Can we get some Dad?'

'Sure.'

Billy grinned his consent. As they crossed the path, Billy spotted his Aunt Maura wrapped in her brown winter coat. A nod of recognition passed between them. The candyfloss vendor, a burly man in an undersized elf hat, greeted father and son before producing a small mountain of red sugar.

'Isn't that stuff usually pink?'

'Ah sure, festive spirit an' all that.'

He handed it over. Adam attacked the snack with relish.

'C'mere boy,' the burly elf grabbed Billy's wrist. 'Have ya tried the Belgian chocolate stall yet?'

'No.'

'They're to die for. It's me cousin's stall. Tell him I sent ya — he'll be sure to share the good stuff.'

'Cheers.'

Turning back towards the swelling crowd, Billy craned his neck up to the darkening night sky and inhaled. The tempting aroma of baked goods, freshly ground coffee and spit-roasted hog wafted from under the eaves of food stalls. A pleasant change from the stale urine and pigeon droppings that usually graced this spot. The council had done a wonderful clean-up job. This was a place he could be proud to bring Adam.

Excited faces, buried under layers of insulation, waddled up and down the temporary plastic paths like contented penguins. Some made their way outside to inspect the artisan craft exhibition in the specially erected marquee, while others queued by the bright lights of the carousel. More still gathered by the foot of the makeshift wooden stage that had been erected next to the imposing ash tree at the centre of the park, in anticipation of Santa's imminent arrival. Billy gazed at Adam, who had grown a sticky red beard. It was finally beginning to feel like Christmas.

'Ah Billy! Merry Christmas! How's it goin' boy?'

Billy turned around to be greeted by his neighbour Tim O'Regan, a hulk of a man whose handshake could shatter diamonds.

'Merry Christmas Tim. On duty?'

Tim patted down the lapels of his sergeant's uniform and winked at Adam.

'I'm always on duty. You know me boy, a one-man-crime-fighting machine.' His considerable belly heaved beneath his luminous jacket as he chuckled. 'It's good to see you out and about again.'

'It's been a tough few months,' said Billy. 'But tonight's a very special occasion. We wouldn't miss it for anything.' He pulled Adam towards him. 'Sure we wouldn't, Adam?'

'Yeah.'

'Good lad.'

Tim clasped both hands behind his back and surveyed the scene as more families made their way to the stage.

'We've got a fine crowd for it. I'm sure I saw your parents earlier.' Tim coughed into his hand. 'You always worry about numbers when you try something new. Those protestors earlier didn't do much for us. But, by Jaysus, we've dealt with that now. If we can keep this up for the week I've no doubt we'll be back next year.'

Tim shot a glob of green phlegm to the ground.

'Jaysus. Feels like there's a box of frogs down the back of me larynx. Sue's at me to wear a scarf, but sure, I'm always telling her they're only for Bangardas.'

Wiping his mouth, Tim noticed the red and green tartan number nestling under Billy's mournful visage.

'Although that's a fairly snazzy one you're sporting there.'

'Grace knitted it for me. She gave it to me the week before she passed.'

Tim leaned forward and patted Billy's shoulder.

'Ah sure, 'tis a fine scarf. I've always said I should wear mine more. God knows, it might do me good.'

Another wad of fluorescent phlegm bulleted from Tim's mouth. He smeared it into the grass with the sole of his shoe.

'Right lads. Must be on me rounds.' Tim rubbed his hands together. 'I think I'll try some of that Belgian hot chocolate to soften me cough. I've heard it's the business.'

Hand in pocket, he knelt down in front of Adam and pulled out ten euro.

'Here's a few bob to buy yourself something nice young man. And remember to keep an eye out for Santa.' With a smile and a cough, he was on his way.

Photo points offering souvenir snaps with assorted elves, reindeer and snowmen dotted the park. A memento of the occasion would be nice. Billy took Adam's hand.

'What d'ya fancy son?'

'A reindeer.'

'How about Rudolph?'

Billy pointed to the left, where a dour man in a reindeer costume and bulbous red nose sat smoking.

'Yeah!'

Rudolph stubbed out his cigarette and posed with the pair in front of a backdrop of snowy meadows.

'Are you really Rudolph?' asked Adam, as Billy paid the photographer.

'Sure am.'

Rudolph grimaced and lit another cigarette.

'What's it like working with Santa?'

'Uh ...'

A loud crackle emanated from Rudolph's waist.

'Hotel Oscar, Hotel Oscar, Hotel Oscar. Come in. Over.'

'Hotel Oscar, Hotel Oscar, Hotel Oscar here. Over.'

'Operation Sierra Alpha November Tango Alpha commencing. Over.'

'Copy that. Over and out.'

Rudolph clicked off his walkie-talkie, reached under the table and slipped into a Garda hi-visibility jacket.

'This is your chance to meet him lad. Santa's coming into the park now. You won't want to miss this.' Smoke steamed through Rudolph's nostrils as he took one last drag. 'Now, if you'll excuse me I've got work to do.'

Adam grabbed his father's hand and led him through the crowd that now swept towards the rear entrance. Santa was about to arrive. Smiling parents led shiny-eyed children. Anticipation built as they reached the rear gates that faced out onto a looming gothic building. Adam peered up in wonder at the towering edifice that housed the local brewery.

Dominated by horizontal black stucco on white walls and a large central arch, the brewery possessed an intimidating quality. A gargantuan black and white clock hung over the main entrance, its wrought iron hands sweeping silently around black Roman numerals. Fully lit, the brewery assumed a nightmarish hue. It was a place that a young Billy had always dreaded passing at night, convinced that Freddy Kruger or Michael Myers was about to leap out from behind the railings.

Now the macabre atmosphere was offset by rows of white fairy lights that hung in parallel rows in the yard. The crowd surged forward as they spotted movement at the brewery entrance. The decaying oak doors swung open. Santa, accompanied by Sergeant Tim.

O' Regan emerged and saluted the crowd before entering the back of a waiting Garda car.

Children cheered and waved as the car made the short journey across the road. Billy hoisted Adam up on his shoulders for a better view. The carollers, who had moved from the front gate, struck up to soundtrack the moment.

*Later on, we'll conspire.*

The car trundled by the park's famous Bruised Heart fountain as it crawled towards the stage. Water gushed through aortas and pulmonary arteries. Dozens of eager revellers beat the car, pressing their hands and faces onto the glass, straining for a glimpse of Santa.

*As we dream by the fire.*

Adam peered through the window as Santa passed by. He looked intimidated by the crowd, his hands held together close to his chest, his neck tucked into his beard. It was almost as if he wanted to disappear.

*To face unafraid.*

'What's wrong with Santa, Dad? He doesn't look happy.'

'That's what happens when everyone wants a piece of you son. Don't worry. I'm sure he'll be fine.'

*The plans that we've made.*

The car finally came to a halt. Sergeant Tim stepped from the passenger seat and doffed his cap at the crowd. A huge cheer went up as the Sergeant opened the door, allowing Santa set foot on the park. Christmas had arrived. The Sergeant took Santa by the elbow and led him onto a large wooden chair at the centre of the stage.

*Walking in a winter wonderland.*

Rudolph came on stage with two elves, clutching large cloth bags full of gift-wrapped presents. Red parcels for girls were placed to Santa's left, silver boys' parcels to the right. Sergeant Tim approached the microphone and held out his hands to request silence from the feverish throng.

'Ladies and gentlemen, boys and girls, on behalf of the City Council and An Garda Siochána, I would like to welcome you to the first night of the first-ever People's Park Winter Wonderland Festival. Before I begin I would like to take this opportunity to thank you all for coming tonight. It is especially encouraging to see so many young families lending their support to what we hope will become an annual event.'

Billy and Adam, who had moved to a vantage point three or four rows back, to the left of the giant Ash, joined in the applause. Glancing down at his son, Billy felt his fingers tingling with anticipation and thought of Grace. He hoped that she was watching.

'I'm sure you're all eager to get on with the festivities, so I won't keep you long. First on the itinerary is the distribution of presents by Santa to all the children who have been good this year. I hope you've all been good! Ho, ho! After meeting Santa, the children will enjoy a Christmas party at the brewery under the care of Santa's little helpers.'

The Sergeant paused to disgorge the contents of his oesophagus.

'This will be followed by a meet-and-greet session for selected adult ticketholders. Once this is finished, we'll have the main event.'

A huge cheer. Billy bit his lip and cast his eyes to the ground.

'Yes, I know we've all been looking forward to it,' chuckled the Sergeant. 'Once the stage is cleared we'll be entertained late into the night by the festive musical stylings of Peter Pendlbury & The Mince Pies. I hope you all have a wonderful evening.'

Sergeant Tim took a step back from the microphone and threw his arms in the air.

'Let the festivities begin!'

The congregation cheered and stomped their feet. Billy knelt down to face his son.

'How're you feeling?'

'Good.'

'Are you ready to see Santa?'

'Yes.'

'And you know what to do?'

'Take the present, smile for the photo and say thank you.'

'That's all. No more than that. Remember what we talked about.'

'Okay.'

'Good lad,' Billy placed his hand on Adam's shoulder. 'Your mother would be proud.'

'Thanks Dad.'

Two snowmen had pushed the crowd back to clear a makeshift path to the stage. Dozens of young boys and girls were already waiting their turn to meet Santa. Billy pushed Adam out to join in the queue.

Despite having hundreds to get through, Santa, Rudolph and his helpers made steady progress. Within ten minutes Adam was at the head of the queue, his excitement mounting with every child that passed clutching large parcels to their chest.

Finally it was Adam's turn. Ushered forward by the snowmen, he made his way to the stage and looked up into Santa's eyes. He didn't look like he did on TV. The Santa Adam knew was a large, jolly man, whose big belly strained against his suit. This Santa was thin and scruffy. His red and white costume sat limp around his shoulders. Giant bags hung from under his mournful eyes, and his fluffy white beard did little to conceal the red sores and scratches that marked his face.

Santa beckoned Adam onto his lap with long, nicotine-stained fingers. Adam obeyed and perched as best he could on his bony lap.

'Ho, ho, ho! What's your name son?'

'Adam. Adam Murphy.'

Santa flinched. Adam could feel hot cigarette breath on the back of his head. Rudolph poked Santa in the ribs with a baton, prompting him to continue.

'Have you been a good boy Adam?'

'I have.'

Santa was trembling.

'And what do you want Santa to bring you for Christmas?'

Adam wanted to ask Santa if he was alright, but held back, not wanting to upset his Dad.

'A new bike, a PlayStation game and a surprise.'

'Well, let's see what I have in my sack.'

An elf handed Santa a silver parcel for Adam. Smile. Flashbulb. Exit.

As he left the stage, Adam glanced back at Santa, whose body shuddered as he raised his right arm to shield his face.

Billy grabbed his son upon his return.

'What did he say to you?'

'Nothing really. Just asked what I wanted for Christmas.'

'That's all?'

'Yeah, he did get a bit funny though.'

'In what way?'

'He got all shaky when I told him my name.'

'Never mind,' Billy rubbed his son's shoulder. 'I expect he's just tired from having to visit so many children around the world. Why don't you open your present?'

Adam ripped open the silver paper. Within lay a friction-powered speedboat, a snowman key ring and a novelty mobile phone that squirted water at the unsuspecting.

'Wow!' Adam was pleased with his haul. 'That phone looks just like Mom's.'

'It certainly does.' Billy gave a tight smile.

Off to his right, snowmen and elves marshalled a growing group of children, who compared presents and giggled in anticipation of the soft drinks and sweets to come.

'Are you ready for the party?'

'Yeah!' Adam punched the air, 'I hope they have nachos!'

'I bet they do.'

Billy took Adam by the hand and led him over towards the other children. Adam waved and brandished his phone at cousins further up the queue.

'Now be good and enjoy yourself. I'll be over to collect you later.'

'I will, Dad.'

Billy kissed his son on the cheek and watched as the snowmen led him away to the brewery.

Once all minors had been removed, the park underwent a rapid transformation. The red and white fairy lights were dimmed. The music was cut. Candles were placed and lit around the stage. Two giant spotlights clicked into life; one on Santa's chair onstage, the other on the giant ash tree. Santa shielded his eyes as Rudolph pushed him under the first spot.

Sergeant Tim ambled to the microphone clutching a glass of mulled wine.

'Time to get down to business, folks. Could I please call on all members and friends of the Murphy family to step forward?'

Billy retreated through a mass of expectant bodies and watched through the silent gloom as the crowd parted in two to form a walkway to the stage. Scores of familiar faces emerged from the gloaming to form a line facing directly towards Santa. A reindeer passed along the line, distributing and lighting ceremonial candles.

One by one they went forward: Grace's sister, her mother, other family members and friends. They were followed by his family, his parents and other family members including Aunt Maura. Each approached Santa in turn, exchanged some brief words, and turned to take their place on the edge of the stage.

Within minutes the stage had filled with dozens who had known and loved Grace. Each stood, head bowed, candle clutched to their chest.

'Very impressive, I must say.'

Sergeant Tim gave the baleful looking group a thumbs up.

'Right. Could Billy Murphy please join us on stage?'

Billy stepped forward from the shadows. Hundreds of pairs of expectant eyes scrutinized his every move. He advanced into the walkway. Arms patted him across the back and shoulder. Voices shouted words of encouragement. Blinking in the darkness, he strained, without success, to indentify the faces of his supporters. Each step lasted forever. Beads of sweat trickled down his back. An awful self-consciousness gripped his body. He swallowed hard and continued to shuffle forward towards the stage. Finally, he reached the edge of the stage. It was his turn to meet Santa. Suddenly, all the lights went out.

Billy blinked, adjusting his eyes to a park illuminated only by candlelight. Sergeant Tim came to meet him at the edge of the stage. Presenting him with a large candle, he lit it and guided him towards Santa. No sound echoed through the park save the hum of traffic from the road outside.

'Stay calm, Billy. I'm here if you need me.'

The Sergeant offered him a reassuring pat on the back.

Santa's mouth trembled as Billy approached. His hands were cuffed together, and his beard had been removed, exposing his badly cut face. Billy laid his candle to the side and stared into his eyes. He couldn't have been more than twenty-five.

'Do you know who I am?'

Santa nodded.

'You met my boy earlier. He seemed to like his present.'

Santa emitted a little squeak.

'Funny thing is,' Billy removed his jacket, 'he got a toy phone as part of his parcel.'

'I'm sorry.'

'Yeah, looked just like the one you killed my wife for.'

Billy rolled up the sleeves of his sweatshirt and punched Santa hard in the gut. Then he did it again, and again, and again.

'Ironic, isn't it?'

Sergeant Tim stepped in.

'That's enough, Billy.'

He held a length of rope in his left hand.

'It's time to finish this.'

Rudolph took the rope from the Sergeant and spent several minutes manipulating it into a noose. Once finished, he stepped into the spotlight and raised the noose above his head with a flourish. The mob responded with a deafening cheer that was sustained as Rudolph hung the noose from a branch of the great ash. On stage, an elf brought the PA system to life. A muzak version of Silent Night wafted across the park, prompting sections of the crowd to sing along.

Candle in hand, Billy looked on as Sergeant Tim dragged Santa towards the chair that stood waiting in the spotlight beneath the ash. Santa kicked and screamed in a desperate bid for survival.

'Don't do this! Please! I only wanted her phone ... I didn't mean to hurt her.'

'Shut it.'

'Please! It was an accident! Show some mercy!'

'I said, shut it!'

Sergeant Tim swung his elbow through the air and into Santa's head, knocking him unconscious. The mob bayed their approval. Santa's prone body was raised onto the chair and the noose wrapped around his neck. After giving the rope several tugs to ensure tightness the Sergeant nodded at Rudolph and returned to the stage.

Rudolph produced a vial of holy water and a small leather notebook. Pacing around the condemned, Rudolph sprinkled holy water on his clothes and on the surrounding ground.

Cheers and shouts mingled with the continued chanting of Silent Night. Dozens held camcorders and camera phones over their heads as they waited for the moment of impact. Rudolph opened his notebook, licked his finger to turn the page and cleared his throat. He spoke in a hushed, solemn tone.

'Through this holy anointing may the Lord in his love and mercy help you with the grace of the Holy Spirit.'

Sergeant Tim raised his glass to Santa and gulped back a mouthful of mulled wine. Moving towards Santa, Rudolph placed his hands on his head.

'May the Lord who frees you from sin save you and raise you up.'

Billy stood centre stage, head bowed, clutching his candle.

'Amen.'

Rudolph kicked the chair out from under Santa. The mob roared as Santa's legs fell forward and his neck snapped. Everyone on stage, bar Billy, blew out their candles in unison, plunging the park into darkness. Whoops and whistles reverberated off the walls, legs stomped against the ground. Billy closed his eyes and thought of Grace.

The din reached a frenzied pitch as the lights returned. Sergeant Tim stood tall before the crowd, arms outstretched, soaking up the adulation. Once the applause died down, he approached the microphone.

'That's it for tonight folks. Thanks so much for coming along. We've had to endure some negative publicity, but tonight's turnout demonstrates the tremendous level of support we've received for this initiative.'

A few isolated whoops. The Sergeant took his reading glasses from his breast pocket and unfolded a piece of paper.

'I've been asked to remind you that tickets are still available for the rest of this week's Winter Wonderland events. Please check our website for further details. Family discounts are available. Thank you again for your support, and a special thank you to all members of the Murphy family.'

The Sergeant paused to allow a lingering round of applause.

'The night is still young, folks, and I hope you'll all stay to enjoy the musical stylings of Peter Pendlbury and The Mince Pies. I'll see you tomorrow night.'

Sergeant Tim departed with a wave. As the band began to set up Billy remained on stage, surrounded by family and friends. The candle still burned in his hands. In his pocket he could feel his phone vibrating. Smiling, he blew out the candle and answered his son's call.

# The School Bag
## Caron Mc Carthy

The old woman's eyes flickered when she heard the front door click open. The silence was disturbed by the familiar sound of high heels on the tiled hall floor.

"Is that you, Cliona?"

"It's only me, Gran," the young woman responded as she entered her grandmother's room.

"I can only stay a minute. I've so much to do today and the day's nearly gone already. I just dropped in to make sure you were alright".

"Come in, come in, sit down for a minute. Isn't it lovely to see you? How's little Clare?"

The old woman maneuvered herself in her bed to receive her visitor.

"Oh, she's fine. I had to leave her into Breda for a couple of hours to get into town. Would you believe it, Joe wouldn't even take her for a while and he knows how much I have to do. He's gone off to some football match. Mind you, Breda owes me. I'd her lot for the whole day last week. How are you, anyway Gran?"

Cliona sat on the side of her grandmother's bed and reached into her bag for her cigarettes. She didn't wait for the old woman's reply.

"I don't believe it, I've no light. Gran, do you have a light?"

"On the mantelpiece there in front of you."

The old woman took note of her granddaughter's agitated state.

"All that rushing around will do you no good, you know. Rest for a while and draw your breath."

Cliona lit her cigarette, took a long drag on it and stared straight ahead into the empty fire grate.

"Do you want me to light a fire for you while I'm here? Are you cold?"

"No, I'm grand for the time being. Tell me, dear, what is your big hurry today?"

Cliona took a few short drags out of the end of her cigarette and cast the butt in the direction of the fireplace.

"It's Clare. She's starting school on Monday and I have to get her a school bag. I thought I told you that last week. And as usual, I've left everything to the last minute. That town will be chaotic on a Saturday. Queues everywhere, and you can never get what you want. I'll tell you what, Gran, I'll make us a quick cup of tea before I head off. Would you like that?"

"Do, do, that would be nice."

Cliona left the room.

The old woman lay back on her pillow and listened in silence to the domestic sounds coming from the kitchen.
After a short while Cliona placed two mugs of tea on her grandmother's bedside table.

"A lovely hot cup of tea, Gran. Now, isn't that nice?"

"Lovely, lovely."

The old woman leaned over to take a sip of her tea. Cliona lit another cigarette. Finished it. Gathered her bag, cigarettes and her grandmother's lighter.

"You'll be alright for a while so, Gran. I'd better make a move."

She looked down into her grandmother's teary eyes and felt a pang of pity.

"I'll call into you again on my way home, alright."

"Will you sit back down there for a minute and rest? You haven't even finished your tea. Besides, I want to tell you a little story."

"What? Are you joking? Have you been listened to a word I've said? I haven't the time for stories. You are really losing it lately, I told you I'm in a hurry. This is it. Isn't it? This is the way old people go when they're near the end." The old woman's expression did not change.

"Oh but I have been listening and it's you that has the time. Now sit down there for a minute like a good girl." Cliona threw her arms in the air and stared at her grandmother.

"It might be worth your while," the old woman added as she lowered her head and looked up at her granddaughter with that air of authority that comes with age and an astute mind.

Cliona knew that look well. It made her feel like a child again, being scolded for some misadventure or other. Her temper was disarmed almost immediately and she knew she was going to wait for the story, however long it took. Cliona sat back down.

"I suppose another few minutes won't make that much difference. I'll have one more cigarette, but then I really do have to go, Gran."

"That's better," the old voice said. "Now, I remember…"

'Here we go, this is going to be a long one,' Cliona thought as she sat anxiously thinking about her own situation, trying her best not to say anything else that she'd regret.

"Yes, go on, Gran, I'm listening."

"Well, when I was Clare's age, I had to go to school too, you know. Education is a very important thing, my dear." The old woman looked up at her granddaughter who was now starring straight ahead of her at the mantel piece with a look of resignation on her face and a cloud of smoke around her.

"I know, Gran, that is why I'm trying to get Clare ready for school."

"And you will, dear, and you will. Now, let me continue....

"I'm not saying anything."

Cliona blew a long line of smoke towards the fireplace.

"Yes, I remember it like it was only yesterday. We were all sitting at the kitchen table. My father was having his boiled egg, as usual, for breakfast when all of a sudden he announced to my mother,

'I'm taking Jane to town today.'

Well, my eyes lit up. He was a man of very few words, my father, but when he said something he meant it, and to go to town with him was always a treat. I was so excited. Before I knew it I was all buttoned up in my good wool coat and he was holding my hand going down the hill outside our house to town. I was skipping along to my fathers stride. He was such a big man, you know, or at least he seemed that way to me at the time."

Cliona turned her head to look at her grandmother and could see that she was lost in thought.

"Anyway, to make a long story short.."

Cliona couldn't resist a half smile.


"...Didn't he stop, all of a sudden? He looked down at me and with a half wink he directed his head towards an open door,

'We'll pop in here for a minute.'

I looked and all I could see was darkness inside but by then he had already stooped his head and entered, dragging me behind him. There was a huge counter made of wood right inside the door and there was a funny smell. My father's elbow was resting on the counter and he was talking to someone but he was still looking at me. He started to laugh when I reached my two hands as high as I could to the top of the counter and tried to lift myself up to see who he was talking to, scuffing my good shoes against the wood at the same time.

'We'd better let her in on the action,' my father said as he lifted me up onto the counter to view my surroundings.

'You'd better,' the other man joked as my legs dangled over the side. The two of them smiled and winked at each other and I was happy just to be with them."

Cliona lit another cigarette and looked at the clock on the mantle piece.

"...So, there I was in this dark room with a funny smell. There was a funny little man inside the counter, I remember he was wearing one of those shirts that you call 'grandaddy shirts' today and it didn't look very clean but he had the brightest sparkly eyes. He leaned over to me and said 'so this is the little one that's starting school, is it?'

'It is,' my father replied.

'And what age is she now?' the little man said looking at me.

'She'll be four soon.'

'Gosh, doesn't time fly.'

Then the little man looked straight at me and said.

'Tell me this, little one, what's your name?'

'Jane,' I said.

'Well, Jane, my name is Paddy, 'and he put out his hand to me.

'Say hello to Paddy,' my father interrupted.

'Hello, Paddy,' I said and I shook his hand. I remember thinking it felt like bones.

'And come here to me, Jane, I hear you'll be needing a new schoolbag for your big day?'

'I will. Daddy said we were going to go to town today for one.'

'Well, Jane, there'll be no need for that because Paddy here knows where there's a very special schoolbag, just for you.'

'You do?'

'I do. You just leave that to Paddy.'

Paddy's eyes sparkled in the half-light. They made me smile back at him. I looked over at my father and he was smiling at me. He lifted me off the counter then and said it was time I got home to my mother."

Cliona looked at her grandmother who was now reclining back in her bed with a cheerful, almost youthful look in her eye. She could tell that she was enjoying her reverie.

"Well, gran did you get your bag?"

"I did, wait until I tell you. Didn't we go back down to Paddy's a few days later…"

"If you don't tell me soon, Clare won't get her bag at all."

"…As I was saying, we went back to the shop. This time my father lifted me straight up onto the counter. The same little man, Paddy, was still there. It was like as if he'd never left and he had the same shirt on. This time he greeted me first or at least I thought so.

'Jane,' he said, he'd remembered my name, 'just the girl I want to see. I've got something for you.' And with that he disappeared into the darkness at the back of the shop. He reappeared holding the most beautiful schoolbag I'd ever seen, or was ever to see again.

'Now Jane, didn't I tell you Paddy'd have a special bag for you when you came back. Paddy won't let you down.' That's what he said.

I couldn't take my eyes off the bag. It was leather, you know, a white leather with lovely black stitching around the edge and two shiny black leather straps at the back that went around my shoulders and tied at the front with a shiny metal clasp.

'Let's try it on for size,' then he said gleaming at me. He was as happy as I was. I tried it on and it was perfect. It smelt like Paddy's shop.

'Don't you look clever with your new schoolbag,' my father said as he looked at me proudly 'she won't talk to us at all now, Paddy' he joked and they both laughed. 'Say thank you to Paddy, Jane, for such a lovely bag.'

'Thank you, thank you Paddy,' I said. 'It's beautiful, it's the best bag ever.'

Then Paddy whispered in my ear,

'Jane, do you not want to open it and see what's inside?'

I took the bag off my shoulders and released the little black strap that fastened it at the front. Inside there was a big pocket and a small pocket to the front. There was a little copybook in the big pocket and two red pencils in the small pocket.

'That'll get her started nicely,' my father said.

'Thank you, Paddy.' I smiled up at him.

'That's not all that's in it, Jane. There's something else in there too.'

'What?' I said with curiosity.

'A little man,' he said.

'Where? I don't see any little man. Where is he?'

I looked back into the bag and searched all the pockets. Then back at Paddy with my mouth open.

'I don't see him, Paddy, I kept saying.'"

The old women chuckled in the bed.

"Aren't children so innocent at that age, Cliona."

Cliona smiled at her grandmother and remained silent.

"'A little man,' he said. He was so serious.

'Yes, a little man, oh he's in there all right, but you'll never see him. He's too smart. He disappears once you open the bag.'

I was looking at Paddy in amazement. He kept talking,

'Yes, but he can see you and he'll mind you, Jane, when you're in school and he'll even help you with your lessons if you ask him but don't tell anyone else about him. It'll be our little secret. He gets annoyed when other people know about him. He might even decide to move to another bag.'

'I won't, Paddy, I won't tell anyone about him. Then I thought for a minute and said, Paddy what's his name?'

I remember my father and Paddy started laughing when I asked that.

'Oh, I don't know, Jane, that's up to you to put a name on him, sure isn't he in your schoolbag.'

I looked over at my father for inspiration. He just smiled and said

'He's your little man, you name him.'

I looked back at Paddy.

'Is it alright if I call him Paddy, after you?'

'Well, now, wouldn't that be an honour. Of course you can, Jane.'

I couldn't wait to take Paddy and my new schoolbag to school the following week."

"That's a lovely story, Gran."

"It's more than a story, Cliona. You see, I still have it."

"What? The bag? Sure that must have been eighty years ago. How could you still have it for so long?"

"Well, we took care of things in our day. Not like your generation that throw things away like tissues."

"Can I see it?"

"That's the whole point. I want you to see it. Take out my old suitcase in that press over there."

Cliona looked at the clock on the mantle piece.

"It's getting late. I'll get it for you when I get back. I really must go."

"Just do as I say, like a good girl, bring it out here to me."

Cliona threw her hands in the air in exasperation and did what she was told.

"That's better," she could hear her grandmother say in the background as she struggled with the old brown battered case in the press.

"Open it," her grandmother ordered quietly.

Cliona opened it and all she could see inside were old rolled up parchments and some photographs, photographs of her grandmother receiving her degrees.

"Well, where is it then? All I see is papers and stuff."

"Underneath the lining. You'll have to get a scissors."

Cliona got a scissors from the kitchen and opened the lining of the suitcase carefully. She reached in and took out an old paper bag.

"Is this it?"

"Bring it over her to me."

Cliona handed her grandmother the paper bag. The old woman took the paper off it. Cliona couldn't help staring at the little white leather bag.

"It's beautiful, Gran. Just like new."

The old woman held the bag close to her face and smelt it.

"It still smells the same, just like Paddy's shop."

She looked up at her granddaughter and smiled. "Now why don't you run along and get Clare and we'll introduce her to little Paddy?"

Cliona stood looking at her grandmother with her mouth open.

"Oh, Gran, she'll love it."

"I know she will," the old woman said, still looking at the little leather bag in her hands.

*"I know she will."*

Caron Mc Carthy

## The Perfect Cup of Tea
### Trevor Conway

Lately, I've been obsessing over tea. I know it sounds strange, but it's taken me thirty-five years to realise it isn't easy. If I counted all the bad cups I've had over the years, they'd outnumber the good cups by about 4/1. All these years, I've been content to drink sub-standard tea. The only word I can think of to describe it is 'rusty'. It has an orange tinge, a dead taste. Awful.

This naturally leads me to the question: what is it that makes a perfect cup of tea? Well, I know the colour: browny-beige. I've decided it depends mainly on two factors: the strength of the tea (a direct result of the squeezing action) and the amount of milk added. The teabag should be squeezed for six seconds against the bottom of the mug — just a gentle squeeze. I prefer to add the milk before squeezing; it allows for the sight of brown swirling through the white liquid, turning it beige.

Teapots are a whole different story. Brewing tea is a guaranteed good result, but it takes a while. I couldn't do it; it'd feel like cheating. Besides, I have no one else to make tea for. It'd be pathetic, brewing a whole pot for myself.

These were my thoughts as a knock came on the door. It was my brother Andy. We get on okay, but we have very little in common. He's interested in football and cars. I'm more at home with films and books.

Anyway, we sat down in the kitchen. He flicked the switch on the kettle, as usual. I tried to look interested.

'We've got a great team this year. A few new young fellas. I think they benefit from playin' with someone like me, someone more experienced,' he began.

'You're probably right,' I replied.

'We're playin' the semi-final Saturday. You should come up an' have a look. Get outta the house. You'll enjoy it.'

*Don't patronise me. I can spend as much time as I like in the house. There's nothing wrong with it.*

I poured two cups of rusty tea.

'So, have you done anythin' about goin' on holidays?' he asked.

'No. Don't know if I'll bother goin' anywhere.'

'We're thinkin' of Portugal for the honeymoon. Simone's brother's got a free apartment over there.'

'Sounds nice.'

I just wasn't in the mood.

Our conversation was silenced for a moment as we both watched a little bird swoop down and land on a tree branch — a little tree, the only one I have in my garden. It was a robin. Stout little fellow. Big red beer-belly. He was looking at us through the window, I think, no more than ten feet away. It's hard to tell with birds — their eyes are on the side of their heads so they have to face away from what they're looking at. I can't help but feel it's a bit sly, somehow. It's a strange thing, the importance of eye contact. Most people feel offended if you stare at them. How do famous people cope with it? Models, especially, have to deal with it on a grand scale. A camera is worth a thousand eyes. Eye contact is a *very* serious thing in gorilla society. If you look the silverback in the eye you're likely never to do so again. You might as well have said, 'Your mother's a low-ranking chimpanzee'.

'Have you got any bread?' Andy asked.

'Yeah. It's up in that press,' I said.

He took two slices from the pack and tore them up into little pieces. He wetted them under the tap and placed each of them, one by one, out on the window sill. He stepped back and we watched — barely five feet away — as the bird swooped down on the window sill. He began to peck at the bread.

'Why are robins so friendly? Most birds are shy,' Andy asked.

I would have used the word 'timid'.

'I don't know. Strange, isn't it?'

I took out a packet of biscuits from the press. Digestives, the poor man's biscuit. I offered one to Andy. The cup wasn't big enough. He forced the biscuit into the cup, took it out and bit off the thin soggy strip at the bottom. Then he turned it around and dipped from the other side. When he'd finished eating it, he said something that really took me by surprise.

'Anyway, the reason I came over was to ask you somethin'.'

'Yeah?'

'Would you like to be my best man?'

I know it isn't strange for a groom to ask his brother to be his best man, but it *was* strange for Andy to ask *me*. I hadn't really thought about it, but I suppose I'd assumed he'd ask one of his friends. He's closer to them than he is to me. I was shocked. He realised it, too.

'Sure. I'd love to,' I told him.

I have to admit, on thinking it over later, I found it a bit daunting. I'd have to give a speech, make sure I didn't drink too much. I'd have to think of funny things to say; good jokes, not dry ones. Avoid clichés. I'd probably feel uncomfortable with the attention. All the same, I felt honoured. There was a certain raw emotion from that point on in the conversation. He didn't stay much longer.

When he left, I found myself thinking of him in a totally different way, almost as if he had matured a great deal. To be honest, I looked down on him, to a certain degree. Maybe I'm just jealous of him, being so outgoing, getting married when I'm not even in a relationship at all.

I took my obsession to new heights that evening: *Tayra ... TB ... Tbilisi ... Tchaikovsky ... Tea!*

It was an old book, one of a set of encyclopedias given to my parents years ago. They never really used them, so I took them with me when I moved out. I learned some interesting facts:

Tea is the most popular drink in more countries, more popular than any other beverage.

Ireland consumes the most tea per person — 1,600 cups per person in a year.

India grows the most tea per year.

There are three main kinds of tea: black, green and Oolong. (The difference is in the processing of the leaves.)

The earliest known mention of tea appeared in Chinese literature of about 350 AD.

Interesting, you ask. Well, it's interesting to me. But I don't see any information on how to make *good* tea, the *perfect* cup. I'll just keep trying, I suppose. I wonder if they'll serve good tea at the wedding reception.

## Statue
## Brid Buckley

It's a funny thing when you've all the time in the world to stand and think and keep very, very still. Things go slow, very, very slow, but if you listen carefully you can still make out the sound of your own heartbeat above the bustle of the crowd. You notice things more. I often think it's like those stories you hear of how, when someone goes blind, their other senses sharpen, only with me it's movement I've lost. I'm a mime, see. A dying breed of artist. I guess no one notices us nowadays as much as they used to. I remember when we would draw the crowds; our sketches would be in the newspapers, the applause would ring out so loud it took all I had in me to keep my face straight. A child would look up at me entranced, and if his gaze should falter for a moment, there I'd be when it was returned a half second later, in a different pose, and he'd howl with awe and delight.

No respect for the old arts these days; it's all about movement and speed, cheap jokes and cheap tricks, nothing's real anymore. See this guy next to me, this so-called magician, *he* gets all the laughs, their eyes, a few minutes from their busy schedules they couldn't spare me, and their money too. And what does he do? What grace or poise or patience does he possess? He can juggle a ball, something a mere monkey can do, and placate them with petty tricks, *plámas* them with false interest.

'So where you from, what's your story?' he drawls in his television accent.

Yet never a word does he offer me, only ever a cold critical stare as if I wasn't even there. Art these days is all about the viewer, what it can tell them about themselves, what lies they would like to hear to make themselves feel important. Nothing is heard about truth, about distance,

119

about something untouchable. And the stench off him! He comes in stinking of food and drink and sweat. It makes my head faint. And I each day immaculate, pristine, no crack in my makeup, no tear on my jacket. He's drawn these blasted pigeons too, with the smell off him. They've gotten bold enough to perch on *my* shoulder and I've to sit blood boiling, resigned not to dampen my professionalism by shooing them.

It wasn't always like this, mind you. I'll never forget the staring matches I used to have. My opponent always started out with the upper hand, trying to make me laugh with a pulled face or rude noise or a favourite joke, whereas all I had to fall back on was the power of my will. Just when my laughter would be at bursting point in my throat my opponent would surrender. The children loved it. Now they sail right past me with scarce a glance thrown my way, straight to that trickster. Why can't anyone see that he doesn't know the first thing about magic?

Only lately, the strangest thing, there's this girl, you see. She passes me every day, but unlike the others, she looks at me, she sees me, her steps slow with hesitance. The first few days I tried to awe her with a stony stare, a glower of intimidation. She returned my gaze, not with a stare of competition, but with her eyebrows slanted in compassion, and her chin tilted up in puzzlement. She'd just look at me, not saying anything, not asking anything of me but then suddenly she'd lower her eyes away from mine, embarrassed, and trail slowly away. She moves much slower than other people in every gesture that she makes. Always dressed in black, her clothes are strung ill-fitting over her body like cobwebs over a portrait. She gives the impression of being from another time and place except for the Galway School of Art's fresher bag she carries, slung awkwardly over one shoulder. I seem to have lost my power of will lately in her presence. No matter how hard I try, I cannot hold her gaze; my eyes dash to the floor, abashed. She has grown more willsome of late, stands closer to me, gazes at me for longer than before, sighs with the intimacy of one who is alone. I find myself thinking of her after she has left, each time wondering will she return, yet when she does I am stupefied, paralysed.

Hush, here she is. She walks right over to me. For the first time she says something.

'You are very beautiful,' she whispers in a voice made of shadows. 'May I draw you?'

I try to answer but it's only now I realise it's been so long since I've last spoken that I've lost the power of speech. I feel silly, inadequate now in all my grey makeup; I wish she could see my face underneath. As if hearing me, she touches my face softly. It does not give like human flesh but retains its expression, solid like stone. I want to tell her how it's been hard to hear my heartbeat lately. I want to tell her...

*Poetry*
*Jimi McDonnell*

## A to Z

Assertively, bravely, crazily
dance. Embrace feverishly
gymnastic hubris.

I jump knowing little matters
now only pirouettes, quick racing
steps that usurp vicariousness.

Why x-ray your zaniness?

## Ireland

Ireland I've been here too long but I'm not ready to leave.
Ireland 317.47 DR, July 6th, 2010.
I can't shut myself up.
Ireland when will you stop voting Fianna Fail.
You scratch my back and I'll punch you in the face.
Fuck this, I'm taking to the bed.
Send me a text but don't call me.
Ireland why can't you be honest?
When will you smile at yourself in the mirror?
I'm sick of your whinging.
When will you stop overcooking red meat?
Ireland the kingdom and the power and the glory is ours.
Surely we can sing our way out of this mess?
Colum McCann lives in New York and he's never coming
home.
Ireland I'm in no hurry.
I don't know if I know what I'm talking about.
Ireland we're watching each other die.
I sit at my desk and I want to fall asleep.
Why are you looking at me like that?
I refuse to say fair play to Westlife.
I won't confess to almighty anyone.
I have seen God in The Crane Bar, Galway.


Ireland did I ever tell you that I stole a bag of pine nuts
from Tesco?
Yes I said something!
Are you going to live your life by Joe Duffy?
I love Joe Duffy.
I listen to him every day.
His voice is chamomile laced with valium.
I put the show on when I'm alone in my car.

It's always about people being annoyed. They couldn't get
seats at Barbara Streisand.
    Why should they get a TV licence for their mobile
home? Everyone's annoyed but
      not me.
Sometimes I think I am Joe Duffy.
Good afternoon to me.


Argentina is calling me.
I don't even have the bus fare to Longford.
I should really do the H. Dip.
Previous experience includes working the night shift at a
Statoil in Tuam and singing
    Dean Martin over the tannoy. I have also installed an
air conditioner in a Jewish
      woman's apartment on East 56th Street.
I want to be a teacher, seriously.
My stated aim is to be president of St. Jarlath's even though
I'm no longer a Catholic.


Ireland stop laughing I'm serious.
I will go on like Jim McDaid driving down the wrong side
of the dual carriageway.
Ireland I will fill your ghost estates with poems.
Ireland love your immigrants.
Ireland when I was six I went to a Progressive Democrats'
rally with my father it was
    great they gave me a paper hat with their logo on it I
thought Des O'Malley was
    class then when I went to college I joined the Socialist
Workers' Party but only
    went to three meetings and my locker was full of black
and white posters I never
    put up anywhere.
Ireland you're not really neutral.

Ireland there are men in jumpsuits shackled in Shannon.
Ireland, go me leith sceal tá mo gaeilge uafasach.
Ireland stop laughing.
Ireland we're in some state.
Ireland this is what I have learned from George Hook.
OK I'll stop messing.
You're right I haven't a notion of becoming a teacher – I
don't even listen to myself.
Ireland I'm putting my hairy head down and getting to
work.

## Jeannie Baker's *A Walk Through Hyde Park*

The man with the sandwich board that says
'Psychiatry is an evil it must be banned'
is softly spoken and carries
a brown leather satchel. It only contains
two things: a cheese sandwich and a picture of his wife.

A dog cocks his leg, claiming the park
while his owners lie a few feet away.
They look at each other, his head
in her lap while she sits up. She is wearing
an orange dress. Their conversation is serious.

A young woman in a floral-printed skirt
considers her sketch pad. A handbag
flops beside her, forgotten. The pencil reprises
its movement, a battle for clarity
between dark grey and white.

The man standing nearby
is wearing a suit that is two sizes too big.
A paper fan is open just below
his toupeed head. A black, white and red
checked shopping bag dangles from his left arm.

He is only a few steps from the young woman.

Look again.

She is sketching him, his insouciant smile, his steady hands.

## My Friend The Pharmacist

His zero nine Nissan
His savage gas cooker
His Curb Your Enthusiasm boxset
His guitar playing
His charity work in India
His sound system – there's speakers in the roof!
His Magimix
His marriage
His kids
His mellow parents
His terraced house in Dublin
His ease with decency

## The Flying Pig Hostel

When I was in Amsterdam
I was stuck in a beanbag

Then Tom helped me up
No he didn't

He made me tea
When I was in Amsterdam

And I drank four cups
At least, or more

When I was on the beanbag
It wanted to eat me

Or at least that's how it felt
When I was in Amsterdam

So I had to lie down
In a dorm with twelve beds

And I was a pane of glass
With a person at each end

Making waves like they
Were making a bed

And I thought
-bang bang bang bang-

That I would shatter
When I was in Amsterdam

# Boats Passing
## Ciara O'Dowd

The last couple agreed to come inside when the rain got so
heavy, the parasol over their table gave way. It creaked
loudly before collapsing, and a torrent of water soaked both
them and their plates of seafood cataplana. People on the
promenade shrieked and scattered, splashing through
puddles. Below, in the darkness, teenagers ran up the sand
looking for cover, kicking through half-demolished sand
castles with their arms over their heads.

The waiter kept smiling as he ushered the two men up
the steps into the white-washed taverna. A party of English
men clapped as they entered, greeting the last diners to
leave the teeming veranda. Cool and a little damp, the
cramped room had low ceilings. Some of the diners had
found seats and tables; others crowded into benches by the
walls, peering out the porthole windows into the night.

Behind the bar, the waiters had gathered, laughing and
chattering loudly in Portuguese. Then the eldest man, stout
and silver-haired, pulled rank and shouted some
instructions. Dry, starched linen appeared as if by magic
and over-full wine buckets were emptied and replaced.
Dishes were whipped back to the kitchen to be reheated and
glasses patted dry. People pulled their tables closer to allow
more seating; some relished the chance to chat to strangers
while others huddled closer to their partners and whispered
remonstrations.

At the doorway, two waiters took scissors to some black
sacks, fashioning raincoats for a beleaguered family. They
bowed ceremoniously as they handed them over. Beneath
the chatter and clinking of glasses, there was still the steady
stream of rain outside, flooding the cobbles and making the
sea dance.

In a nook in the corner, sat a girl fresh-faced enough to be a teenager. Alice was almost twenty-one, wearing sparkly shoes and a short skirt. She'd been glum all night but now a smile twitched at her lips, amused by the waiters' antics. Her mother noticed it but said nothing. Secretly hoping for a turnaround, she topped up their wine glasses.

'The storm will clear the air,' Joan told her daughter. 'Sunshine tomorrow.'

'I hope so. Otherwise I'll be going home half a stone heavier.'

Joan put her knife and fork back down, staring at the remaining potatoes on her plate. They were cold anyway. She watched her daughter pick at her tuna.

'Then he'll really have no regrets about dumping me,' Alice added. Joan didn't have the energy to reply.

Nearby, Terry reached over to put his hand on Adam's. Both had wet hair, Adam's now slicked back with a comb he carried in his pocket. Adam's shirt was damp, clinging to his shoulders and his torso and Terry couldn't help feeling a little grateful for the rainstorm. Adam had the most beautiful hands of any man he'd dated. Long and thin, the nails were gleaming and so well shaped they could have been manicured. And the most beautiful face: high cheekbones and skin so pale it was almost translucent. Such a fragile, beautiful boy. If only he could show some sense of humour at the absurdity of the situation. Instead, he wore an expression of utter melancholy. All day Adam had worn that expression — when they sat in the shade by the pool, when they had a glass of wine on the balcony of the hotel, when they returned to their room for a siesta and to change their clothes before dinner. It was the same expression that had drawn Terry to him at the dinner party, an urge to comfort and console, to hold the fragile face in his hands. Terry finished his glass of wine and motioned to the waiter for another bottle.

In the centre of the restaurant, the waiter cleared his throat and clapped his hands.

'I would like to offer you all dessert, as they say ... on the house.'

A cheer went up. In the corner, Joan patted her stomach and hoped the offering would please her daughter. On the plane over, while Alice sobbed and stuffed herself with Maltesers like a toddler in a tantrum, she'd chewed nicotine gum and wondered how a responsible mother was supposed to deal with this, how she could help her mature. All she wanted was to shake her daughter and tell her to grow up, to point out her own wobbly thighs and wrinkly chest, the stretch marks on her stomach. Remind her she had her whole life ahead of her. But a responsible mother wouldn't have felt a stab of jealousy when the waiter had called her daughter *principessa* and held out the chair for her.

Terry was topping up his own wine glass again. He held the bottle over Adam's and raised his eyebrow, searching for a reaction. Adam tilted his head; he had no idea what the gesture meant.

'You drink a lot when you're away, don't you?' Adam said.

Terry let the question go, watching the hubbub behind the bar. He bit his lip.

Joan sipped her water, rubbed her bare arms and looked out at the storm when Alice stood to go to the Ladies. She had offered her daughter her cardigan, pointing out her goose bumps, and Alice had taken it without a murmur. Depressed and bored, she was trying to resist the descending smog of self-pity. She was angry with herself; so desperate for pity, she wanted to unburden her problems on her naïve daughter.

'Excuse me?'

The man at the next table leant over with a smile.

'But this is a rather expensive bottle of wine and we're not going to finish it, would you like a glass?'

Her glass was empty and she'd noticed there wasn't much conversation at his table.

'Sure. It feels like that kind of night.'

'Doesn't it?' Terry said as he tipped the bottle over her glass. He checked his companion's expression out of the corner of his eye. Arms folded, lips tight.

Joan felt a flicker of delight when Terry returned the bottle to his table without offering any to Alice. He was barely middle-aged, she surmised. Well kept, with a designer sports jacket over his shirt and a healthy tan. She complimented the wine. The extra glass brought up rosy apples on her cheeks as she waited for her daughter to return.

All over the restaurant, deserts were being dropped onto the tables like swooping birds of prey. Gigantic slabs of cake, bloated profiteroles, and tottering ice cream sundaes. Terry took his dish with his customary grace and, in a low voice, enquired about taxis.

'It's a Saturday night sir, and with the weather as it is … Can I get you another spoon for that?'

Terry looked at Adam, who was sipping his water and studying an ink drawing on the wall with a look of disdain.

'I don't think that will be necessary.'

He dug the spoon in, and it chimed off the plate. Adam flinched at the noise, excused himself and headed for the back of the restaurant.

Terry turned to the lady at his side and pushed the plate over.

'Dessert on your own is no fun.'

Joan twiddled her coffee spoon, considering it.

'Maybe just a taste.'

Alice had gone to the door, hoping for a better reception on her mobile phone. The waiter passed by, looked for a sign of approval and they both nodded. Terry raised his glass. A red-haired woman was searching for her jacket, and asking her companion how exactly she was meant to cover her sandals. He wasn't paying attention and she looked disgruntled. Terry noticed her gaze.

'You're trying to be sympathetic,' he said.

In the candlelight, he could see that Joan was older than she'd first appeared. There were deep worry lines etched under her eyes and around his mouth.

The couple were clearly bent on escaping. He was portly, with a swagger; she clung to his arm as they weaved through the tables to the door.

'Pity,' Joan said. 'There was going to be a row there.'

Somebody in the corner was asking the waiter if anyone had a guitar and Alice was holding her phone up and waving her arm out of the doorway in the rain. A brightly-coloured umbrella passed and the woman pushed Alice out of the way and leaned out in vain hope, but it was gone.

Terry handed Joan a napkin and then wiped the cream off his own chin. Adam still hadn't returned.

'Is he okay?' She gestured at Adam's vacant seat. And then she asked, 'Do you smoke? Do you think there's somewhere we could -'

'I'll keep you company,' he offered.

Terry was calling over the waiter. She sat back and watched their exchange, unable to hear the negotiations; her head now a little woozy from too much wine. As she stood up to follow him, he offered her his arm and she was grateful for the support. Alice was still busy with her phone.

Terry led her down a steep staircase at the back of the restaurant and out a fire exit. A waiter looked surprised to see them, then stubbed out his cigarette and went back upstairs.

'Is this allowed?' Joan asked.

They were in a narrow alley, dark and cobbled, and there was a smattering of stars in the sky. Overhead, the rain played on a corrugated iron sheet and there was a stench of fish and stale cigarette smoke. Terry pulled a napkin from his pocket and wiped down a rickety chair. She perched on it, mindful of a wobbly leg and sucked on the cigarette he lit for her.

Joan had never known such rain in a place like this, and despite her fears of having to spend the next day cooped up with Alice, there was something refreshing about the storm. The door was open just a crack and in the dim light, Terry looked thinner than before. He stood as straight as a dancer, his feet turned out.

'We'll go back to them in a minute,' he said after a brief silence.

'Do we have to?' she asked.

Terry had seen her at the pool during the day. He had watched her potter around the pool with a strained look on her face. He had seen her go to the bar after getting a phone call, had seen her throw back the brandy and root in her beach bag for change to leave a tip, and a napkin for the tears. He let out a long sigh, leaning against the wall and also enjoying the cigarette more than he'd like to admit.

'Adam won't be pleased,' he said. 'You didn't bring any mints, did you?'

'Let's go for a walk on the beach. In the moonlight.'

He laughed and patted her hand.

'You're tipsy. And it's dangerous down there, with the waves so high.'

Joan imitated Alice's pout, and stood up to look out at the storm.

'We could pretend to be young lovers!'

She fixed her arm under his and they stepped out into the rain together. The water seeped into her sandals and as a dart of lightning ripped open the sky, they fell back, laughing.

'Why do we try so hard?' she asked, when the giggling had subsided.

He let the question hover in the cigarette smoke.

'Is he gone?' Terry asked after a moment. 'Your husband?'

She looked a little startled. And then, 'No. But she's pregnant.'

There was a rumble of thunder overhead. In a flare of lightning, she saw the look on his face and laughed.

'Not Alice. My husband's mistress.'

'Bastard,' he spat out the word.

'Is it over with Adam?' she asked.

'Never started.'

He peered out into the alley and scanned the sky for more lightning. Then he smiled, saying, 'We should run off together.'

She let the cigarette drop into a puddle. When they'd stood arm in arm, he was warm, with the hint of expensive aftershave. At the far end of the alley was a cocoon of light: another bar, or a house. She tried to picture it, the pair of them stealing away together, hand in hand.

'Another cigarette?' he asked.

'I should go back.'

She wondered if Alice had found a reception and was calling her Dad.

'Come on then!' he offered her his arm again.

She wrinkled her nose.

'You're supposed to say not yet.'

'Let's go for a walk tomorrow!' he suggested.

There was something in his smile that brought her back to herself. Understanding. Pity. Indulgence. She pulled at her hair and arranged the chain around her neck.

Inside, the lights had gone out again and candles had been put on all the tables, some just an inch of wax.

'Where were you?' Alice asked.

She knew instinctively that Terry wasn't behind her, that he'd wound a different path through the tables to conceal their entrance. But as she sat back in her seat and asked if they'd served coffee, she noticed the table next to them was empty. The glass of wine was full and a napkin had been left, carefully folded into a tiny square parcel. Terry was in an altercation with one of the waiters, pushing a wad of cash into his hands. Alice followed her gaze.

'Please tell me you weren't flirting with him. Mum! I think he's gay!'

The waiter had produced an umbrella and Terry was testing the catch. It wasn't too sturdy, and the waiter was reminding him about the howling wind. Joan hoped he'd look back but Terry was buttoning his jacket and turning up his collar. Alice's face had withered into a petulant frown and the anger came crashing over Joan like a wave.

'Come on!' she pulled her wrap around her shoulders and stood up. 'We'll walk.'

As they paid the bill, the waiters produced two more black sacks and Joan stood impatiently while they ripped the plastic and offered the cloaks. Water ran down the plastic and down their necks as they sloshed through the puddles in silence, until the wind thrust its fingers up Alice's skirt and she screamed. They held out sodden arms as taxis sped past, up the winding streets.

Alice let out a whoop of delight when they rounded the corner and saw up ahead the familiar amber lights of the complex. As they trudged up the final hill, Joan's vision was blurred and she couldn't read the name of the apartments. There was a line of palm trees being battered by the rain and on the street in front of the gate, a lake had formed in an oversized pothole. By the kerb, there was an upturned umbrella. It had blown inside out and the wires were broken, so it sat in the puddle like an oddly-shaped boat. A royal blue boat. Joan stopped for a moment, catching her breath, and tried to remember the colour of Terry's umbrella.

## A Failure of Recognition

You walked into the store today
addressed all aspects of the weather
purchased milk and rashers
claiming to be fifty per cent better than before.

I could not place your face
you'd been somewhere in the sea of faces in the wave of black.

I'm not sure if you placed me either;
I'd been returned to the wrong aisle in your mind
So many seasons since had spun and been cut down
weaving and unravelling like spiders webs
until nothing's left.

He had fallen with the corn
and you had been somewhere in the sea of faces in the wave of black.

Not when shock stopped heart a moment to bring me close to father
you'd supped tea on haybales with
Me bringing the sandwiches,
you telling me I'd grown taller
smiling proud as punch
and looking up to see if he was too
Yes you were somewhere in the sea of faces in the wave of black.

The haydust clears
and checkout beeps awake me to his death
like the hospital machines that could have jolted him back to life had he had the chance
but we had slept through alarm bells we hadn't known were set;
they'd gone off so soon.

I catch my breath when I look at you a second time and recognise
you'd been somewhere in the sea of faces in the wave of black.

It's grey now, hard to see you in this altered light
but it'd been black then
blacker than the word black
blacker than the night-sky's yawning
blacker than the fullest nothing
blacker than these last drops of midnight oil my mind
tries to fill the white page with
only to find the words illegible to ghost and child
And you, you are somewhere in the sea of letters in the wave of black.

## I am Dressing

I am dressing
I am placing a sign on my door
that says *do not disturb*
I am dressing
donning stockings that won't warm your cold feet
clasping wire and cloth across where your cheek
never felt my heart beat.

I am dressing
I am turning a key in my door
to lock your naked face out
I am dressing
pulling trousers over grazed knees
I won't allow you to see
tightening my belt round the waist
where your hand had been.

I will be disciplined.

I am dressing
I am raising the music to
lower my thoughts
I am dressing
zipping my coat up high
to stop my heart's sleeve-slide
stepping into boots steel-capped
so I won't feel the glass.

I am dressing
I am placing a sign on my door
that says *do not disturb*
I am dressing
my face
to cover the cracks
painting a smile
over my gauzed words.

I am keeping this to myself.

I am fastening buttons
scraping back hair
tipping my hat
winding on scarves
wearing my thickest layers
I am dressing up warm and yet
I am colder than when my skin was bare
I am trying to accept that you will never undress me.

# Nativity
## Jennifer McCarrick

You were meant to love babies, especially your own.
Everybody knew that. But what happened when you didn't?
What happened when the thing came out after months of
waiting and wondering and excitement and you looked at it
and it seemed like it was not your own but someone else's
— perhaps even the spawn of some other species
altogether?

Ellen had loved being pregnant. She'd had no sickness,
no tiredness, barely an ache or pain. Everyone said she had
never looked better. Radiant was the word they most often
used. It ought to have followed that motherhood would be a
breeze. Instead, she found she was frightened of the child
from the moment it was born. She held it awkwardly and
winced when it cried. The midwives shook their heads and
whispered together and she knew she was an unfit mother
and wished they'd take the baby away someplace so she
wouldn't have to be reminded. She could have another
when she felt more ready and hopefully it would be a little
girl, a small, sweet creature who would love her and be
satisfied with her efforts. It didn't really sink in that she
was stuck with this big lump of a boy until the hospital
discharged her and she had to take it home with her. She
cried for days, the child roaring along with her until the two
of them were red eyed and spent. Saddled with each other,
that's how it was, and the baby resented it as much as Ellen
did. She could tell by the way it glared at her from behind
its soggy bib, its big round eyes full of reproach for her
weakness. To revenge itself on her it gulped air with its
milk and kept her awake all night screaming so that she had
to walk the floor eternally with it slung over her shoulder,
patting it on the back to make it burp.

Perversely, it was as quiet as a mouse whenever anyone called and visitors thought it a perfect angel and commiserated with it — over what Ellen couldn't make out. She only knew that it irked her unbelievably to listen to her mother-in-law cooing, 'Poor babby, poor little boy,' all the time, as if his arm had fallen off or something, when anyone could see that the little bastard was in the rudest of health.

Worse than anything else was the lack of sleep. It made her stupid and forgetful. She put washing up liquid in the fridge and towels into the oven. She served chicken still raw in the middle while her potatoes turned to mush in the pot. Once, she'd even scorched the front of Jim's uniform — although if he'd told her once he'd told her a million times to put a towel over the jacket when she ironed it. He roared like a bull when he saw it and made her cry, which only made him angrier. What was wrong with her at all, he wanted to know, and could she not 'pull her socks together' and just deal with the situation like other women did. His own mother had reared eight children without a single complaint and the house was always immaculate and dinner on the table at the same time every day. They'd never heard of colic in those days either by God, probably because — he suspected — it was nothing more than a made-up ailment modern mothers used as an excuse to moan to each other. Ever since they'd lifted the marriage bar women just weren't content doing their duty in the home anymore; that was his own opinion anyway and the fellows down at the barracks all agreed. Now there was talk of there being sent a woman recruit next year and who knew what the world was coming to at all. Sure what use would a woman be on a Friday night after fair day when the rolling drunks had to be locked up for their own good? None at all, was what. De Valera had had the right idea, God rest him — a saint of a man and no mistake. They didn't make them like that anymore.

'Thanks be to God for that,' was Ellen's tearful response, but as usual Jim didn't hear her.

'No, they do not,' he finished, and went back to reading his paper.


Somehow it was December already. Where had October and November got to? Two months had been lost in a haze of washing and feeding and sleepless nights. She remembered how she had looked forward to Christmas all summer long as her stomach swelled, padding about in a motherly fashion, knitting little cardigans and blankets, planning the special meals she would make for their first Christmas together as a family — a nice fat goose, three types of potatoes, the pudding and brandy butter. She was a good cook. She'd get a nice big tree and decorate it with tinsel and red bows, put a wreath on the door, a bit of holly over the sacred heart pictures to liven them up a bit. Now there was no time for these things. The pantry was empty. No presents had been bought. She'd forgotten entirely to order the goose and Jim's mother, the judgmental auld bitch, would be there to criticize her at every turn. She had eight children, but she just had to land herself on Ellen for the holiday.

The day before Christmas Eve she began to panic in earnest. She wrapped the squalling baby in two blankets and lodged it in the pram for the walk into town, just remembering to take the housekeeping money (what little there was of it) from the tin on her way out the door. The streets were mobbed, everyone smiling at her when they passed as if it was all great craic, this pushing and lumbering about like a herd of cattle at a mart. Her face and hands were frozen by the time she reached the butchers shop and squeezed herself and the pram through the door.

Just as she expected the queue was half a mile long. She waited her turn, fighting back tears of sheer exhaustion. The women were all turning to stare at her, probably wondering why she made no effort to quiet the baby, who'd started whinging as soon as they stopped moving. Well, let them. She was past caring what they thought. They were all the same — culchies. She knew they found her stand-offish and put it down to her being from Dublin. She was a blow-in and a flibbertigibbet and that's all she'd ever be if she lived to be a hundred and never left Ballyhinch again, which was likely. Eventually Farrell the butcher motioned her to approach the counter.

'Well Mrs. Kehoe, what can I do for you?'

She looked over her shoulder, fearful of her mother-in-law until she realized it was herself he was addressing.

'I wanted a goose,' she said.

'Did you now?' he roared over the baby's screams, 'and hadn't you right to order it a week ago when we could've got one for you?'

'You haven't one then?'

'I haven't.'

He seemed very pleased with himself, considering he couldn't help her. She asked for a ham and stuck it in the pram with the child. It would have to do. She'd get some sprouts and potatoes to go with it and maybe she could buy a shop cake for dessert. The old bag would have something to say about that no doubt, but as far as Ellen was concerned she could take a running jump for herself.

Mahoney's the greengrocer was nearly as bad. She bought the few vegetables and some oranges and got out again as quickly as she could. The shop-girls' festive cheer depressed her, as did their loud and chirpy attempts at conversation. She decided to drop into the church before she set off for home. She'd go in and say a quick prayer —

anything to get off the cold and crowded streets and sit down for a few minutes.

Inside it was cool and quiet and all aglow with candlelight. The statues looked down on her benignly from their perches, baring their bleeding hearts with good grace. That's what faith did for you; it made you suffer your injuries without rancour and smile on your aggressors. Ellen didn't know if that was really a blessing or not; she thought it was better not to suffer at all if you could help it. She wheeled the pram around the pews slowly until she came upon the nativity scene set into the alcove beside the door. The Madonna looked so lovingly upon the plaster baby in the manger that for a moment Ellen felt her heart would burst with sadness. But then, the infant Jesus was so placid with its knowing smile and rosy cheeks — the perfect child.

'No crying it makes,' she whispered, reaching out to draw a finger along the shiny surface of its face. No wonder it moved even the barnyard beasts to wonder and awe. Once more she felt the weight of her own burden and fought back despair. Quickly she crossed herself and prayed to God to give her peace, to lift this cloud that clung to her and let her love the baby. He was hers, after all, her own flesh and blood, and deserving of love like all human beings. It was true she was a bad mother but she would try to be better from now on.

As she left behind the gloomy hush of the church Ellen realized with a start that she could hear her own thoughts clearly for the first time in months. There wasn't a sound from the pram. The crying had stopped.

Feeling two tons lighter she trudged home as fast as she could through the snow, pulling the cold air deep into her lungs. At last she could breathe again. It was the sweetest thing in the world to come back home and leave the baby in its pram to sleep while she tidied up the house and got the dinner on. And then to make herself a cup of tea and put her feet up and listen to the radio for a whole hour while she smoked one woodbine after another. Absolute bliss. She didn't realize she had fallen asleep until the sound of the door slamming jolted her back to wakefulness. Then, like a nightmare she saw Jim's red face looming an inch above hers, saw his mouth moving and knew he was shouting before she felt the drops of spittle land on her nose. She saw him lift her by the collar of her blouse and pull her out of the chair like it was happening to someone else, and then the sound returned and she heard him roar at her.

'I said, what the hell have you done to the child?'

She couldn't understand what was wrong with him. The child was fine.

'He's sleeping,' she tried to tell him. 'He's in the pram.'

He threw her roughly to the ground.

'In the pram, is he? In the feckin' pram!'

He kicked the thing with force so that it toppled onto its side and the baby fell out onto the carpet. She screamed, but the child didn't make a sound. Jim picked it up with one hand and flung it against the wall, cracking its plaster head so that its nose broke off.

'You mad bitch you — where is he?'

Her baby, her beautiful baby was destroyed. She crawled over to it and cradled it in her arms. She was crying.

'Poor darling, poor little babby. Shhh, Mammy's here, sweetheart. Mammy loves you.'

## The End
### *Joe Jennings*

I am that aneurism in your artery.
I am that malignant tumour in your brain.
I am that blood in your urine.
I am that wrinkle in your skin and
that cough in your chest and
that blur in your vision.
I am that bend in your spine.
I am that stiffness in your fingers and
the tightness in your throat.
I am that silence in your ear.
I am that word you never speak of and
the notion you always think of and
the fear that burns deep inside you.
I am growing while you shrink.
I am near you when you sleep.
I am flowing through your veins and
in your soggy breath and
in your salty tears.

# ABOUT THE AUTHORS

## Brid Buckley

Brid Buckley is a poetry and fiction writer from Cork. She moved to Galway in 2009 to do the MA in Writing in NUIG. Before this she studied English and Psychology, and subsequently Film in UCC. She has read and emceed O' Bheal poetry nights in the Long Valley in Cork. She is published in the 2008 Five Word Challenge anthology, as well as Measured Words. A guest speaker at Over the Edge in Galway City Library, she has also read her work at Tuam and Ballyferriter's Art Festivals as well as at the Whitehouse Limerick. In 2010 she co-wrote and produced the Smedia nominated radio drama College Road as part of the Mighty Student collective.

## Colm Byrne

Colm Byrne's plays have been performed Off-Broadway, Los Angeles, Edinburgh, Vienna and Galway. The *New York Times* said his work offers 'Wisdom in its comments on the world' and *Citysearch* called him 'a master of dialogue.'

He is a recipient of the Bay Area Critics Outer Circle award and was a writer in residence for the LA Writer's Centre. He conceived of and was show-runner for the Smedias nominated radio drama College Road. Recent Irish stagings and readings include Galway Theatre Festival, the Flatlake Literary Festival, Dublin Book Festival, and the Electric Picnic. This is his first adventure in short form.

## Trevor Conway

Trevor Conway, from Sligo, writes poetry, fiction, songs and scripts. Currently he is recording an album of his songs with Athenry singer Sandra Coffey. His work has appeared in magazines and anthologies across Ireland, Austria, the UK, the US and Mexico, where his poems will be translated into Spanish. His first collection of poems will be published by Salmon Poetry in 2012.

He offers freelance editing and other services for aspiring writers http://www.trevorconway.weebly.com.

## Elizabeth Cox

Elizabeth Cox grew up in Multyfarnham, was educated in Galway, and is currently living in Cambridge. Will write for scones.

## David O'Doherty

David is a fiction writer whose main areas of interest are black humour and satire. His work has been published in ROPES, Wordlegs and Cheerreader. A native of Cork, David is currently working on his first novel.

## Davnet Heery

Twenty years ago Davnet first began writing poetry in workshops with Anne Kennedy. Bit by bit poems from three series: *Connemara Views*, *Poems For My Daughter, Father Poems* appeared in the Writing in The West pages of the Connacht Tribune then edited by Eva Burke. Some poems also appeared in small magazines in Co. Clare and Co. Galway. These magazines have since disappeared. For a decade nothing was heard of her. Sightings were reported of her wandering the boglands of lower Connemara muttering to herself. She has been heard too along the shores of Chois Fharraige singing plaintive songs to the seals, who seem to respond. There are rumours that she now thinks she's an umbrella, and this could well be her in this anthology's cover image, hovering over the High Nellie!

## Joe Jennings

Joe Jennings was born in Galway in 1987. His interests lie mainly in poetry and fiction.

## Jennifer McCarrick

Jennifer loves fiction of all kinds and hopes to write the Great Victorian Novel sometime in the next decade - if she has time. She currently lives in County Galway with her partner, two children, a cat and three chickens. She plans to get a dog this summer.

## Caron Mc Carthy

Caron Mc Carthy is an archaeologist from Galway City. She enjoys writing fiction, non-fiction and being inspired. She is currently finishing her first novel, a thriller entitled *Noone*.

## Jimi McDonnell

Jimi McDonnell is a native of Tuam, Co.Galway. He cites his family, Tom Murphy and footballer Ja Fallon as pivotal influences. From 2007 to 2011, Jimi was the music correspondent for the Connacht Tribune. He has read his work at Listowel Writers' Week, the Over The Edge Series in Galway and Tuam Arts Festival. In 2010 Jimi was awarded an Individual Artists' Bursary from Galway County Council, part of which he used to fund a week at the Tyrone Guthrie Centre in Annaghmakerrig, Co. Monagahan. One of Jimi's proudest moments was having his poem A to Z selected by Upstart, a Dublin-based collective which hung artistic work alongside political posters during the 2011 General Election campaign. You can keep up with Jimi's writing on jimihair.blogspot.com.

## Ciara O'Dowd

Before completing the MA in Writing at NUI, Galway, Ciara studied Drama Studies and English Literature in Trinity College Dublin and the University of Glasgow. Her first play *The Tree Experiment* was performed at the Flat Lake Literary Festival in Monaghan, and she has completed an internship with *Blue Raincoat Theatre Company* in Sligo. She has spent the last five years trying to disprove the theory that chartered accountants are devoid of imagination.

## Anna O'Leary

Anna O'Leary, North Kerry writer, lived in the Middle East for seventeen years. Her fascination with the area has continued unabated. Her poetry, fiction and non-fiction are imbued with a sense of the Middle East.

Her short story was published in ROPES, and launched at Cúirt 2011. As a journalist she has written for Al Jazeera.net. She has appeared on the satellite channel, Press TV, as a Middle East commentator. She won a short story prize at K.I.S.S. (Kerry International Summer School) in 1996. Her poetry is published by Kerry Literary and Cultural Centre.

Anna worked on the Bin Laden family's private jet; was a guest of Saddam Hussein in Baghdad; and lived in a royal palace in Riyadh. An award winning Interior Designer she executed palace projects. Anna's first book in progress, Saudi Arabia: Axis of Power, tells of her meeting with Osama Bin Laden.

After Iran's revolution she moved to Kuwait and to Egypt. In her second book in progress, Iran:Axis of Power, she paints a rich canvas of pre revolution Iran, and of Egypt caught in the turmoil of Anwar Sadat's assassination. She was flying the Peace Route for Egypt. In Egypt she met Israel's one eyed general, Moshe Dayan. She frequently went horse riding with the late Prince Ali Reza Pahlavi of Iran.

Anna has an MA in Writing from NUIG and is preparing for a Ph.D. in Middle East politics.

**Visit us at** http://www.bicyclesumbrellas.org  v2.6